Sacred Gifts and Worldly Treasures

SACRED GIFTS AND WORLDLY TREASURES

Medieval Masterworks from the Cleveland Museum of Art

Edited by Holger A. Klein

Texts by Holger A. Klein, Stephen N. Fliegel, and Virginia Brilliant

THE CLEVELAND MUSEUM OF ART 2007
DISTRIBUTED BY ABRAMS, NEW YORK

❖ The Cleveland Museum of Art Board of Trustees ❖

Published by the Cleveland Museum of Art and
distributed by Abrams, New York
ISBN: 0-978-940717-91-6
Library of Congress Control Number: 2007925346

Produced by the Publications Department of the
Cleveland Museum of Art to accompany a traveling
exhibition on view at the J. Paul Getty Museum, 30
October 2007–20 January 2008.

Editing: Barbara J. Bradley and Kathleen Mills
Design: Laurence Channing
Production: Charles Szabla
Photography: Howard Agriesti and
Gary Kirchenbauer
Digital scanning: David Brichford
Digital retouching: Ellen Ferar
Printed in Italy by Amilcare Pizzi, Milan

The Ohio Arts Council helped fund this exhibition
with state tax dollars to encourage economic growth,
educational excellence, and cultural enrichment for all
Ohioans.

❖ Contents ❖

To a museum all gifts are sacred. Medieval treasuries, formed from donations, are a prototype of modern museums, which rely largely on the generosity of donors. The early Cleveland benefactor J. H. Wade, for example, helped to secure important medieval objects crucial to the development of the collection of the Cleveland Museum of Art. But all treasures cannot be said to be worldly, since among them number the spirit of service to others, the artist's skill, and the moral and aesthetic force of the objects we study and care for.

The earliest objects in this exhibition represent the cosmopolitan aesthetic of Roman art, dimmed with the decline of the empire but never quite extinguished. At the beginning of this period the polities of Europe faced a crisis more grave than any since. Whereas the great wars of later centuries left recognizable borders and political entities, the political landscape of Europe in the middle of the first millennium was a lawless wasteland in which widely scattered monasteries sheltered what remained of classical culture, as well as the seeds of what would become the lofty achievements of medieval art, scholasticism, and humanism.

As we study these objects we can hear tremendous events in the background as the nations of Western Europe began to form and, over all, the music of innumerable choirs. Christian faith was the unquestioned foundation of all artistic and intellectual activity, not only the subject of art but also its validation. Many of the most precious objects created during the Middle Ages were made to serve devotional and ecclesiastical purposes, with a twofold audience: clergy and laity, whose understanding of the art of their time is very different from ours. In the 12th century, Abbot Suger wrote that the beauty of precious gems transported him to a higher spiritual plane. Though Suger was one of the greatest art patrons of his time—he directed the reconstruction of the church of Saint-Denis, a seminal development of Gothic architecture—his writings emphasize the value of religious experience through precious materials rather than artistic skill or inspiration. His colleague Bernard of Clairvaux, a more puritan sensibility, inveighed against the church sculpture we prize today as an irreverent distraction from meditation on the laws of God. And what of art that failed to address Christian themes at all? Another notable 12th-century author, Bishop John of Salisbury, the lieutenant of Thomas Becket in his struggle with Henry II, referred to ancient statues brought from Rome to England as "idols, carefully made by the heathen in the error of their hands."

Today the heathen regard art primarily as an individual aesthetic response to existence, which medieval observers would have considered impious futility. Though their art displays plenty of humor and love of life—as may be seen in the margins of many illuminated manuscripts—all sensory experience was part of an ontological reflection of God's presence and agency in the world, and their difficulty in separating the aesthetic from other kinds of value was not due to didactic puritanism, but to their vision of existence completely integrated by the centrality of God. It has been centuries since humanity could enjoy the security of the unified cosmos described by the fifth-century author who took the name of Paul's convert Dionysos the Areopagite—a reconciliation of Christianity and Neoplatonic philosophy that would permanently inform Christian theology, holding that in the relation of the material world to God all things, creatures, and actions are combined in a marvelous unity. But despite the revolutions in thought and taste that have intervened since the Middle Ages, the works of art in this exhibition remain precious today, and not only because of their beauty. They are the inheritance of all heirs of European culture, and the past we glimpse through them is our own. Whether preserved in church treasuries, buried in the ground, or forgotten in some chest or unvisited corner, objects of the medieval period are survivors of a lost age. Yet for everyone raised among the arts of the West the experience they offer is one of recognition as much as discovery. Across the centuries their voices are still clear.

Medieval art played a dramatic role in the early years of the Cleveland Museum of Art. The first major medieval accession, a collection of armor intended to gild the opening in 1916, was lost on a railway siding until recognized by the museum's first director, Frederic A. Whiting, from his berth in a sleeping car, and, once hastily delivered, reassembled from a pile of dismembered ironmongery on the floor of the Armor Court by a redoubtable curator of armor from the Metropolitan Museum of Art. This collection is still one of the museum's most popular.

The size and quality of the medieval collection is due to general recognition of its cultural legacy as well as the openness of William M. Milliken, a curator who became the museum's second director, to the artistic profundity of what we call the decorative arts, and to the taste and generosity of some early donors, particularly J. H. Wade. In 1930 and 1931 Milliken's acquisition of some of the Guelph Treasure, originally some 140 objects donated to a cathedral treasury in Saxony, was made possible by the persuasive young curator's scholarship and the generosity of a few trustees; Milliken later wrote "almost no comparable objects such as these pieces . . . could ever come on the market again," and few have. Milliken had already secured some important early ivories and the unique *Table Fountain,* one of the few truly secular objects in the collection, which, still encrusted in the dirt in which it had been buried, had been rejected by the Louvre. Pristine today, this object, and the interactive digital reconstruction showing it as it operated to delight some pleasure-loving 14th-century courtiers, amply invoke the "happiness and gaiety" Milliken ascribed to it. Under his successors many other distinguished works were added, especially under Robert P. Bergman, the museum's fifth director, whose passionate interest in medieval art discovered aesthetic potential in objects that might previously have been considered of only ethnographical interest.

The growth of the collection fostered by William Milliken and his successors forced the physical plant to increase, and the latest renovation—a spectacular reinvention of the museum by Rafael Viñoly—allowed Charles Venable, Deputy Director for Collections and Programs, to send several collections out into the world as ambassadors for Cleveland. The organization of the medieval exhibition gave Holger A. Klein, Robert P. Bergman Curator of Medieval Art, an opportunity to focus what might have been merely an aggregation of splendid objects into a disciplined, sharply defined presentation of the highpoints of a millennium of culture. Holger and his colleagues Stephen N. Fliegel, Curator of Medieval Art, and Virginia Brilliant, Cleveland Curatorial Fellow for Medieval Art, brought new method and focus to planning the exhibition and interpreting its riches to the public. Thanks to the partnerships they forged with Dr. Renate Eikelmann, Director, and Dr. Matthias Weniger, Curator of Painting and Sculpture before 1550, of the Bayerisches Nationalmuseum, and Michael Brand, Director, Antonia Boström, Curator of Sculpture and Decorative Arts, and Jeffrey Weaver, Assistant Curator of Sculpture and Decorative Arts of the J. Paul Getty Museum, the exhibition will travel to Germany and California, where these institutions' rich collections of related material will add luster to ours.

I hope that visitors to this exhibition in Munich and Los Angeles will someday enjoy a reunion with these objects in their new galleries in Cleveland, as part of an extraordinary collection represented here by only a small, though choice, sample.

Timothy Rub, Director

❖ Acknowledgments ❖

This exhibition, which presents an extraordinary selection of more than one hundred masterworks of Early Christian, Byzantine, Western Medieval, and Early Renaissance art, would not have been possible without the help and support of many staff members, colleagues, and friends in Cleveland, Munich, Los Angeles, and elsewhere. As the organizing curator of *Sacred Gifts and Worldly Treasures,* I would like to take the opportunity to thank a number of people from the Cleveland Museum of Art for their contributions, help, and expertise.

The complicated logistics of organizing a major exhibition and its tour were skillfully managed by Heidi Domine Strean, Director of Exhibitions, and Morena Carter, Exhibitions Coordinator. Under the direction of Mary Suzor, Director of Collections Management, extraordinary pains were taken to equip our rare and fragile objects for the road. Gretchen Shie Miller, Associate Registrar for Loans, coordinated the myriad transportation and insurance details, and Larry Sisson, Packing Specialist, not only designed the shipping crates and packed the objects, he also went to Munich and Los Angeles to unpack them.

Many of the objects have been freshly treated by Bruce Christman, Chief Conservator, and Sari Uricheck, Associate Conservator of Objects. My thanks also to Jim George, Robin Hanson, Juliette Jacqmin, Joan Neubecker, Dana Norris, Moyna Stanton, and Marcia Steele, who prepared the objects, paintings, and textiles for travel and exhibition. In the photo studio, I am grateful to Howard Agriesti, Chief Photographer, and Gary Kirchenbauer, Associate Photographer, for their excellent photographs, and Bruce Shewitz for his help and patience with a plethora of last-minute photo and printing requests. Editor Jane T. Panza prepared the labels and exhibition texts. For what is not visible, I would like to acknowledge our mount makers Philip Brutz and Dante Rodriguez, whose elegant work never ceases to amaze me. Thanks are also due to Mark McClintock and Joe Blazer for their care in handling even the heaviest and most difficult objects, and to Tracy Sisson for coordinating the transportation of objects within the museum and for her help in making objects available for study even on short notice.

Not least among the opportunities presented by this exhibition was the chance to publish these treasures with the éclat they deserve; many have not appeared in print for many years. The catalogue, edited by Barbara J. Bradley, Senior Editor, attempts not only to celebrate the objects but also to place each within the context of its time; the design by Laurence Channing, Director of Publications, enhances their visual splendor. Yet no picture can do more than remind us of the experience of encountering the objects themselves.

My colleagues William H. Robinson, Curator of Paintings, and Louise Mackie, Curator of Islamic Art and Textiles, willingly agreed to include some extraordinary objects in this exhibition that do not fall under the immediate care of the Medieval Art Department. Finally, I would like to extend my heartfelt thanks to Elizabeth Saluk, Curatorial Assistant in the department of Medieval Art, who with great energy and skill maintained the checklist for the exhibition, coordinated the ordering of comparative photographs for the catalogue, helped to compile the glossary, and kept an eye on all administrative issues during the preparation of the exhibition and its catalogue.

Holger A. Klein, Robert P. Bergman Curator of Medieval Art

The Cleveland Museum of Art has a special quality among American museums for each object which it contains has been bought because it was loved. —Bernard Berenson

In the last quarter of the 19th century American cities discovered that pre-eminence required a museum of art, and in Boston, New York, and Washington museums in stately neoclassical buildings had already begun to build collections when a timely gift of land catalyzed the final negotiations that made possible the incorporation of the Cleveland Museum of Art. A bustling city fortunate in a location rich with iron ore and on major transportation routes, Cleveland possessed the requisite private wealth and public generosity, but almost four decades were needed for lawyers, politicians, and connoisseurs to weld three estates into a single institution.

Many ambitions—cultural, architectural, educational—persuaded the trustees of the new institution to embark on a venture far from defined or fully funded. Yet when they leaped the net appeared: funds in the nick of time, an ingenious land swap with the city to site the building properly, and resourceful people whose skills seemed to be called forth by the very problems they solved. (The daring of the founders became a tradition, still vital almost a century later, when Rafael Viñoly's vision of an expanded museum elicited exactly the same willingness to commit whatever it takes.)

Of course everyone agreed that, like those in Boston, New York, and Buffalo, the new museum building would be neoclassical, a style especially influential in Cleveland because of the Group Plan, a city plan for downtown commissioned from the Chicago firm of Burnham, Brunner, and Carrère in 1903. Daniel Burnham had supervised the architecture of the 1893 Chicago World's Fair, the "White City" of splendid Beaux-Arts structures. When presenting his plan for Cleveland to the mayor, Burnham explained that it was to be based on "the historic motives of the classic architecture of Rome,"[1] and the fluted columns with their Ionic capitals and the massive architrave seemed to represent a solid permanence, the timeless legacy of classical culture.

Hubbell and Benes, a local firm, created a firmly symmetrical plan: a series of galleries and courts centered on a rotunda, modeled on a Greek temple, the home of an ancient god adapted to shelter modern society's most precious objects. Classical design aimed not only at elegance, but also moral seriousness that would encourage the visitor to approach the museum in a spirit of reverence, and its symmetry provided a format apt for an exposition of art history. For the first time in an American museum, the service and office areas were carefully planned, neatly housed in a ground floor beneath the galleries.[2]

Plaster model showing the south facade, Cleveland Museum of Art building,
Hubbell and Benes, 1912.

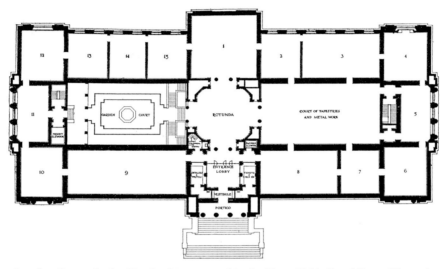

Plan, first floor as built, Cleveland Museum of Art building, Hubbell and Benes. The main
exhibition level has a series of galleries and courts that flow off a central rotunda.

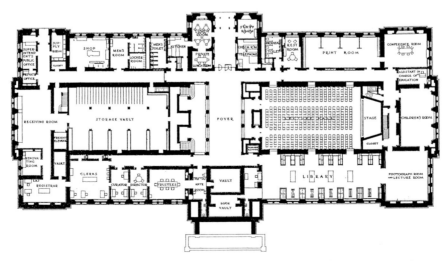

Plan, ground floor as built, Cleveland Museum of Art building, Hubbell and Benes. This
level housed support services as well as the library, classrooms, and a lecture hall.

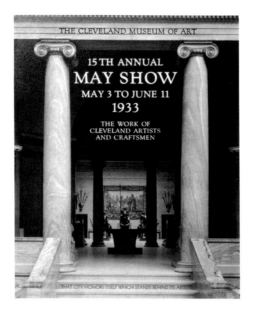

The contents of the gallery floor were less clearly defined. In painting, Colonial American portraits—a bargain compared to Old Master painting—were the initial targets, representing the virtues the museum hoped to encourage in its visitors. The museum's first director, Frederic Allen Whiting, also believed strongly in exhibiting contemporary art, both local and national, and began an annual series of exhibitions that became Cleveland's principal contemporary art event for 75 years. Whiting's ambition for a museum of world culture modeled on Boston and New York

The Armor Court in 1916 showing the Severance Collection of arms and armor and the tapestries presented by Mrs. Dudley P. Allen during the *Inaugural Exhibition*.

led to the creation of a world-class collection. Without the financial resources of Boston and New York, however—the Boston Museum of Fine Arts spent more on acquisitions between 1895 and 1904 than the total cost of the entire Cleveland building—the most stellar European objects were out of reach, except as donations. Further, the intellectual legacy of the Arts and Crafts movement encouraged the acquisition of objects that would instruct a largely immigrant work force in the aesthetic importance of the industrial arts. (Whiting had led the Boston Society of Arts and Crafts, which aimed at improving society through crafts.) Just as the museum was about to open its doors in 1916, a large collection of armor, considered by Whiting to be especially appropriate for an industrial city, was purchased from another collector through the generosity of local industrialist John Long Severance.

Spectacular Objects and Perceptive Donors

When the Cleveland Museum of Art opened to the public, its medieval collection consisted of little more than the newly acquired Severance Collection of arms and armor (nos. 108–11, 113). Works of art collected by Jeptha Homer Wade II began entering the collection a few years later, but it was only with the appointment of William Mathewson Milliken, a former curator of decorative arts at the Metropolitan Museum of Art in New York, that a focus on the decorative arts took deep root in the museum, to bear fruit many years later. Milliken had attended Princeton University, where Early

The Armor Court has remained a perennial favorite with children, who visit regularly with school groups, as shown here in photographs from the 1930s and 2005. Casual visitors and art students also enjoy the space.

Plaques from a Portable Altar: Christ and the Apostles, mid 1000s. German, Lower Rhine Valley.
Walrus ivory, 5.1 x 16.5 cm (largest plaque). Gift of J. H. Wade 1922.307.a–c.

Christian and Medieval art was a prominent field of study and where students could scrutinize original works of art, as well as casts. Further, he was on staff at the Met when J. P. Morgan's extensive, extraordinary collection was on view in 1914–16. This firsthand contact with medieval and Renaissance objects further shaped Milliken's attitude toward the era, and once in Cleveland he set about building a collection.

Milliken's first major medieval acquisition was a set of three 11th-century German walrus ivories, which he acquired in 1922 from Emile Rey of Arnold Seligman, Rey, and Company in New York, who had been closely associated with Henry Walters, Morgan, and other important American collectors. J. H. Wade backed Milliken on this first important purchase (as he did on many others to come), confirming the curator's judgment that there was indeed "nothing as fine of this type in the Metropolitan."[3] A year later Milliken secured for the museum through funds from Wade the *Spitzer Cross* (no. 53), a very fine late 12th-century enamel cross from Limoges. In 1924, he acquired not just one, but two spectacular objects: the rare Middle Byzantine ivory casket with scenes of Adam and Eve from the Bethune collection in Ghent (no. 25), for which funds had been provided by Wade, Severance, William Gwinn Mather, and Francis F. Prentiss; and the 14th-century French *Table Fountain* (no. 68) that had allegedly been found in a palace garden in Istanbul. Milliken had discovered the fountain, encrusted in a ball of earth, in Raphael Stora's gallery in Paris. Because the outcome of the cleaning process was uncertain, Jean Joseph Marquet de Vasselot (then curator at the Musée du Louvre in Paris) did not consider the fountain for purchase, but Milliken brought it to Cleveland, where it was soon exhibited in its original beauty. In 1925 he recommended yet another masterpiece for the fast-growing collection, the famous Byzantine ivory *Enthroned Virgin and Child* from the Stroganoff collection (no. 19). Paul Sachs, then director of Harvard's Fogg Art Museum, later described this acquisition as "a triumph for all concerned. Every serious student and every lover of truly *great* things must now visit The Cleveland Museum of Art if only to see this one object."[4]

Other magnificent objects—the exceedingly beautiful enamel pendant from the Meuse region (no. 45), a Venetian rock crystal cross (no. 95), and the sculpture *St. John Resting on the Bosom of Christ* (no. 84)—were acquired during the following years, establishing a pattern for collecting medieval art that Milliken later summarized: "The pattern was to buy quality, never to fill in a gap in the collection. If the proper piece came so much the better. If not, a gap was far more important than a mediocre work of art."[5] Yet, Milliken's crowning acquisitions were still to come.

In the aftermath of World War I, the German aristocratic house of Braunschweig-Lüneburg, which owned the famous Guelph Treasure, began disposing of parts of its art collection.[6] When rumors emerged in 1928 that at least some of the objects in the Guelph Treasure were up for sale, the government tried to step in but was unable to raise the required funds. As a result, the treasure was sold to a syndicate of German dealers (Julius R. Goldschmidt, Z. M. Hackenbroch, and Saemy Rosenberg); in the summer of 1930, it was put on view in Frankfurt and later in Berlin. After securing financial support from his director and board of trustees, Milliken traveled to Frankfurt to see the treasure. As he later recalled, "The thrill of seeing such objects, the knowledge that it was possible for Cleveland to acquire some of them, was tremendous."[7] Deciding which to choose proved difficult, but he did acquire six stunning objects, including the *Cumberland Medallion* (no. 35), the *Paten of St. Bernward* (no. 39), the *Arm Reliquary of the Apostles* (no. 38), the *Horn of St. Blaise,* and the book-shaped reliquary with the Ottonian ivory of Christ's miracle at Cana (no. 40).[8] These objects were shipped to Cleveland following the exhibition in Frankfurt.

The remaining pieces of the treasure arrived in the United States in the fall of 1930 for an exhibition in the newly established Goldschmidt and Reinhard galleries in New

Horn of St. Blaise, 1100s. Siculo-Arabic, Palermo. Ivory, 12 x 49.5 cm. Gift of the John Huntington Art and Polytechnic Trust 1930.740.

Cleveland's exhibition of objects from the Guelph Treasure was the museum's first blockbuster. Each object was accorded its own small gallery, and adults and children alike crowded around the display cases.

York. Cleveland's six objects arrived by train, accompanied by four of the museum's trustees. The exhibition then went on the road; in Cleveland it broke all visitor records: from 10 January to 1 February 1931 nearly 97,000 people saw the Guelph Treasure, making the exhibition the most successful and dramatic event in the museum's short history.[9] On the opening day alone, nearly 8,200 people stood in line—30,000 in the first week.[10] It took an hour and a half for the crowd to move in a double line

Clevelanders waiting in line to see the Guelph Treasure, 11 January 1930. In the middle ground are the dealers who brought this great medieval treasure from Europe. Left to right: Saemy Rosenberg (hands in pockets), Julius R. Goldschmidt, and Z. M. Hackenbroch (dark hair and moustache).

past the objects. The education department organized 182 events around the history of the treasure, which were attended by 15,000 people. Given the success of the show, Milliken made yet another pitch to the trustees to acquire more objects, and his wish was favorably answered: with help from the Huntington and Wade funds and with gifts by Mrs. Edward B. Greene (Wade's daughter) and Mrs. R. Henry Norweb (granddaughter of Liberty E. Holden, Cleveland financier and journalist and chairman of the museum's original Building Committee) it was possible to secure three of the treasure's most famous early objects: the 11th-century *Portable Altar of Countess Gertrude* (no. 36), a true masterpiece of Early Medieval craftsmanship, and two ceremonial crosses that formed part of Gertrude's original donation to the church of St. Blaise in Brunswick (see p. 116).

Director Milliken

Shortly before the Guelph Treasure arrived in Cleveland, Milliken was appointed the museum's second director, succeeding Whiting, who went on to become the president of the American Federation of the Arts in Washington. While the new director relinquished his responsibilities as curator of paintings, he remained curator of decorative arts until he retired in April 1958 and continued securing masterpieces.[11]

Inspired by the museum's acquisition of some of the most important objects from the Guelph Treasure, during the 1930s Milliken began broadening the holdings in German medieval art. Through Saemy Rosenberg, Milliken became aware of a series of German illuminated miniatures—three single and two double pages—that had been removed from their original manuscripts and bound together by the bibliophile Count Christoph von Kesselstatt, a canon at the cathedral of Trier. One of the single leaves, produced in Helmarshausen Abbey in the last quarter of the 12th century (no. 37), was closely related to other manuscripts produced for the Guelph Duke Henry the Lion of Saxony, one of the great benefactors of the church and treasury of St. Blaise. Purchased with proceeds from the J. H. Wade Fund, these leaves joined a small but steadily growing collection of exquisite illuminated manuscript leaves established in 1924 through the generosity of Jeptha Wade himself (nos. 51, 103, 105).[12]

Other significant additions to the medieval collection during the 1930s included an important panel from a diptych by the Master of Heiligenkreuz (no. 87), which had been exhibited at the museum's *Twentieth Anniversary* exhibition in 1936 and remained in Cleveland as a gift of friends of the museum in memory of John Long Severance, who had died earlier in the year.[13] The acquisition of this panel was followed two years later by the purchase of two masterpieces of German Gothic sculpture from the Schuster Collection in Munich, which Milliken had seen in the mid 1930s.[14] He later recalled:

> I knew little enough about German sculpture then and always wanted to learn more. Curiously there was almost no representation of first class things outside Germany. French Gothic sculpture had usurped the field. What a chance it was, for in 1938 came word that the [Schuster] collection would be auctioned in Munich. The Catalogue arrived and bids were sent in care of a friend, Dr. Wolfgang Krönig. He attended the sale on the day of the Anschluss, when Germany marched into Austria. The Cleveland Museum was fortunate in securing the fine Crucifixion by Leinberger [1938.293], bidding against the Museum in Landshut. Only later did we learn that the German Museums had known that Landshut was bidding and held off. They were upset when they learned that an American Museum had bought it instead. The second purchase was the wonderfully preserved Pietà by the Master of Rabenden [no. 93], with all its original polychromy.[15]

A year later, these purchases were supplemented by yet another exceptional work: the small statuette *Mourning Virgin from a Crucifixion Group* by Veit Stoss (no. 92).

Great acquisitions for the medieval collection continued to be made during the Second World War and its immediate aftermath. In the late 1930s, four mourning figures from the ducal tombs of Philip the Bold and John the Fearless at the Chartreuse of Champmol (nos. 73, 74) in Burgundy appeared on the New York art market. They had passed from the distinguished collection of Baron Arthur de Schickler at Martinvast in France into the possession of Clarence H. Mackay at Roslyn, Long Island. Upon Mackay's death in 1938, the trustees of his estate appointed Germain Seligman to dispose of his art collection.[16] Milliken had been notified about the availability of the sculptures by Seligman's business partner César de Hauke. While the Rijksmuseum in Amsterdam and the collector Jacques Matoussian had been interested in acquiring the four figures, the outbreak of the war and subsequent occupation of the Netherlands put both out of the competition. As Milliken later recalled, "This tragic conjunction of events meant that Cleveland could act and act she did, immediately. Two of the figures were brought to Cleveland by Mr. de Hauke, one figure from the Tomb of Philip the Good, the other from the Tomb of John the Fearless. They were actually purchased and the offer accepted on the tragic day of the Fall of France."[17] While Milliken regretted the fact that he could not purchase all four mourners, his wishes to bring them to Cleveland were eventually granted for the other two mourners had secretly been bought by Leonard C. Hanna Jr., the museum's vice president, who had been present when the statuettes were first seen in New York and had been "as much moved by their beauty as the Museum had been."[18] After Hanna's death in 1957, they joined their fellow mourners in Cleveland.

Milliken's acquisitions during the later 1940s reflect his interest in broadening the existing collection of medieval art as much as they betray his wish to strengthen particular fields within it. His purchases during these years include such fine works as a 14th-century French ivory *Mirror Case* (no. 66), an intricate 12th-century bronze altar cross with stand from Hildesheim (no. 49), an important Middle Byzantine gospel book with two inserted evangelist portraits from another manuscript associated with Empress Katherine Komnene (no. 23), and the exquisitely carved alabaster statuette *St. Jerome and the Lion* by Tilman Riemenschneider (no. 90). When Milliken first saw this delicate statuette at the firm of Rosenberg and Stiebel, there was no question in his mind "that it too was indicated for Cleveland, with its small but brilliant group of German sculptures. But it was the ever present question. How? If it had not been for the unfailing generosity and thoughtfulness of Rosenberg and Stiebel, it could not have been possible. They allowed it to stay in Cleveland until sufficient funds had accumulated."[19]

Another object acquired during the early 1940s, but outside of Milliken's immediate curatorial purview, was the small panel *The Adoration of the Magi* by Giovanni di Paolo (no. 98). This work had been in the possession of Mrs. Alice Kerr of Baltimore, a descendant of Thomas McKean, one of the signers of the Declaration of Independence, and had escaped the attention of scholars for decades. It was bought "for a mere song,"[20] as Milliken later wrote, by Harry G. Sperling of Kleinberger and Company in New York, passed to Arnold Seligman, Rey and Company, and was offered to Cleveland in 1942, where it was identified as belonging to the predella of an altarpiece, of which four other panels were already known.

The last decade of Milliken's tenure as director saw a steady increase in acquisitions not only in the field of Western Medieval art, but also in Early Christian and Byzantine art. Interest in the arts and culture of the Byzantine Empire had grown considerably among American scholars, museum curators, and private collectors in the 1930s, following a major exhibition in Paris in 1931 and the founding of the Byzantine Institute of America by Thomas Whittemore. Later in the 1930s and 1940s, Whittemore restored the mosaics of Emperor Justinian's church of Hagia Sophia as well as the mosaic and fresco cycles of the late Byzantine monastery of Christ of the Chora (Kariye Camii) in Istanbul (formerly Constantinople).[21] In 1950 a fine single leaf excised from a Middle Byzantine psalter and New Testament on Mount Athos (Pantokrator 49) (no. 24) joined the museum's Byzantine gospel book and evangelist portraits acquired earlier through the New York dealer Dikran Kelekian. As Milliken noted, "Fine Byzantine objects had seemed to have been off the market, or at least they had not gravitated to Cleveland. Yet, fine objects in one field have an inevitable attraction for others in the same field."[22] Indeed, later the same year the museum acquired an important ecclesiastical silver treasure originally made for the church of St. Sergios in the Syrian village of Beth Misona (no. 9). This acquisition was followed in 1951 with an important Early Byzantine ivory *Pyxis* (1951.114) and a Byzantine steatite icon of the Virgin Hodegetria (no. 20), which was later identified as having formed part of the cathedral treasury of Aachen in Germany, where it had been revered at least since the 17th century as one of the pendants found around the neck of Charlemagne when his tomb was opened by Emperor Otto III in 1000. Empress Josephine, wife of Napoleon Bonaparte, received it as a gift of Bishop Marc-Antoine Bartolet of Aachen, and it remained in the possession of her family until becoming part of the Daguerre Collection in Paris; the Paris dealer César de Hauke then owned it and offered it to Cleveland. Later in the 1950s, Milliken was able to add other significant pieces to the collection of Early Byzantine art, among them an exceptional treasure of domestic silver (no. 6) as well as precious phylacteries, gold necklaces, and other objects of personal adornment (nos. 14, 15).

Milliken's interest in Byzantine art grew during the 1940s and 1950s, but he did not neglect Western Medieval art. Under his supervision, Henry S. Francis, the museum's curator of paintings, acquired a number of significant works for the collection, among them the mid 15th-century Schlägl altarpiece (no. 88) and the beautiful *Annunciation* (no. 69) from the collection of Arthur Sachs, both bought with funds left to the museum exclusively for the acquisition of paintings by Julia Morgan Marlatt in memory of her late husband, William H. Marlatt, in 1939.

A Legacy Continued

"One of the happiest things for a curator is to see his interests go on."[23] In 1958 Milliken greeted the arrival of William D. Wixom, his successor as the museum's curator of decorative arts (under director Sherman E. Lee), with those words. Indeed, Wixom continued his predecessor's legacy both in terms of his wide range of interests

St. Stephen, 1508–10. Tilman Riemenschneider (German, about 1460–1531). Polychromed and gilded lindenwood, 93.5 x 35 x 23.5 cm. Leonard C. Hanna Jr. Fund 1959.43.

and in the consistently high quality of his acquisitions. Born in Philadelphia and educated at Haverford College and New York University's Institute of Fine Arts, Wixom was hired as assistant curator of decorative arts in 1958, promoted to associate and then full curator, and eventually made curator of medieval and Renaissance decorative arts. During his 20-year tenure, which ended when he accepted the position of chairman of the Department of Medieval Art and the Cloisters at the Metropolitan Museum of Art in 1979, he was responsible not only for a number of special exhibitions, including *Gothic Art 1360–1440, Treasures from Medieval France,* and *Renaissance Bronzes from Ohio Collections,* but also for the acquisition of some of the museum's most treasured masterpieces. One of his many important purchases, Riemenschneider's statues of saints Lawrence (no. 91) and Stephen, was made early on in his career. In fact, they became the subject of Wixom's dissertation under Harry Bober at the Institute of Fine Arts in 1963.[24] They were followed in short succession by a number of equally important works: *The Gotha Missal* (no. 78), *The Hours of Queen Isabella the Catholic* (no. 83), and *The Hours of Charles the Noble* (no. 79), thus continuing the tradition of collecting fine illuminated manuscripts and single leaves on the highest level. Other important purchases followed, most notably that of the *Jonah Marbles* (no. 1) in 1965, which added significantly to the museum's holdings in the field of Early Christian art. Apart from a number of smaller Byzantine works acquired during Wixom's tenure, one later purchase must be singled out for its exquisite craftsmanship: the fragment of a Middle Byzantine silver processional cross (no. 22) reportedly commissioned by a monk and presbyter called Nicholas and dedicated to St. Sergios.

Notable acquisitions in the realm of Early Western Medieval art included the ivory plaque *Christ's Mission to the Apostles* (no. 41), a work that can be attributed to an ivory workshop active in Milan during the reign of Emperor Otto the Great, and another ivory plaque, *Journey to Bethlehem* (no. 42), made by a workshop located in or around Amalfi in Southern Italy.

While many areas of the Cleveland museum's collection of Early Christian, Byzantine, and Western Medieval art benefited from Wixom's expertise and connoisseurship, his contribution was particularly strong in the fields of Gothic sculpture and decorative arts, an area that grew steadily in quality and number under his watchful eye (nos. 56, 61, 62, 63, 75, 77).

Wixom's departure left a void, but the museum quickly appointed Philippe Verdier as consulting curator of Early Western art in July 1979. A highly respected French-born medieval art historian, Verdier had held various academic and curatorial positions in the

Crucifix with Scenes of the Passion, 1230–40. Italian, Pisa. Tempera and oil with gold on panel, 186.6 x 160.7 x 12.7 cm.
Leonard C. Hanna Jr. Fund 1995.5.

United States since the 1950s. It was at his recommendation that the museum acquired the corpus of a 12th-century French crucifix (no. 57), which stands out among works of the period for its fine carving and the serenity of Christ's facial features. Verdier assumed the position of consultant curator at the Menil Foundation in Houston in 1980, but he was succeeded during the same year by Patrick de Winter, who in his six-year tenure added a number of significant works to the museum's distinguished collection of illuminated manuscripts and objets d'art (nos. 64, 65). The curatorial position in the Department of Early Western Art remained vacant from 1986 until the mid 1990s, but the German art historian Renate Eikelmann conducted research on the collection from 1988 to 1991 in order to write a catalogue, appointed by the museum's fourth director, Evan H. Turner. It was not until Robert P. Bergman, a renowned specialist in the field of Early Christian and Medieval art, assumed the directorship in 1993 that the fortunes of the Department of Western Art, as it was then called, once again changed. Guided by his leadership, the museum was able to acquire the exquisite octagonal pendant and spacers associated with Emperor Constantine the Great and his family (no. 4) as well as an important painted cross from Pisa. Since 1996, Stephen N. Fliegel has been serving the Department of Medieval Art in a curatorial position, further adding to the museum's holdings a number of precious objects such as the beautifully preserved Visigothic *Belt Buckle* (no. 33), an important manuscript leaf attributed to Simon Marmion (no. 82), and, most recently, the so-called Caporali Missal (no. 106).[25] His collection catalogues of the museum's arms and armor and the Jeanne Miles Blackburn collection of manuscript illuminations, and the exhibition catalogue *Art from the Court of Burgundy* continue a long tradition of scholarly publications in medieval art, setting a high standard for future explorations of the museum's holdings in this field.[26]

With its endowment in 2004 of a chaired curatorial position in medieval art, named for Robert P. Bergman, the Cleveland Museum of Art has renewed its commitment to the collection and study of medieval art and charted a course for the future. Sharing its medieval masterpieces and their stories with audiences around the world is part of this commitment and an invitation for everyone to see and explore the beauty, significance, and meaning of the museum's most sacred gifts and worldly treasures.

Holger A. Klein
Robert P. Bergman Curator of Medieval Art

Notes

1. Cleveland 1986, 24 n. 2.

2. For the history of the Cleveland Museum of Art and its collection, see Cleveland 1991 and Leedy 1991.

3. William M. Milliken, *The Cleveland Museum of Art Collections* (unpublished), 15.

4. See Cleveland 1991, 21 and 25 n. 11.

5. Milliken, *Cleveland Museum Collections,* 54.

6. For a summary account of the modern history of the Guelph Treasure, see De Winter 1985B, 128–37; Dietrich Kötzsche, "Der Welfenschatz," in Braunschweig 1995, vol. 2, 511–28.

7. Milliken, *Cleveland Museum Collections,* 73.

8. Milliken 1930, 163–77. The sixth object, a portable altar with Byzantine frame (now Staatliche Museen Preußischer Kulturbesitz, Kunstgewerbemuseum, Berlin, W4), was returned to the dealers in 1931 as a partial payment for the altar and cross of Countess Gertrude.

9. Wittke 1966, 85; Milliken, *Cleveland Museum Collections,* 89, cites 89,000 visitors.

10. Wittke 1966, 85.

11. Milliken had originally hoped to retire after fulfilling 40 years of service at the museum. See Milliken 1975, 185–86.

12. Milliken later commented: "The purchase funds of the Museum were small except for the Wade Fund. The income of that fund had to cover so many fields, and for the moment, Mr. Wade desired that it be used in areas other than painting. One thing however did seem possible, and that was the purchase of Illuminated Miniatures. With these one could savor whole sections of European pictorial art which could not by any possibility be touched in any other way. Superlative things of Cleveland quality could be secured at modest prices." See Milliken, *Cleveland Museum Collections,* 27.

13. The Friends of the Cleveland Museum of Art was established in 1926 "to aid in the development of the collection by augmenting the purchasing funds of the Museum." Chaired by John L. Severance and Leonard C. Hanna, the group existed for ten years. The last painting acquired with its funds was the panel of the Master of Heiligenkreuz. For further information, see *CMA Bulletin* 14 (1927), 6–7; Cleveland 1936, 82, no. 198; Cleveland 1991, 62–63.

14. For the Schuster Collection, see Böhler 1938 and Wilm 1937.

15. Milliken, *Cleveland Museum Collections,* 126.

16. On Clarence Mackay and the sale of his art collection, see Seligman 1961, 214–17.

17. Milliken, *Cleveland Museum Collections,* 134.

18. Ibid., 135.

19. Ibid., 137.

20. Ibid., 165.

21. On the Paris exhibition, see Paris 1931. On Thomas Whittemore and the Byzantine Institute of America, see N. Teteriatnikov, "The Byzantine Institute and Its Role in the Conservation of the Kariye Camii," in New York 2004B, 43–60. On the growing interest in Byzantine art among private collectors, see R. S. Nelson, "Private Passions Made Public: The Beginnings of the Bliss Collection," in Athens 2005, 39–51.

22. Milliken, *Cleveland Museum Collections,* 199.

23. Ibid., 29.

24. Wixom 1963D.

25. Stephen Fliegel served the department as a curatorial assistant from 1982 to 1995. In this position he assumed responsibility for the care of the medieval collection during the early to mid 1990s.

26. Fliegel 1998; Cleveland 1999; Dijon/Cleveland 2004.

CATALOGUE

The advent, rise, and spread of Christianity across the vast territory of the Late Roman Empire was a phenomenon that, by the beginning of the third century, started to have a noticeable impact on Roman life, society, and culture. Having emerged in response to the life, teachings, and death of Jesus Christ in Roman-occupied Palestine around 30 AD, Christianity, like other Eastern religions and mystery cults, was able to take advantage of the empire's well-developed infrastructure and religious pluralism to attract a great number of followers not only in the cities of Syria-Palestine and Asia Minor, but also further west in Greece, Italy, and beyond. Despite repeated persecution during the first centuries of its existence, the success of the new religion can be measured by the steady rise of its urban membership, the development of a highly efficient administrative structure and ecclesiastical hierarchy, and, finally, its growing appeal among the wealthier members of Roman society. By the middle of the third century Christian communities included senators, high-ranking court officials, and even members of the imperial household.

The popularity of the new religion among converts with fully Romanized cultural and religious backgrounds had, by the beginning of the third century, already resulted in a change of attitude by some theologians toward the visual arts. While some early Christian writers such as Tertullian of Carthage spoke out categorically against any use of images in order to prevent idolatrous behavior, others such as Clemens of Alexandria began to acknowledge the reality of Christians living in a world of images and openly reflected upon the appropriateness of the Christian use of symbols such as anchors, boats, doves, or fish on seal rings, which were interpreted by the faithful in decidedly Christian terms. The image of the sheepbearer, for instance, which had long been established in Roman art as an idyllic representation of bucolic life, was interpreted in terms of the parable of the Good Shepherd (Luke 15:3–6) and Christ sacrificing his life for that of his flock (John 10:11–15).[1] The underground cemeteries in Rome, the so-called catacombs, provide ample evidence for the use of such images in the context of Christian burials. Like their non-Christian neighbors, wealthy Christians of the early third century began to decorate their *cubiculae* (burial chambers) with painted images that expressed the deceased's hope for salvation and alluded to a peaceful afterlife. In some cubiculae less specifically Christian images such as that of the sheepbearer are joined by early images of the Old Testament stories of Jonah (see no. 1), Daniel (see no.

58), or the Three Hebrews in the Fiery Furnace, leaving no doubt about the religious affiliation of the deceased and the Christian meaning of the images depicted.

Early evidence for the Christian use of images depicting biblical events, however, is not limited to paintings in the Roman catacombs. Around the middle of the third century, the Christian community at Dura Europos, a city located in Syria on the eastern fringes of the Roman world, decorated the baptistery of the house in which they gathered with frescoes depicting Old Testament events such as the Fall of Adam and Eve, and miracle scenes associated with the life and ministry of Jesus. During the second half of the third century, Christian iconographic themes such as the story of Jonah also begin to appear on marble sarcophagi, and in the unique case of the Jonah Marbles (see no. 1) as an independent statuary group, thus revealing the refined taste of members of a distinct segment of the Roman upper class who had adopted the Christian faith without giving up their identity and traditions.

Following a new wave of persecution under Emperor Diocletian and Galerius, his co-emperor, between 303 and 305, the fortunes of the young religion took an unforeseen turn in 312, when Emperor Constantine (see. no. 4) defeated his rival Maxentius in the battle at Saxa Rubra, better known as the Battle of Milvian Bridge, and attributed his victory to the Christian God. Constantine's interest in the Christian faith was sparked, at least in part, by his mother, Helena, who was rumored to have become a follower of the new religion long before her son discovered its potential usefulness for his political aims. Over the next two decades Constantine's favorable disposition toward Christianity took on a variety of forms, ranging from the edict of toleration issued in Milan in 313 to imperial support for a number of prestigious ecclesiastical building projects such as the Lateran Basilica and St. Peter's in Rome, the Church of the Nativity in Bethlehem, and the Church of the Holy Sepulcher in Jerusalem (see no. 11). Among the emperor's foundations, the churches in the Holy Land soon emerged as major destinations for Christian pilgrims from all over the Roman world, keen to visit the sites of Christ's suffering and resurrection from places as far away as northern Italy and western France. Unfortunately, Constantine's Church of the Holy Sepulcher no longer exists. It was, as so many of his foundations, rebuilt time and again in later centuries. What remains, however, is a letter in which Constantine informs Bishop Macarius of Jerusalem about his plans for the building: "Not only shall this basilica be the finest in the world, but everything else, too, shall be of such quality that all the most beautiful buildings of every city may be surpassed by it . . . for it is fitting that the most wondrous place in the world should be worthily adorned."[2] While Christianity was still only one of many religions practiced within the boundaries of the Late Roman Empire, the fact that it had gained imperial favor and public support resulted in a surge in membership, conversions, and public building projects all across the empire. Constantine's decision in 324 to move the empire's capital from Rome to Byzantion (Byzantium)— a city located on the Bosphorus, the strait that connects the Black Sea and the Sea of Marmara—and rename it Constantinoupolis (City of Constantine) laid the foundation for the emergence of a Christian Roman Empire that flourished for more than a thousand years. In 391, some 60 years after Constantinople was established on 11 May 330, legislation was passed that prohibited all pagan cult practices, thus making Christianity the official religion of the Roman state.

The triumph of Christianity had a deep impact on the development and dissemination of Christian art during the fourth and fifth centuries. Painted funeral chambers, marble sarcophagi, and luxury objects of personal use and adornment have survived in sufficient numbers to attest to the continuities and changes in the tastes and beliefs of the Christianized empire's social and political elite. By the sixth century, Christian symbols, narrative cycles of Old and New Testament stories, and iconic representations of Christ, the Virgin, and saints (see nos. 18–21) formed an established feature of the visual and material culture of the Late Roman Empire, now commonly referred to as the Byzantine Empire after the city that became Constantine's new capital. The proliferation of Christian religious imagery, both in the public and private sphere, and the increase of superstitious devotional practices during the sixth and seventh centuries no doubt contributed to an unprecedented outbreak of iconoclasm in the Byzantine Empire, a period of intense political and theological debate over the justification for and use of religious images that lasted for more than a hundred years (from 726 to 843) and ultimately resulted in the triumph of the iconophile (icon friendly) faction over those who had promoted a more spiritual, imageless version of Christianity.

The victory of the orthodox, or icon-friendly, cause resulted not only in a codification of the proper use of religious images, but also in a golden age of Byzantine art and court culture that can best be measured in the exquisite and technically refined icons produced during this period in all sizes and media: painting, ivory carving (see no. 19), mosaic, textile (see no. 18), and precious metalwork. Reigning as Christ's representative on earth, the Byzantine emperor considered himself the only legitimate heir of the

Roman Empire and ruler of the Christian world, an attitude that was finally shattered when Crusader forces captured Constantinople in 1204 and established it as the center of a Latin empire that lasted about two generations. A final flowering of Byzantine art began in 1261 when Constantinople was recaptured by Emperor Michael VIII of the Palaiologos family, whose immediate successors started to rebuild the empire and its capital despite the loss of much of its former territory and most of its sacred treasures, among them the relics of Christ's Passion, which had been brought to Paris and deposited at the Sainte-Chapelle during the Latin occupation. After sustaining many assaults by the Ottoman Turks, Constantinople was finally conquered on 29 May 1453, and the empire that had been founded by Constantine the Great ceased to exist. What remains of it is the culture of icons that still characterizes the world of Orthodox Christianity and many artifacts, ecclesiastical and secular, of utmost beauty and refinement. HAK

1. All biblical references are based on the Douay-Rheims version (Baltimore, 1899), as reproduced by Tann Books and Publishers, Inc.

2. Translation of Eusebius, *Life of Constantine,* after Cameron/Hall 1999, 134–35.

The Jonah Marbles

ABOUT AD 280–90; LATE ROMAN, ASIA MINOR?

MARBLE

The story of the Old Testament prophet Jonah was one of the most popular subjects in Christian art during the third and fourth centuries. Cast into the sea from a ship and swallowed by a sea monster after disobeying the Lord's command to proclaim judgment to Nineveh, Jonah spent three days praying in the stomach of the beast before being cast ashore again. When asked a second time, Jonah obeyed the Lord and fulfilled his mission. However, Jonah became displeased when the Lord decided to spare the repentant city. Having pleaded for Nineveh's destruction, Jonah went outside the city to await its destiny. He laid down to rest in the shadow of a large gourd that grew above him on a vine. But the Lord infected the gourd with a worm and it wasted away, exposing the prophet to the burning sun. When Jonah started to lament the withering of the gourd, the Lord rebuked him for his grief over the gourd while asking for the destruction of the mighty city of Nineveh and its inhabitants.

Acquired by the Cleveland Museum of Art in 1965, this sculptural ensemble, commonly known

as the Jonah Marbles, depicts the story of the prophet in four distinct scenes: Jonah being swallowed and then cast up by the sea monster; Jonah praying or pleading with the Lord; and Jonah resting under a gourd vine. Allegedly found together with a statuette of the Good Shepherd (opposite page, far right) and three pairs of portrait busts of an aristocratic Roman couple (see no. 2), the group is unique among Late Antique "mythological" sculpture not only because of its Christian subject matter, but also because it can be dated fairly accurately based on the style and coiffure of the accompanying portrait busts. As such, the Jonah Marbles are a rare testimony of the refined taste and religious leanings of a growing segment of the Roman upper class at the end of the third century.

While the location and the circumstances of the ensemble's discovery remain elusive, the entire group was reportedly buried in a large *pithos* (jar) and unearthed together. This claim is supported by the fact that all the sculptures share certain stylistic characteristics, are carved from the same highly crystalline white marble, and show a yellowish-brown patina with incrustations. Technical analysis has helped to identify the Roman imperial quarries at Dokimeion in ancient Phrygia (near the modern Turkish city of Afyon) as the source for the marble. Given the wide distribution of marble sculptures throughout the Mediterranean, it is difficult to determine, however, whether the workshop responsible for the ensemble was located in this region of Asia Minor or elsewhere. The same is true

for the identity of the Roman aristocratic couple whose likenesses have been preserved with the Good Shepherd and Jonah Marbles. While we cannot say who they were and where they lived, their sculptural commission betrays their indebtedness to both the cultural traditions of the Roman world and the religious imagery of the new faith.

For Christians of the third and fourth century, the story of Jonah held a much deeper significance than the Old Testament narrative may suggest: it was seen as an allegory of Christ's death and resurrection (Matt. 12:38–40) and thus understood as a story of hope, salvation, and the redemptive power of prayer and repentance. It is not surprising, therefore, that the story of Jonah was often chosen to decorate the walls and ceilings of Christian burial chambers in the Roman catacombs or the sculpted fronts and sides of marble sarcophagi. That the statuettes in Cleveland were meant to serve a similar decorative function in a funereal context—a burial chamber, family mausoleum, or grave garden—has often been suggested. However, they may likewise have been intended to decorate the house or garden of an affluent Christian family, thus replacing the gods and heroes of classical mythology with their Old and New Testament counterparts. HAK

John L. Severance Fund 1965.237–240

DIMENSIONS: Jonah Swallowed, 50.4 x 15.5 x 26.9 cm; Jonah Cast Up, 41.5 x 36 x 18.5 cm; Jonah under the Gourd Tree, 32.3 x 46.3 x 18 cm; Jonah Praying, 47.5 x 14.8 x 20.3 cm

BIBLIOGRAPHY: Hannestad 2007, 284–87; Bergmann 1999, 23, 59; Provoost 1994, 187–201; Kitzinger 1993, 2: 117–39; New York 1979, 406–11, no. 364–68; Wixom 1967, 67–68.

38

2

Pair of Portrait Busts of an Aristocratic Couple

ABOUT 280–90; LATE ROMAN, ASIA MINOR?

MARBLE

These two marble portrait busts of an aristocratic Roman couple are part of a set of three closely related pairs that were acquired with the so-called Jonah Marbles (see no. 1) and a statuette of the Good Shepherd (see p. 37, far right). Reports that the busts and statuettes were found together and may thus be considered a sculptural ensemble are supported by the fact that all 11 figures are carved from the same fine-grained marble and have the same yellowish-brown patina with incrustations. Each bust is made from a single block of marble, hollowed out on either side of a central supporting stem in the back, and set on a circular base with a blank index tablet. Given the close physiognomic similarities among the three male and female portraits, it seems highly likely that the pairs represent the same individuals, presumably a husband and his wife.

While the Cleveland busts are unique in representing a single Roman couple three times with only minor variations in costume, multiple statues of the same private individual are known to have existed in Roman art. What distinguishes the Cleveland busts from other multiples is the fact that the variations in dress and accessories seem too insignificant to characterize different aspects of the couple's public and private persona. Consequently, their original display context and intended function remain a mystery. While a separate presentation of each pair in similar overall settings seems more likely than a display of all three pairs in a private portrait gallery, it is also possible that they were not meant to be displayed together at all, but intended for distribution among members of the same family. The alleged discovery of the portrait busts with the Jonah Marbles and the Good Shepherd complicates matters further as it raises the question of whether the statuettes and portraits together formed part of a funereal or domestic context or whether their joint survival indicates something else. It has been suggested, for instance, that the figures survived as an ensemble because they were stored together by a workshop or a patron before they could be distributed. Given the limited information available about the circumstances of the ensemble's discovery, however, other scenarios are equally likely. HAK

John L. Severance Fund 1965.246 (woman), 1965.245 (man)

DIMENSIONS: 33.2 x 20 x 14 cm, 35.2 x 21.5 x 12 cm

BIBLIOGRAPHY: Hannestad 2007, 284–87; NewYork 2006B, 124–27, no. 47–52; Dahmen 2001, 183–84, no. 148–53; Alföldi-Rosenbaum 1996, 105–16; Kitzinger 1993, 2: 17–39; NewYork 1979, 406–11, no. 362–63; İnan/Alföldi-Rosenbaum 1979, 323–27, no. 320–25; Bergmann 1977, 188–90; Wixom 1967, 67–68.

Tapestry: Fragment with Satyr and Maenad

4TH CENTURY; LATE ROMAN, EGYPT

PLAIN WEAVE WITH INWOVEN TAPESTRY WEAVE; DYED WOOL AND UNDYED LINEN

This tapestry fragment from Egypt originally formed part of a much larger luxurious tapestry hanging with representations of Dionysos (the Greek god of wine, mystic ecstasy, and fertility) and members of his *thiasos* (entourage). At least one, perhaps even two other fragments of the same tapestry are now preserved in the Museum of Fine Arts, Boston (1973.290) and the Abegg-Stiftung in Riggisberg, Switzerland.

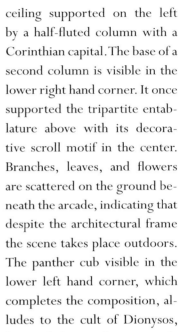

In contrast to the fragment in Boston, which represents Dionysos with a cornucopia (inset), and the one in Riggisberg, which shows one of the god's female followers (a maenad playing the kithara), the Cleveland tapestry has a pair of Dionysiac revelers with wreaths in their hair and bright haloes: a satyr, identified by his greenish faun-skin costume as well as an inscription; and a dancing maenad at his side. Except for an orange mantle suspended behind her back, a golden necklace with a green pendant, and bracelets around her wrists, upper arms, and ankles, the maenad is entirely nude. While she is moving away from the satyr in a pose that suggests dance, the satyr holds her back by the wrist and draws her face closer to his by touching the nape of her neck. Both figures are placed underneath a vaulted arch with a coffered ceiling supported on the left by a half-fluted column with a Corinthian capital. The base of a second column is visible in the lower right hand corner. It once supported the tripartite entablature above with its decorative scroll motif in the center. Branches, leaves, and flowers are scattered on the ground beneath the arcade, indicating that despite the architectural frame the scene takes place outdoors. The panther cub visible in the lower left hand corner, which completes the composition, alludes to the cult of Dionysos, whose entourage often includes panthers, animals sacred to the god.

Whether this costly tapestry was commissioned for use in a cult setting or the home of an affluent devotee of Dionysos in Late Roman Egypt remains uncertain, but it was likely made before the end of the fourth century, when the cult of the god still flourished and its mysteries were celebrated publicly in the region. HAK

Purchase from the J. H. Wade Fund 1975.6

DIMENSIONS: 139 x 86.4 cm

INSCRIBED: CATYPOC (Satyr)

BIBLIOGRAPHY: Rutschowscaya 1990, 82–87; New York 1979, 144–46, no. 124; Shepherd 1976, 307–13; *CMA Bulletin* 63 (1976): 70, no. 149. For the fragment in Boston, see Arensberg 1977, 4–25; for the fragment in Riggisberg, see Schrenk 2004, 37–39, no. 3.

Octagonal Pendant and Two Spacers

This octagonal pendant, made of sheet gold and decorated with pierced openwork known as *opus interrasile,* is one of the finest works of gold jewelry to survive from late antiquity. It once formed the centerpiece of a sumptuous gold necklace that originally consisted of five closely related pendants—one octagonal, two round, and two hex-agonal in shape—and at least four column-shaped spacers. The necklace was probably an imperial gift for a high-ranking court official or member of the imperial family. Except for a missing chain and possibly two spacers, all other elements of this necklace seem to have survived and are now preserved in various public and private collections.

Like the other surviving coin mounts, the Cleveland pendant is set with a rare double solidus of Constantine the Great (r. 306–37). The first Christian emperor, he founded Constantinople (modern Istanbul), the Roman Empire's new capital on the Bosphorus, which connects the Black Sea with the Sea of Marmara. Constantine appears in left profile on the coin's obverse, or front. Wearing a cuirass (body armor) and a paludamentum (military cloak), the crowned emperor is shown holding a globe in his left hand and raising his right in salutation. The reverse shows the facing busts of his sons Crispus and Constantine II, each wearing consular garments and holding a globe and eagle-tipped scepter. The encircling inscription indicates that the coin was struck in 324 in the imperial mint of Nicomedia (modern Izmit in Turkey) to commemorate the third consulship of the two Caesars.

Held in place by a circular collar and set in an elaborate octagonal frame, the central coin is surrounded by eight small medallions with exquisitely executed busts of alternating male and female figures in high relief. While some of these busts have been identified as mythological figures, the overall iconographic program of the five pendants and the necklace remains elusive. The same is true for the necklace's place and date of manufacture. Since the central coins of all five pendants can be dated between 321 and 324, it has been suggested that the necklace was made between 324 and 326, the year Crispus fell into disfavor with his father—he allegedly became involved with his stepmother, Fausta—and was executed by Constantine's order. It has likewise been argued that the style of the busts may indicate a date during the reign of Theodosius I (379–95), a time that saw the revival of a distinctly classicizing style in imperial sculpture and luxury arts. The fact, however, that the coins in all five pendants were struck to commemorate the joint consulships of Constantine's sons seems to weigh strongly in favor of the earlier date. If this assumption is correct, the imperial residences at Sirmium (modern Sremska Mitrovica in Serbia) and Nicomedia, where the double solidi were struck, are the most likely places for the necklace's manufacture. HAK

Leonard C. Hanna Jr. Fund 1994.98.1–3

DIMENSIONS: 9.7 x 9.4 cm (pendant), about 6.5 x 1.9 cm (spacers)

INSCRIPTIONS: obverse: D[ominus] N[oster] CONSTANTINVS MAX[imus] AVG[ustus] (Our Lord Constantine the Great, Augustus); reverse: CRISPVS ET CONSTANTINVS NOBB [nobilissimi] CAESS [caesares] COSS [consules] III (Crispus and Constantinus, the most noble Caesars and three-time consuls); in the exergue: SMN (Sacra Moneta Nicomediae)

BIBLIOGRAPHY: Yeroulanou 1999, 36, 225, no. 120; Deppert-Lippitz 1996, 30–71. For related objects in general, see Christie's 1970, lots 197–202. For British Museum objects, see London 1994, 26–27, no. 2; Buckton 1983, 15–19; and Frankfurt 1983, 424–25, no. 38. For Dumbarton Oaks objects, see Ross 2005, 141–59, nos. 180–81; Bruhn 1993, 16–22; and New York 1979, 304, no. 276. For Musée du Louvre objects, see Duval 1973, 367–74.

5

Spoon: St. Paul as an Athlete

ABOUT 350–400; LATE ROMAN, PERHAPS SYRIA

SILVER, GILDED SILVER, AND NIELLO

Silver spoons with swan neck handles were popular in both the eastern and western parts of the Late Roman Empire as various fourth- and early fifth-century treasure hoards from Scotland (Traprain Law), England (Canterbury), and Switzerland (Kaiseraugst) attest. Locating the workshops responsible for their execution with any certainty is thus difficult. Such spoons could have been manufactured and decorated in one of the major centers of the empire such as Rome or Constantinople and exported to the provinces, or manufactured and decorated locally in the provincial capitals of Antioch, Trier, and Milan, for instance, or in any other imperial city with sufficient means and artistic talent.

This elegant spoon formed part of a larger silver treasure discovered in northern Syria in the early 1960s. The treasure, which may have been the fine tableware of a well-to-do Roman family residing near Antioch in Syria before being buried for safekeeping, originally included six objects, all preserved in various public and private collections: a silver plate decorated with a lion hunt; three spoons; a bowl with a beaded brim; and a hunting horn. Unlike any spoon in this or other Late Roman silver treasures, the one in Cleveland is decorated with a nude figure of a victorious athlete, characterized as such by a well-established iconography showing him holding a palm branch in his left hand and reaching with his right for a floral crown on his head.

The most intriguing, unusual decorative aspect of the spoon, however, is a Latin inscription in niello identifying the figure as "Paulus." While no other object from the treasure holds any Christian significance, it is tempting to interpret the juxtaposition of the name with a classical representation of an athlete as a subtle allusion to a passage in St. Paul's first letter to the Corinthians (1 Cor. 9:24–27), in which the apostle characterizes himself as an athlete of Christ and asks: "Know you not that they that run in the race, all run indeed, but one receiveth the prize? So run that you may obtain. And every one that striveth for the mastery, refraineth himself from all things: and they indeed that they may receive a corruptible crown; but we an incorruptible one." While such a reading may tell us something about the religious affiliation of the object's owner, it does not imply a liturgical use. Like the other silver objects in the hoard, the spoon likely served in a purely secular context—as an object for display and fine dining. HAK

John L. Severance Fund 1964.39

DIMENSIONS: 12.2 x 5.6 cm

INSCRIBED: PAVLVS

BIBLIOGRAPHY: Rumscheid 2000, 65, 170, no. 118; New York 1979, 336–37, no. 316; Engemann 1972, 170–71; Wixom 1970B, 141–48; Ross 1967–68, 59–61. For related objects from the same treasure, see Gonosovà/Kondoleon 1994, 180–83, no. 58 (Virginia Museum of Fine Arts), and Dodd 1973, 31–32, no. 9–10 (Abegg-Stiftung).

6

Lamp and Stand

LATE 4TH CENTURY; EARLY BYZANTINE, SYRIA
SILVER

A great number of oil lamps of various shapes and sizes have survived from the Late Roman and Early Byzantine periods, some made with chains for suspension (see no. 7), others with a stand for greater flexibility of placement. While the majority were produced in clay or bronze to serve a basic utilitarian function, a few examples such as this one have survived in silver, reflecting their owners' wealth and original use in either an upper-class home or a richly endowed ecclesiastical foundation.

The most striking feature of this lamp, which is characterized by the simple elegance of its design, is probably the handle, which takes the form of the head and neck of a horse. Visually separated from the lamp's smooth body by a profiled collar, the neck curves upward over the round filling hole with the head facing toward the spout. The four-sided spike that emerges from the center of the fluted reservoir is hollow and allows for a secure placement of the lamp on its stand. It also creates the illusion that the spike of the stand protrudes right through the center of the lamp. With its elegant tripod base, baluster shaft encircled by five loose rings, and deep beaded pan, all cast individually, the stand is an excellent example of Early Byzantine craftsmanship.

The silver lamp and its stand are said to form part of a silver treasure allegedly found near the ancient city of Laodicea (modern Latakia) in northern Syria. Nine other objects from the same treasure were also acquired by the Cleveland Museum of Art. They include a large bowl with a beaded brim (1954.259); two smaller bowls, one with a fluted exterior (1956.29), the other with an ornamental medallion in its center (1956.30); a mirror (1956.31); a spouted pitcher (1956.32); a ewer (1956.33); a ladle (1956.34); and two spoons (1956.35–36). Since all objects in this treasure are secular in nature, one may assume they formed part of the property of a wealthy individual or family and were buried for safekeeping in a time of crisis. HAK

Purchase from the J. H. Wade Fund 1954.597.a–b

DIMENSIONS: 9.2 x 16 x 7 cm (lamp), 42.6 x 16 x 16 (stand)

BIBLIOGRAPHY: Ball 1980, 212; Milliken 1958, 35–41. For other objects in the same treasure, see Worcester 2000, 191, no. 76; Strong 1966, 201, 203; Downey 1963, 214.

7

Lamp with Griffin-head Handle

4TH–5TH CENTURY; EARLY BYZANTINE

BRONZE

Bronze oil lamps with griffin-head handles and Christian symbolic decoration are common from the fourth through the sixth century and have been found all over the Mediterranean world in considerable numbers. The continuing popularity of griffins, ancient mythological creatures with the body of a lion and head and wings of an eagle, is probably rooted in their traditional role as powerful guardian figures and protectors. On this Early Byzantine bronze lamp, the griffin seems to have functioned similarly as a guardian of the flame and a keeper of the light.

Like many griffin-head lamps, this elegant example features hooks with chains for suspension as well as a circular base that serves as a stand. While cast in one piece, the lamp has a distinct tripartite design that highlights its main functional elements: a tubular spout with a scalloped octagonal lip that surrounds the hole for the wick; a bulbous body with a filling hole for the oil on top; and the griffin-head handle with its long curved neck. Visually, these elements are joined together by two neck rings and collars of upturned leaves that nestle against the lamp's body from both sides. The griffin's neck, with its spiked mane, grows from a similar collar of slightly smaller leaves, developing into a fierce-looking head with a pointed beard, sharp beak, and staring eyes. A *staurogram* emerges from between the griffin's pitched ears. This early Christian symbol that combines the Greek letters T (tau) and P (rho) alludes to the Crucifixion of Christ. Two similar staurograms in relief decorate the lamp's body on both sides. The Greek letters α (alpha) and ω (omega) are shown hanging from their horizontal bars in allusion to the apocalyptic vision of Christ as "Alpha and Omega, the first and the last, the beginning and the end" (Apocalypse 22:13).

While the simultaneous presence of ancient mythological imagery and Christian symbols has sometimes been interpreted in religious terms as a Christianization of pagan themes and emblems, the combination of different protective devices may rather be considered an effort to enhance the efficacy of utilitarian objects through an accumulation of both pagan and Christian apotropaic symbols. HAK

Gift of Mrs. Chester D. Tripp in honor of William Mathewson Milliken on his 85th year 1974.77

DIMENSIONS: 14.7 x 22.6 x 7 cm

BIBLIOGRAPHY: *CMA Bulletin* 62 (1975): 98, no. 33; *CMA Bulletin* 61 (1974): 382. For similar objects in other collections, see Munich 2004, 228–29, no. 340; Paderborn 2001, 211–12, no. II.6; Munich 1998, 90–91, no. 87; Gonosovà/Kondoleon 1994, 250–51, no. 85; Ross 1962, 31–32, no. 30; Baltimore 1947, 62, no. 238–39.

Floor Mosaic: Fragment with Adam and Eve

LATE 5TH OR EARLY 6TH CENTURY; EARLY BYZANTINE, NORTHERN SYRIA
MARBLE AND STONE TESSERAE

Once forming part of a much larger mosaic that decorated the floor of an Early Byzantine church in northern Syria, this mosaic panel represents the Fall of Adam and Eve. Set in front of a light background made of cream-colored tesserae, Adam and Eve are depicted sharing the forbidden fruit while covering their pudenda with large leaves. Branches of the forbidden tree are still partly visible on the right; the small patch of grass with blooming flowers below indicates that the scene is set in paradise. The Greek inscription at the top of the panel alludes to the passage describing the Fall in the book of Genesis (3:7–8) and highlights the two moments that are simultaneously depicted here.

Despite a certain awkwardness in the rendering of the human body and its proportions, the naïve beauty of the figures' faces, with their large eyes, softly modeled cheeks, and small mouths, reveals a high degree of accomplishment on the part of the artist, whose composition successfully reinforces the consequences of the couple's disobedience. As Eve is handing the fruit to Adam with her right hand, her breasts are left exposed to the viewer, stressing both her nakedness and the fruitlessness of her attempts to conceal it.

The provenance of this and other related panels acquired by the Minneapolis Institute of Arts and Cleveland (inset) in the late 1960s unfortunately cannot be determined with certainty. All allegedly came from the same source, a town near Antioch on the Orontes (modern Antakya in Turkey). Antioch rivaled Rome, Constantinople, and Alexandria in importance and was one of the most prosperous provincial capitals in the Late Roman Empire.

Since representations of the Fall are not otherwise attested among Syrian floor mosaics from the fifth and sixth centuries, it is difficult to assess whether this mosaic panel formed part of a larger pictorial cycle. A floor mosaic in the north church (Michaelion) at Hūarte (Syria) that depicts Adam enthroned, naming the animals in paradise (Gen. 2:19–20), may suggest that this panel likewise formed part of a nave mosaic of an Early Byzantine church. HAK

John L. Severance Fund 1969.115

DIMENSIONS: 142.9 x 107.3 cm

INSCRIBED: κ[αι] ἐφαγον ἐγυμνώθη[σαν] (and he ate [and they] were stripped naked)

BIBLIOGRAPHY: Donceel-Voûte 1988, 487–89. On the representation of the enthroned Adam at Hūarte, see Wisskirchen 2002; on a group of related mosaics at the Minneapolis Institute of Arts, see McNally 1969.

The Beth Misona Treasure

6TH–7TH CENTURY; EARLY BYZANTINE, CONSTANTINOPLE OR SYRIA

SILVER

These four liturgical silver objects, three chalices and one paten, form what is now called the Beth Misona Treasure, named for the village in northern Syria for which they were originally made. While nothing is known about the circumstances and exact location of the treasure's discovery, the objects themselves hold important clues as to their provenance and early history.

The hammered and lathe-turned silver paten, used to hold the pieces of bread to be consecrated during the liturgy, is decorated at its center with an engraved Latin cross and surrounded by a dedicatory inscription that records not only the name and affiliation of the donor, a certain Domnos, but also the names of his father, the village, and the church to which it was offered in fulfillment of a vow. It is

likely that the village of Beth Misona, named in the inscription, is the modern Msibina, located about 30 miles southwest of Aleppo.

The three chalices are closely related in shape, physical make-up, and decoration. Supported on a flaring foot with a knob made of overlapping leaves, each chalice has a broad cup decorated with four repoussé medallions containing portrait busts of saints Peter and Paul between a youthful Christ and the Virgin in her *maphorion* (veil). Two of the chalices are further decorated with a braided band at the bottom of the cup and a broad frieze of stylized egg-and-palmette motifs at the rim. The third chalice has instead a dedicatory inscription that runs around the cup immediately below the rim. It names not only the donor of the vessel and his father, but also the patron saint and priest of the church that received the pious gift. That Kyriakos, the donor of at least one if not all three chalices,

was the son of Domnos, named as the donor of the paten, cannot be determined with certainty. The fact, however, that the objects in the treasure form a coherent liturgical set makes such a possibility at least highly likely.

Unlike other pieces of Early Byzantine silver, none of the objects in the Beth Misona Treasure was stamped by the office of the "comes sacrarum largitionum" (minister of finance), a practice first introduced by the Byzantine emperor Anastasius I (r. 491–518) and commonly attested into the reign of Constans II (641–68). The objects can therefore be dated only broadly to the sixth or seventh century. Like other Christian communities in Syria and Palestine, the people of the village of Beth Misona were probably forced to bury their church silver in an effort to hide it from the Persians or Arabs, who conquered their lands in the first half of the seventh century. HAK

Purchase from the J. H. Wade Fund 1950.378–81

DIMENSIONS: 17.1 x 14.9 cm overall (chalices); diam. 32.2 cm, depth 3.5 cm (paten)

INSCRIBED: on the paten: ΕΥΞΟΜΕΝΟC ΔΟΜΝΟC ΥΙΟC ΖΑΧΕΟΥ ΠΡΟCΗΝΕΝΚΕΝ ΤΩ ΑΓΙΩ ΣΕΡΓΙΩ ΧΩ[ρίου] ΒΕΘ ΜΙCΩΝΑ (Having vowed, Domnos, son of Zacheos, has offered [this paten] to [the church

of] St. Sergios of the village of Beth Misona); on one of the chalices: ΠΡ[εσβύτερος] ΚΥΡΙΑΚΟC ΥΙΟC ΔΟΜΝΟΥ ΤΩ ΑΓΙΩ ΣΕΡΓΙΩ ΕΠΙ ΖΗΝΩΝΟC ΠΡΕCΒΥΤΕΡΟΥ (The priest Kyriakos, son of Domnos, [offered this chalice] to St. Sergios under Zeno the priest)

BIBLIOGRAPHY: Worcester 2000, 211, no. 98; Mango 1986, 228–31, no. 57–60; New York 1979, 608–9, no. 544; Dodd 1973, 17–23; Downey 1953, 143–45; Bréhier 1951, 256–64; Milliken 1951, 142–45.

Pilgrim's Ampulla

LATE 6TH OR EARLY 7TH CENTURY; EARLY BYZANTINE, PALESTINE
TIN-LEAD ALLOY AND FRAGMENTS OF LEATHER

One of the most striking religious phenomena associated with the triumph of Christianity in the early fourth century and its spread across the Roman Empire is the idea of pilgrimage, which often involved long-distance travel to holy sites that were considered spiritually significant through their association with events recorded in the Old and New Testament or with the life and death of a specific saint or holy person. Following the example of Emperor Constantine's mother, Helena, who went to Jerusalem searching for traces of the life and Passion of Christ and allegedly discovered the so-called True Cross, the material remains of the cross on which Christ was crucified, Christians from all parts of the Roman Empire started similar journeys to Palestine to see the places described in the Bible and venerate the relics considered proof of the veracity of the gospels' account.

Guided by the belief that physical contact with holy matter would result in the transfer of its miraculous powers, pilgrims not only desired to touch and kiss sacred relics at each holy site, they also tried to preserve and carry with them substances that could claim some physical contact with the sites they had visited or the sacred relics they had seen and venerated. These substances, frequently referred to as *eulogiai* (blessings) in contemporary pilgrim accounts, often included wax from candles or oil from lamps that had burned at holy places. Depending on the pilgrim's financial resources, these substances could be collected and carried away in small ampullae (flasks) of pewter,

lead, terracotta, or more precious materials such as silver, which were all offered for sale on site.

This lead ampulla belongs to a small but well-known group of Early Byzantine eulogia flasks from the Holy Land known as Monza or Bobbio ampullae, so called because the largest group of such objects has been preserved in the cathedral treasuries of Monza and Bobbio in northern Italy. Like other examples, the Cleveland flask is decorated on both sides with images of central events from the life of Christ, namely the Crucifixion (obverse, illustrated here) and the Ascension (reverse). The inscriptions surrounding these images reveal that the flask once contained "oil of the wood of life," namely oil that had been brought into contact with the relic of the True Cross. An anonymous pilgrim from Piacenza, who visited Jerusalem around 570, records how this was achieved:

In the courtyard of the basilica [at Mount Golgotha] is a small room where they keep the Wood of the Cross. . . . At the moment when the Cross is brought out of the small room for veneration . . . , a star appears in the sky and . . . stays overhead whilst they [the pilgrims] are venerating the Cross, and they offer oil to be blessed in little flasks. When the mouth of one of the little flasks touches the Wood of the Cross, the oil instantly bubbles over, and unless it is closed very quickly it all spills out.

HAK

John L. Severance Fund 1999.46

DIMENSIONS: 6.3 x 4.6 x 1.5 cm

INSCRIBED: on the obverse: + ΕΛΑΙΩΝ ΞΥΛΟΥ ΖΩΗΣ ΤΩΝ ΑΓΙΩΝ ΧΡΙΣΤΟΥ ΤΟΠΩΝ (+ Oil of the Wood of Life from the Holy Places of Christ); reverse: + ΕΥΛΟΓΙΑ ΚΥΡΙΟΥ ΤΩΝ ΑΓΙΩΝ ΤΟΠΩΝ (+ Blessing of the Lord from the Holy Places)

BIBLIOGRAPHY: Engemann 2002, 157–58, no. 4; Gustafson 1999, 778. For related pilgrim's flasks, see Engemann 2002, 153–69; Kötzsche-Breitenbruch 1984, 229–46; Vikan 1982; Engemann 1973, 5–27; Grabar 1958. For the quote, see Wilkinson 1977, 83.

Mold for a Eulogia Bread

7TH–10TH CENTURY; EARLY OR MIDDLE BYZANTINE, PALESTINE?

WOOD

Building on Egyptian, Greek, and Roman traditions, stamping loaves of bread with special molds made of wood, stone, terracotta, or metal became a common practice among Christians. Depending on whether the bread was intended for ordinary use in a Christian household, ritual use in the Eucharistic liturgy, or distribution among the faithful on specific feast days and other occasions, the decoration could vary. Many surviving Early and Middle Byzantine bread stamps are decorated with Christian symbols—the cross, simple inscriptions such as "Fruit of the Lord" or "Life/Health," and abbreviations for "Jesus Christ, Son of God," "Jesus Christ conquers," or "Christ grants grace to Christians." Inscriptions and images on other bread stamps seem to indicate that they were used for loaves of bread destined for distribution as *eulogiai* (blessings) among participants of certain church festivals or visitors of specific pilgrimage sites.

Representing what seems to be a faithful depiction of Emperor Constantine's Church of the Holy Sepulcher on Mount Golgotha, the hill outside Jerusalem on which Christ was crucified and entombed after his death, this wood mold was likely used for loaves of bread distributed to pilgrims in Jerusalem, providing them with a portable token of sanctity and an image commemorating their pilgrimage. The buildings depicted here include most of the significant elements of the fourth-century complex of the Holy Sepulcher, which aimed to isolate the sites of Christ's crucifixion and entombment, and to provide a suitable place for Christian worship and veneration. The long colonnade visible in the lower foreground likely denotes the entrance to the church from the colonnaded street that stretched along the complex's eastern end. Behind it rises a structure that can clearly be identified as the Martyrium, the magnificent five-aisled basilica commissioned by Constantine in 326. The domed structure at the far right represents the Anastasis, the centralized structure that housed the tomb of Christ. While it is difficult to determine the exact date of the Cleveland eulogia mold, the small crescents that decorate the front and back gables of the basilica may indicate that it was made between the Arab conquest of Jerusalem in 637/38 and the destruction of much of the Holy Sepulcher under the Fatimid Caliph Al-Hakim in 1009. HAK

Thirty-fifth anniversary gift of Mr. and Mrs. Paul Mallon 1951.152

DIMENSIONS: diam. 8.8 cm

BIBLIOGRAPHY: New York 1979, 598–99, no. 528; Duval 1978, 38–39; Galavaris 1970, 153–61; Galavaris 1966, 751; Baltimore 1947, 37, no. 89.

12

Pilgrim's Flask: St. Menas

6TH–7TH CENTURY; EARLY BYZANTINE, EGYPT

TERRACOTTA

Apart from sites in the Holy Land, which were directly associated with the life and Passion of Christ, other locations in Italy, Greece, Asia Minor, Syria, and Egypt also gained popularity as destinations for pious pilgrims. As in Rome, where the apostles Peter and Paul and other early followers of Christ were persecuted, killed, and commemorated as martyrs since the middle of the first century, pilgrimage centers also developed in other areas of the empire where Christian martyrs and holy men had preached, lived, healed, or were buried. One of these places was the shrine of St. Menas near Alexandria in Egypt. According to one version of the saint's legend, Menas was an Egyptian soldier serving in Asia Minor (modern Turkey), where he was martyred under Emperor Diocletian (r. 284–305). When his remains were later brought back to his native Egypt, the camels carrying his relics at one point refused to go any farther, thus indicating the final resting place the saint had miraculously chosen for himself. Attracted by the saint's miracle-working powers, Christian pilgrims soon started to visit the site, making the cult of St. Menas one of the most popular in the Christian Mediterranean.

The popularity of St. Menas can be measured best by the large number of surviving terracotta flasks that bear the standard image of the saint with his hands raised in prayer and camels kneeling to the right and left at his feet. Produced in large quantities and sold on site, these flasks could be filled with holy water, oil, or earth from near the saint's tomb. The possession of and contact with those substances, sanctified through their physical contact or immediate proximity to the saint's holy body, was believed to grant the owner the saint's blessing and protection. Accordingly, pilgrims carried such *eulogiai* (blessings) around their necks or fastened them to their belts, thus ensuring immediate access to the saint's miracle-working powers and protection from sickness and imminent dangers. HAK

Gift of Bruce Ferrini in memory of Robert P. Bergman 1999.230

DIMENSIONS: 10.2 x 6.6 x 2.3 cm

BIBLIOGRAPHY: for similar pilgrim flasks in other collections, see Witt 2002; Kaminski-Menssen 1996; and Metzger 1981.

13

Pilgrim's Medallion: St. Symeon the Younger

ABOUT 1100; MIDDLE BYZANTINE, SYRIA

LEAD

While traveling to the Holy Land, pilgrims passing through Syria and Palestine were frequently attracted by other pilgrimage sites on their way. During the fifth and sixth centuries, two of the most popular such destinations were those associated with St. Symeon the Elder (about 389–459) and his homonymous imitator St. Symeon the Younger (521–92). Both gained celebrity status and were venerated as holy men during their lifetimes for their decision to lead a life of extreme asceticism and seclusion on a small platform atop a column (*stylus* in Greek). Symeon the Elder, the first stylite saint, spent the last 36 years of his life atop such a column, located prominently near the highway from Antioch to Berroia (modern Aleppo).

Inspired by Symeon the Elder and other stylites, Symeon the Younger ascended his first pillar at the age of seven near Seleukia Pieria, the port city of Antioch. Around 541, he moved to a rocky outcrop overlooking the Orontes River a few miles southwest of Antioch, where a pilgrimage complex and monastery soon developed around him. In 551, Symeon ascended his last and highest column, located at the very center of the monastic complex. He died there in 592, having spent more than 40 years standing on top of this column.

The site of Symeon's column, which became known as the Wondrous Mountain, attracted many pilgrims from all over the Roman Empire during and after his lifetime. These pilgrims often carried home with them small *eulogiai* (blessings) made from reddish earth collected around the base of Symeon's column and imprinted with his image. Numerous miracle accounts in Symeon's *Vita* attest to the protective power and medicinal efficacy of these tokens. While the Wondrous Mountain remained a popular pilgrimage destination even after the Arab conquest of Syria-Palestine, the large-scale production of eulogia seems to have ceased in the early seventh century. It was revived after the Byzantine reoccupation of the region in the tenth and eleventh centuries, however, using variants of images and inscriptions featured on earlier tokens.

This lead medallion is an example of a eulogia token from the period of the cult's revival in the late 11th century. Meant to be worn around the neck as a pendant, it shows on the obverse the half-length image of St. Symeon, haloed and dressed in monastic garb, within an enclosure atop his column and two angels of God, one ascending via a flight of stairs with two crosses, the other flying toward the saint with a chalice. Flanking the column are two figures identified through inscriptions as the saint's mother, Martha, and his disciple Konon. Their hands are raised toward Symeon in intercessory poses, thus forming a link between the pilgrim holding the token and the saint presented in his miracle-working image. The reverse of the medallion features a cross with flaring arms and round finials. Decorated with arabesque designs, it equates Symeon's standing on the column with Christ's suffering on the cross and alludes to the latter's life-giving quality. HAK

Norman O. Stone and Ella A. Stone Memorial Fund 1972.52

DIMENSIONS: diam. 5.7 cm

INSCRIBED: on the obverse: + + ΕΥΛΟΓΙΑ ΤΟΥ ΑΓΙΟΥ ΣΥΜΕΩΝ ΤΟΥ ΘΑΥΜΑΤΟΥΡΓΟΥ + ΑΝΕΙΤΕ ΤΟΝ Θ[ΕΟ]Ν ΕΝ ΤΟΙΣ ΑΓΙΟΙΣ ΑΥΤΟΥ ΚΥΡΙΟΣ ΑΓΑΠΑ ΔΙΚ(ΑΙ)ΟΥΣ (+ Blessing of Saint Symeon the Miracle-Worker + Praise God in his saints. The Lord loves the righteous);

ΑΓΓΕΛΟΥ [sic] Θ[ΕΟ]Υ (angels of God); ΟΑΓ[ΙΟΣ] ΚΟΝΟΝ (Saint Konon); Η ΑΓΙΑ ΜΑΡΘΑ (Saint Martha)

BIBLIOGRAPHY: New York 1997, 385–86, no. 255; Vikan 1982; Verdier 1980; *CMA Bulletin* 60 (1973): 67, 108, no. 82. On the iconography of Saint Symeon the Younger, see Volbach 1966, 293–99, and Lafontaine-Dosogne 1967, 169–217. On the medicinal function of "Symeon tokens," see Vikan 1984, 65–86.

14

Mounted Rock Crystal

5TH–6TH CENTURY; EARLY BYZANTINE

GOLD, QUARTZ, AND ALMANDINE

When this precious gold object was acquired by the Cleveland Museum of Art in 1953, it was identified as either a receptacle for holy oil or another sacred relic or substance. However, a close examination of the object reveals that the central rock crystal, once thought to be the container of holy matter, is devoid of any cavity that would allow for such a purpose. While the original designation of this object as a phylactery, or relic container, is thus questionable, alternative explanations for its original purpose are not readily available.

The core of this puzzling object is a hexagonal rock-crystal prism fastened between two gold mounts: a closed cap at the top and an open collar at the bottom. Enclosing the rock crystal between them, these mounts are held together by a gold wire that is threaded through a series of granulated loops at the bottom and four granulated bosses of different shapes at the top. A third gold wire wound around each of the four double strings holds the crystal in place. Extending up from the center of the cap is a gold rod on which are threaded, like beads on a string, four individual perforated seg-ments of differing shapes and sizes, all decorated with granulation: a drum with a rhomboid surface pattern, an openwork filigree basket, a small granular tube, and a flat lozenge with a rhomboid surface pattern. These elements are held together by a finial consisting of a wreath of braided gold wire and four inverted granular pyramids. Together they create the negative shape of a Greek cross, a form that is further emphasized through the use of a quatrefoil almandine pane fastened to the back of the finial. A short chain with a tiny gold fish-shaped pendant is attached just below the cross-inscribed wreath.

While there can be no doubt that the rock crystal, whose naturally formed hexagonal faces Pliny described as "so perfectly smooth that no craftsmanship could achieve the same effect," plays a significant part in the meaning of the ensemble as a whole, its relation to the rest of the decoration, especially the fish pendant with its Christological overtones, remains a mystery. It is possible that the object was thought to carry certain amuletic or medicinal powers and thus meant to protect its owner from evil and mishaps. HAK

Purchase from the J. H. Wade Fund 1953.640

DIMENSIONS: 10.2 x 1.9 cm

BIBLIOGRAPHY: Milliken 1954, 191. For the quote, see Pliny's *Natural History,* bk. 37, chap. 9.26.

15

Necklace with Pendants

5TH–6TH CENTURY; EARLY BYZANTINE, CONSTANTINOPLE?

GOLD AND GARNETS

Continuing Near Eastern, Greek, and Roman metalworking traditions, Byzantine goldsmiths in Constantinople, Antioch, and elsewhere in the Roman Empire commanded a variety of styles and techniques for the production of fine jewelry. This Early Byzantine gold necklace features a chain of the multiple loop-in-loop type, a technique that can be traced back as far as the middle of the third millennium BC. Fastened at its ring-capped ends with a simple wire loop, the chain supports four gold pendants of different shapes and sizes. A gold cross with flaring conical arms forms the central ornamental element. Attached to the chain with a plain suspension ring, the cross is decorated on the obverse at the intersection of its arms with a dark red garnet set in a high circular collet. Two hexagonal gold cylinders, which may have enclosed either magical texts or holy substances, flank the cross. Each is suspended from two plain rings and has beaded borders and rounded caps on either side. The fourth pendant, outfitted once again with a plain suspension ring, is circular in shape and decorated on its obverse with a central garnet.

Wearing richly ornamented gold necklaces such as this one was a common practice among members of the Late Roman and Byzantine Empire's upper class. In addition to their use as objects of personal adornment and symbols of social status, necklaces with cross pendants and amuletic capsules also functioned as powerful protective devices. While Christian theologians were not always comfortable with the use of protective amulets, especially if they contained undisclosed texts or holy substances, their existence is well attested throughout the Late Roman and Early Byzantine periods. One of the earliest records for the use of Christian relics as apotropaic devices in necklaces comes from St. Gregory of Nyssa, who reported that, at the time of her death, his sister Macrina (d. 379) was wearing a fragment of the relic of the True Cross on a chain around her neck. A few years later, Bishop Paulinus of Nola in Italy sent another fragment of the True Cross to a friend in Gaul. It was enclosed "in a small golden tube" that may well have resembled the hexagonal containers on this necklace. HAK

Purchase from the J. H. Wade Fund 1954.3

DIMENSIONS: length 56.5 cm (chain), 4.5 x 3.1 cm (cross)

BIBLIOGRAPHY: Frolow 1966, 44; Milliken 1954, 190–92.

16

Monogram of Christ

6TH CENTURY; BYZANTINE, SYRIA?

GOLD SHEET, GOLD WIRE, AND GARNETS

From the third century on, monogrammatic abbreviations of the name of Christ are frequently encountered in Early Christian art and literature. One of the most popular abbreviations of this kind, commonly known as a Christogram, or Chrismon, is composed of the superimposed Greek letters *X* (chi) and *P* (rho), the first two letters of Christ's name in Greek, XPICTOC. While the letter combination itself had been in use as a literary abbreviation long before the emergence of Christianity, its appropriation by Christians resulted in a wide dissemination of the chi-rho monogram as a powerful symbol and direct visual reference to Christ.

The popularity of this monogram in the visual arts of the fourth through the sixth centuries and beyond can be explained in part by the fact that this very sign appeared to Emperor Constantine the Great before the battle against his rival Maxentius near Rome in 312. According to Constantine's biographer Eusebius of Caesarea, the emperor soon "summoned goldsmiths and jewelers, sat down among them, explained the shape of the sign, and gave them instructions about copying it in gold and precious stones. [On] a wreath woven of precious stones and gold . . . two letters . . . formed the monogram of the Savior's title, *rho* being intersected in the middle by *chi*."

Made of gold sheet and decorated on each side with three garnets, one in the center and two in the loop of the letter *rho,* as well as with border linings of braided double-ply gold wire, the Cleveland Chrismon undoubtedly recalls the victory-bearing sign of Constantine's vision. While it is difficult to determine the monogram's original function, the loops at the terminals of each letter and the fact that the object was meant to be seen from both sides seem to indicate that it once formed the centerpiece of a golden wreath or garland, serving as either a protective emblem or a sign of imperial victory and Christian triumph. HAK

Gift of Lillian M. Kern 1965.551

DIMENSIONS: 14.8 x 12.1 cm

BIBLIOGRAPHY: for similar use of twisted wire, see Elbern 1969, 493–95. Translation of Eusebius, *Life of Constantine,* after Cameron/Hall 1999, 81.

17

Tapestry: Christian Imagery

6TH CENTURY; EARLY BYZANTINE, EGYPT

PLAIN WEAVE WITH INWOVEN TAPESTRY WEAVE; DYED WOOL AND UNDYED LINEN

This rare textile from Early Byzantine Egypt likely served as a decorative wall hanging in a church or a home. Despite its fragmentary state of preservation, it is extraordinary for its richness in Christian symbolism.

The symmetrical composition is dominated by an elaborate arch decorated with interlacing bands of contorted green, red, and yellow loops as well as blossoms and flower motifs consisting of an arrangement of dots. Two columns with similar interlace decoration and stylized capitals support the arch. They, in turn, carry an intricately decorated entablature that divides the pictorial space into two distinct fields. The semi-circular area directly under the arch, the tympanum, features the central symbol of a large *T* (tau) cross flanked by two birds with pearl necklaces; directly above the cross is a wreath. Together the cross and wreath form an ankh, an ancient Egyptian symbol of life that remained popular during the Early Christian period. Below the ankh is a decorative tablet, a *tabula ansata,* flanked by two birds and inscribed with the Greek word "ΙΧΘΥΣ" (fish), an acronym Early Christians frequently used to identify Christ as the Son of God and Savior. The area under the entablature shows three youthful figures, fully dressed, with their hands raised above their heads. This is almost certainly a representation of the Old Testament story of the three steadfast Hebrews who refused to worship King Nabuchodonosor's golden idol and were cast into a fiery furnace; thanks to God's intervention they were unharmed. "The great men of the kingdom being gathered together, considered these men, that the fire had no power on their bodies, and that not a hair of their head had been singed, nor their garments altered, nor the smell of the fire had passed on them" (Dan. 3:94).

Immediately above the scene is a Christogram, formed by a *X* (chi) and *P* (rho), the first two letters of Christ's name in Greek, and an additional cross bar. The monogram is flanked by an *A* (alpha) and an *ω* (omega), the first and last letters of the Greek alphabet, thus alluding to Christ as "the first and the last, the beginning and the end" (Apocalypse 22:13). Another Christogram, with a peacock on either side, appears above the arch, and around it are various stylized trees and animals, some suckling their young.

The significance of the combined use of these images and symbols lies in their invocation of Christ's redemptive and life-giving power. Together, they assure the viewer that Christ, the Son of God and Savior, will bring redemption and eternal life to those who follow his teachings. HAK

John L. Severance Fund 1982.73

DIMENSIONS: 110.5 x 76.8 cm

INSCRIBED: ΙΧΘΥΣ (also used as an acronym for ΙΗΣΟΥΣ ΧΡΙΣΤΟΣ ΘΕΟΥ ΥΙΟΣ ΣΩΤΗΡ [Jesus Christ, Son of God, Savior])

BIBLIOGRAPHY: *CMA Bulletin* 70 (1983): 53, no. 75.

18

Tapestry: Icon of the Virgin and Child

6TH–7TH CENTURY; EARLY BYZANTINE, EGYPT

SLIT AND DOVETAILED TAPESTRY WEAVE; WOOL

This tapestry is one of a very small number of surviving Christian icons that predate Byzantine Iconoclasm, an era of extended political and theological debate over the justification and proper use of religious images that was a reaction to an increasing demand for religious images during the sixth and seventh centuries and the spread of private devotional practices not sanctioned by the church. It ended in 843, with the triumph of the iconophile (icon friendly) faction over those who had promoted a more spiritual, imageless version of Christianity.

While the word "icon," which means image in Greek, is often considered to apply to panel paintings only, the Orthodox definition of what constitutes an icon is much broader in scope and includes, according to the dogmatic decrees of the Second Council of Nicaea (787), "holy images, whether painted or made of mosaic or of other suitable material [and which are exposed] in the holy churches of God, on sacred instruments and vestments, on walls and panels, in houses and by public ways."

One of the earliest references attesting to the existence of woven icons is a passage in a pilgrimage account recorded by Abbot Adomnan of Iona (about 624–704), who relates that among the miraculous things shown to pilgrims in Jerusalem was "a linen cloth . . . said to have been woven by Saint Mary, and is for this reason preserved in a church and venerated by the whole population. Pictures of the twelve apostles are woven into it, and there is also a portrait of the Lord." The abbot's description of the woven icon in Jerusalem suggests that it must have been similar in type and iconography to the Cleveland tapestry icon, which is divided into two distinct picture zones framed by a single garland border that is decorated with various fruits and flowers as well as twelve medallions representing busts of the four evangelists and eight of Christ's apostles.

The lower zone, which occupies about two-thirds of the two-part composition, shows the Virgin Theotokos (God-bearer) dressed in her traditional blue robe with head-scarf. She is seated on an elaborate gem- and pearl-studded throne with a large red cushion and an equally elaborate footstool. Holding the Christ child on her lap, the Virgin is flanked by the archangels Michael and Gabriel and further framed by an aedicula (shrine) consisting of two variegated columns supporting a thin architrave with inscriptions. The attending archangels are dressed in light blue tunics with gold borders and white mantles. Signifying their status as members of the heavenly court, each carries a long golden staff. Gabriel also holds a blue sphere decorated with two half moons, the sun, and a star, symbolizing the universality of Christ's rule over the entire cosmos. In the upper zone, Christ is represented above the stars as the Pantokrator (All-sovereign) within an oval sphere supported by two angels, one on either side. Like

the Virgin and Child in the lower zone, Christ is seated in a gem- and pearl-studded throne with a large cushion and footstool. Holding the book of the gospels in his left hand, he raises his right in a gesture of blessing. While the red background, the starry sky, and the floral patches next to the archangels in the lower zone indicate that both representations take place in a realm beyond this world, the placement of the apostle and evangelist portraits in the frame seems to suggest that a distinction is being made between the realm of Christ as the divine ruler and Christ as the incarnate Logos.

The theological concept of the tapestry icon can thus be considered as twofold. In the upper zone, Christ is represented in his divine nature as the all-sovereign ruler of the universe, while in the lower zone Christ's humanity and incarnation are emphasized through his representation in the arms of the Virgin and his association with the portraits of his disciples and followers. Together, both parts of the image confirm the divinity of the incarnate God and the Virgin's role as the Theotokos as it was decreed by the Third Ecumenical Council of Ephesos in 431. HAK

Leonard C. Hanna Jr. Fund 1967.144

DIMENSIONS: 178.7 x 110.5 cm

INSCRIPTIONS: on the architrave: Ο ΑΓΙΟΣ ΜΙΧΑΗΛ (Saint Michael); Η ΑΗΑ (Η ΑΓΙΑ) ΜΑΡΙΑ (Saint Mary); Ο ΑΓΙΟΣ ΓΑΒ[ΡΙΗΛ] (Saint Gabriel); on the frame: ΒΑΡΘΟΛΟΜΑΙΩΣ (Bartholomew); ΠΕΤΡΟΣ (Peter); ΜΑΘΕΩΣ (Matthias); ΙΩΑΝΝΗΣ (John); ΘΩΜΑΣ (Thomas); ΜΑΡΚΟ[Σ] (Mark); ΦΙΛΙΠΠΟ[Σ] (Philipp); ΙΑΚΩ[ΒΟΣ] (Jakob); ΛΟΥΚΑΣ (Luke); ΠΑΥΛΟΣ ΑΠΟΣΤΟΛΟΣ (Paul the Apostle); [Μ]ΑΤΤΕΟΣ (Matthew); ΑΝΔΡΕΑΣ (Andrew)

BIBLIOGRAPHY: Rutschowscaya 2000, 222–25; CMA Masterpieces 1992, 22–23; Pelikan 1990; Rutschowscaya 1990, 135–37; New York 1979, 532–33, no. 477; MMA Bulletin 1977, 80–81, no. 69; Shepherd 1969, 90–120. For the decrees of the Second Council of Nicaea, see Schaff/Wace 1986, 14: 549–51; a more recent version is Tanner 1990, 1:133–37. For Adomnan of Iona's pilgrimage account, see Wilkinson 1977, 93–116, esp. 98.

Plaque: The Virgin and Child

SECOND HALF OF THE 10TH OR EARLY 11TH CENTURY;

MIDDLE BYZANTINE, CONSTANTINOPLE

IVORY

This ivory plaque, often called the "Stroganoff Ivory" for one of its previous owners, is one of the finest examples of its kind to survive from the Middle Byzantine period, an era that extends from the end of Iconoclasm in 843 through the conquest of Constantinople by Crusader forces in 1204. It has been identified as belonging to a distinct group of related Middle Byzantine ivories named the "Nikephoros group" after an ivory *staurotheca* (cross reliquary) that carries an inscription mentioning Emperor Nikephoros II Phokas (r. 963–69).

The Cleveland ivory represents the Theotokos (God-bearer) wearing the traditional robe and veil. Holding the Christ child on her knees, the Mother of God is seated on a lavishly carved gem-studded throne with a large cushion and a high, multi-lobed back that is decorated with large six-petal rosettes. She is flanked in the panel's upper corners by the busts of two angels who emerge from the background with their hands raised in awe and veneration, drawing attention to the divine child in his mother's lap. Dressed in tunic and mantle, Christ is shown fully frontal, holding a scroll in his left hand and raising his right in a gesture of blessing.

Representations of the enthroned Virgin and Child have a long tradition in both monumental and devotional Byzantine art, stretching back perhaps as far as the first half of the fifth century (for a pre-iconoclastic example, see no. 18). However, its popularity increased considerably after the end of Iconoclasm and the unveiling of a monumental apse mosaic showing the enthroned Virgin and Child in the church of Hagia Sophia in Constantinople in 867. In a sermon held by Patriarch Photios during the Mass that celebrated the mosaic's inauguration on Easter Saturday, 29 March 867, he explained the meaning of the image:

A Virgin with a child reclining in her arms is a Christian mystery. She is both mother and virgin at the same time, but no shame to either condition. Through art we see a lifelike imitation of her. She looks with affection at the child, yet her expression is detached and distant towards the emotionless and supernatural child. . . . Christ was born in the flesh, and is carried in the arms of his mother. This is seen, proved and demonstrated by icons; the observer sees for himself and believes.

Since the Cleveland ivory is missing drill holes on the upper and lower rims of its frame, a common detail on ivory plaques that served as centerpieces of devotional triptychs, its original functional context remains elusive. It may have formed part of a larger ensemble or, considering its impressive size, served as a single devotional icon, visualizing for its pious beholder the mystery of Christ's incarnation. The crudely executed and grammatically inconclusive Greek inscription between the Virgin's footstool and the base of the throne was added by an untrained hand, presumably that of one of the icon's later owners. HAK

Gift of J. H. Wade 1925.1293

DIMENSIONS: 25.3 x 17.2 x 1.8 cm

INSCRIBED: + ΑΛΛΟΝΗΣ ΜΑΡΤΥΡΟΣ ΔΟΥΛΟΣ + (+ Allones Martyr Servant +)

BIBLIOGRAPHY: Athens 2000, 302–3, no. 19; Koenen 1998, 199–227; New York 1997, 140–41, no. 87; Baltimore 1947, 44, no. 126; Goldschmidt/Weitzmann 1979B, 49, no. 79; Milliken 1926, 25–29; Pollak/Muñoz 1911, 2: 161. For Patriarch Photios's Sermon 17, see Mango 1958, 286–96.

Pendant Icon: Virgin Hodegetria

12TH CENTURY; MIDDLE BYZANTINE (STEATITE),
MID 14TH CENTURY; GERMAN (FRAME)
STEATITE, GILDED SILVER, AND PEARLS

Mounted in a gilded-silver and pearl-studded Western medieval frame, this small-scale Byzantine icon was carved from soapstone, or steatite, a material highly appreciated by Middle and Late Byzantine artists for its softness and pale green color. Depicted in the center of the icon is the half-length figure of the Virgin, holding the Christ child on her right arm and pointing toward him with her left hand. This iconographic type, often referred to as Dexiokratousa, forms a variant of the Virgin Hodegetria, named for one of Constantinople's most famous miracle-working icons, the Virgin and Child of the Hodegon Monastery. Allegedly painted by the evangelist Luke in Jerusalem and subsequently brought to Constantinople, the Virgin Hodegetria was, at least from the 12th century on, considered an authentic portrait and thus became one of the most widely copied icon types of this subject. It is not known when and how exactly the Dexiokratousa type emerged. Since it is essentially the mirror image of its prototype, one may assume that it came into being as the result of a direct contact or impression of its prototype. By the Middle Byzantine period, the Dexiokratousa type is well established and frequently depicted on icons of all sizes and media.

Little is known about the date and the circumstances under which this icon arrived in western Europe. It may have been given as a diplomatic gift, looted during the sack of Constantinople in 1204, or acquired commercially at any time between its manufacture, presumably in the 12th century, and the mid 14th century, when it was mounted in its present Gothic frame, presumably by a German artist working in Aachen during the reign of Charles IV (1355–78). As the frame's inscription reveals, the Byzantine icon was, at that time, considered an authentic portrait of the Virgin and Christ child painted by St. Luke, a claim further emphasized by the engraved image of an ox, the symbol of St. Luke, depicted on the frame's reverse (see inset). By the first half of the 17th century, it was considered to be one of three reliquary pendants that had been found hanging around the neck of Charlemagne (r. 800–814) when Otto III (r. 996–1002) opened his tomb in Aachen Cathedral in the year 1000. While this claim can be dismissed as legend on the basis of the steatite icon's presumed date of manufacture, it is not too far-fetched to assume that the pendant once adorned the reliquary bust of Charlemagne, a work commissioned by the emperor's namesake Charles IV for Aachen Cathedral in 1349.

The pendant formed part of the Aachen treasury until 1804, when it was given to Empress Josephine of France as a gift. After her death it passed into the possession of her son Eugène de Beauharnais and from him into the Daguerre Collection in Paris. The pendant was eventually bought for the Cleveland Museum of Art from the Paris dealer César de Hauke in 1951. HAK

Purchase from the J. H. Wade Fund 1951.445.1–2

DIMENSIONS: 5.3 x 4 cm (steatite), 6.7 x 6.3 cm (frame)

INSCRIBED: on the frame: ha[n]c ✳ ymagine[m] ✳ fec[it] ✳ s[anctus] ✳ Lucas ✳ ev[angelista] ✳ ad ✳ si[mi]litudinem ✳ b[ea]t[ae] ✳ mari[a]e (This image was made by Saint Luke the Evangelist according to the likeness of the Blessed [Virgin] Mary)

BIBLIOGRAPHY: New York 2004A, 500, no. 303; Athens 2000, 189, no. 125; Kalaverezou-Maxeiner 1985, 124, no. 32; Grimme 1972, 48–50; Grimme 1965, 48–53; Aachen 1965, 494–95, no. 674; CMA Bulletin 50 (1963): 208, no. 54; Montesquiou-Fezensac 1962, 74.

Cameo: St. George

10TH/11TH CENTURY; MIDDLE BYZANTINE, CONSTANTINOPLE

BLOODSTONE (HELIOTROPE)

Continuing earlier Greek and Roman traditions, Byzantine artists were highly skilled in carving precious and semi-precious stones. A considerable number of finely carved cameos—gems with a raised rather than engraved (intaglio) design—survive from the Middle Byzantine period. Executed in different types of stone such as jasper, bloodstone, sardonyx, amethyst, and sapphire, they attest to the continuing popularity of carved gemstones among the Byzantine Empire's aristocratic and urban elite. The small size of these luxury items as well as their frequent decoration with images of Christ, the Virgin, and popular Byzantine saints suggests that they were meant to serve as objects of both personal adornment and private devotion.

This bloodstone cameo was carved in high relief with the bust-length portrait of St. George, one of the most popular saints in the Byzantine Empire. Like other military saints such as Demetrios, Theodore, and Prokopios, George was frequently represented on small-scale portable icons to serve as a powerful guardian and protector for those carrying his likeness. The Cleveland cameo shows George as a youthful warrior, clean shaven, with short cropped hair and a faint nimbus. Dressed in a tunic with a broad decorated border and a mantle, he holds his sword upright over his right shoulder while carrying a cross-inscribed shield on his left arm. The high relief of the carving and detailed treatment of the saint's features suggests a tenth- or eleventh-century date for this cameo. While its original mount has not been preserved, one may assume that this object, like many others of its type, was once mounted as a pendant and carried around the neck by its owner so it could easily be kissed and touched in moments of distress and crisis. Such close physical contact with a holy image was believed to enhance its effectiveness and create a strong bond between the worshiper and the subject of his devotions. In addition to the powers attributed to a holy image, the stone from which it was cut was often thought to carry magical powers. Bloodstone, for instance, was believed to stop hemorrhages and increase blood circulation. HAK

Dudley P. Allen Fund 1959.41

DIMENSIONS: 3.2 x 2.8 cm

INSCRIBED: ΑΓΙΟ(C) ΓΕΩΡΙΟC (Saint George)

BIBLIOGRAPHY: Wentzel 1960; *CMA Bulletin* 64 (1959): 63; Purgold 1937, pl. 53.

Fragment of a Processional Cross

This fragment of a silver cross is considered the finest of five related processional crosses to have survived from the Middle Byzantine period. Frequently attested in both historical and hagiographic sources, such crosses were intended to be carried in a leading position in military campaigns as well as imperial ceremonies and liturgical processions. While a large number of bronze processional crosses have survived from the Early and Middle Byzantine periods, none of them can compare to the Cleveland cross and its few surviving relatives in terms of the material richness and artistic quality of their decoration.

The Cleveland cross consists of thin sheaths of partly gilded and nielloed silver held together over an iron core by elegant finials at the ends of each cross arm. The front was decorated in the most refined manner with a variety of metalworking techniques. The central medallion with its intricate border of nielloed petals shows the half-length figure of Christ Pantokrator (All-sovereign), raising his right hand in a gesture of blessing. As the source of life, Christ is placed at the center of an elaborate repoussé design that consists of intricate floral scrolls and blossom motifs on a stippled gold ground. At the ends of the horizontal arm are medallions with the repoussé busts of the Meter Theou (Mother of God) and St. John Prodromos (Forerunner), who address Christ with their hands raised in the classical pose of intercession and prayer. Together they form what is often called the "Deesis" (Entreaty), a powerful Byzantine image formula that invokes the Virgin and St. John's intercession with Christ on behalf of humankind. A medallion with the repoussé bust of the archangel Michael, holding a scepter in his right hand and raising the left in a gesture of awe and veneration, completes the decoration on the upper end of the vertical arm. The now-missing lower arm may once have showed a similar image of an archangel.

Both the figural decoration and the recorded and extant inscriptions hold important clues about the cross's history and original function. A recorded inscription on the lost lower arm is reported to have stated: "This precious cross was beautifully worked in the name of our blessed father Sabas by Nicholas, the monk, presbyter, and founder of the Monastery of Glastine." The Cleveland cross can thus be identified as the work of a monk and priest named Nicholas, who made it in honor of St. Sabas, the founder of a famous monastic community outside of Jerusalem in the fifth century. On the back, Sabas is represented in a bust in the central medallion, placed at the intersection of a floral cross, executed in niello on a stippled gold ground, and surrounded by half- and full-length representations of six other Byzantine monastic saints, all inscribed and executed in niello with partial gilding.

While the iconographic program and dedicatory inscription of the cross indicate that it was intended to be used within the liturgical context of a monastic community, it remains unclear whether the cross was in fact made for the otherwise unknown Glastine (?) monastery, mentioned in the inscription, or for another monastic foundation to which the monk Nicholas held close ties. HAK

Leonard C. Hanna Jr. Fund 1970.36

DIMENSIONS: 32.3 x 44.8 cm

INSCRIBED: on the front: IC XC (Jesus Christ); MHP ΘY (Mother of God); O A IΩ O ΠΡΑΜ (Saint John the Precursor); O APX MIX (The Archangel Michael); on the back: O OCIOC CABAC (The Blessed Sabas); O OCIOC ANTΩNIO[C] (The Blessed Anthony); O OCIOC EYΘYMIO[C] (The Blessed Euthymios); O OCIOC EΦPAIM O CYP[IOC] (The Blessed Ephraim the Syrian); O OCIOC IΛAPIΩN (The Blessed Hilary); O OCIOC ANACTACIO[C] O TOY CINA (The Blessed Anastasios of Sinai); O OCIOC IΩ[ANNHC] O KΛIMAKO[C] (The Blessed John Klimax); on the scroll carried by Ephraim the Syrian: OCOI TA TOY KOCMOY MATAIA ΦYΓEIN EΞHΛ (Those who go out to flee the vain things of the world); on the scroll of John Klimax MIMECΘO O TO EAYTOY ΦOPTION (Let him be imitated who owns his own burden)

BIBLIOGRAPHY: New York 1997, 60, no. 24; Washington 1994, 68–75, no. 2; Caillet 1988, 208–17; Mango 1988, 41–49; Wixom 1986, 294–304; Bank 1980, 97–111.

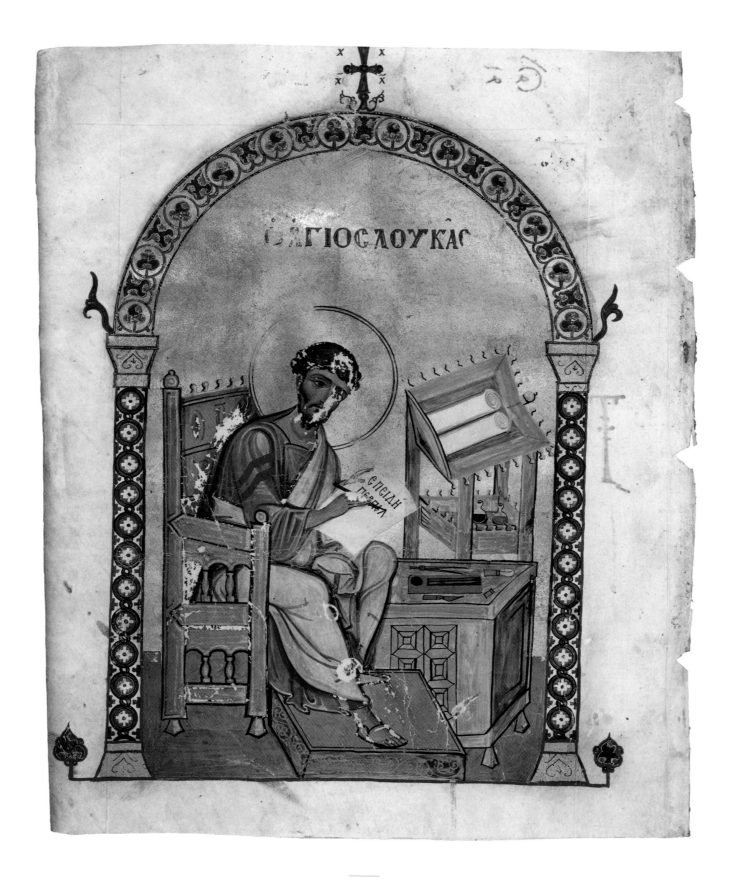

Two Leaves from a Gospel Lectionary: St. Luke and St. Matthew

ABOUT 1063; MIDDLE BYZANTINE, CONSTANTINOPLE

INK, TEMPERA, AND GOLD ON VELLUM

These two manuscript leaves with full-page illuminations of the evangelists Luke and Matthew were excised from a Byzantine gospel lectionary that once belonged to the library of the Phanar School in Istanbul and is now preserved in the National Library of Greece in Athens (Mageles to genous scholes 2). A colophon reveals that the manuscript had originally been presented to the monastery of the Holy Trinity on Chalke, an island off the coast of Constantinople in the Marmara Sea, by Empress Catherine Komnene in March 1063. One of six daughters of Tsar John of Bulgaria (r. 1015–18), Catherine and other members of her family had fallen into Byzantine captivity after Emperor Basil II's decisive victory over the Bulgarians at Dyrrachion (modern Durrës in Albania) in 1018. She later married Isaac Komnenos, one of Basil's generals, and became empress when her husband rose to the imperial throne after a palace rebellion in 1057. Isaac's reign, however, was short-lived. He abdicated in 1059 and became a monk at Stoudios Monastery in Constantinople. As witnessed by the Phanar Lectionary, Catherine took the veil a few years later and adopted the name "Xene" following common monastic practice.

As is often the case in gospel lectionaries, books in which the individual readings (lections) are arranged chronologically for better use during liturgical services, the four evangelist portraits of the Phanar Codex once introduced the lections for each author. Placed before a luminous gold ground and framed by an elaborately decorated arch, St. Luke is seated in a high-backed chair and dressed in tunic and pallium, the classical garments of ancient philosophers. His youthful appearance conforms to the common Byzantine iconographic practice of re-serving older age for Matthew and John. Focusing intently on the parchment leaf in front of him, Luke has just finished writing the first verse of his gospel. The armoire and lectern before him carry the usual tools of an author and scribe: a stylus (for writing, drawing, and engraving), a compass (for transferring measurements), pens, knives, and inkpots. St. Matthew is likewise depicted in the act of writing, sitting within an imposing architectural framework filled with a golden background. Unlike Luke, however, he is not focusing on the text in front of him, but looks into the distance as if waiting for divine inspiration. In the physical context of the Phanar Lectionary, Matthew's gaze formerly rested on the gospel lection on the opposite page, thus giving expression to the divine word he is about to compose. The evangelist portraits in this and other gospel books and lectionaries not only function as author portraits in the traditional sense, but also serve to authenticate the text and remind the viewer of its divine provenance.

While the portraits share certain stylistic similarities, they were undoubtedly executed by different artists who chose different approaches to the composition of the architectural frame and the style of the identifying inscription. Judging from an early photograph of the now-missing portrait of the evangelist John and the portrait of St. Mark (see p. 85), preserved in the Dumbarton Oaks collection in Washington, the group originally consisted of two sets of portraits, which may have been executed independently from the manuscript in which they were placed. Still intact in the early 1920s, the Phanar Lectionary seems to have lost its illuminated leaves by 1931, when the folio representing St. Mark was exhibited in Paris as belonging

ΟΜΑΤΘΑΙΟC

to the Guerson Collection. While the two leaves in Cleveland were acquired in 1942 through the dealer and collector Dikran Kelekian in New York, the Dumbarton Oaks leaf was not purchased until in 1979. The fate of the fourth leaf representing St. John is presently unknown. HAK

Purchase from the J. H. Wade Fund 1942.1511—12

DIMENSIONS: 28.9 x 22.6 cm and 28.8 x 24.3 cm

INSCRIBED: Ο ΆΓΙΟC ΛΟΥΚΑC (Saint Luke); Ο Ά[ΓΙΟC] ΜΑΤΘΑΙΟC (Saint Matthew)

BIBLIOGRAPHY: New York 1997, 103, no. 58A–B; Spatharakis 1981, 1: 26, no. 77; Princeton 1973, 84—87, no. 13—14; Athens 1964, 315, no. 309; Bond 1962, 428, no. 42.1511—12; Baltimore 1947, 137, no. 700; Milliken 1947, 50—56; Clark 1937, 122—23; Diehl 1927, 9; Diehl 1922, 243—48. For the leaf at Dumbarton Oaks, see Kavrus-Hoffmann 1996, 306—7; Vikan 1980; Paris 1931, 173, no. 653.

ΠΕΤΡΟΥ ΕΠΙΣΤ(ΟΛΗ) ΚΑΘΟΛΙΚΗ. Α

Πετρος αποστολος ΙΥ ΧΥ· εκλεκτοις παρεπι
δημοις διασπορας· ποντου· γαλατιας· καπ
παδοκιας· ασιας και βιθυνιας· κατα προ
γνωσιν θυ πρς εν αγιασμω πνς εις υπακοην·
και ραντισμον αιματος ΙΥ ΧΥ· χαρις υμιν
ειρηνη πληθυνθειη· ευλογητος ο θς και πηρ
του κυ ημων ΙΥ ΧΥ· ο κατα το πολυ ελεος αυτου
αναγεννησας ημας εις ελπιδα ζωσαν· δι ανα
στασεως ΙΥ ΧΥ εκ νεκρων· εις κληρονομιαν αφθαρ
τον και αμιαντον και αμαραντον· τετηρημενην
εν ουρανοις εις ημας· τους εν δυναμει θυ φρουρου
μενους δια πιστεως· εις σωτηριαν ετοιμην αποκαλυ
φθηναι εν καιρω εσχατω· εν ω αγαλλιασθε·

ς̅ ξ̅ λβ,   εα
τ̅   εβ:

Leaf from a Greek Psalter and New Testament

1084; MIDDLE BYZANTINE, CONSTANTINOPLE

INK, TEMPERA, AND GOLD ON VELLUM

This leaf was excised from a very fine Byzantine manuscript that combines a psalter and the New Testament in a single codex. The parent manuscript, which still survives, once belonged to the monastery of Christ Pantokrator (All-sovereign), founded on Mount Athos in northern Greece in 1363. Formerly known as "Pantokrator 49," the manuscript was removed from the Holy Mountain at some point between 1941, when it was last studied and photographed within the monastery, and 1950, when the Cleveland leaf was acquired on the New York art market. In 1962, the codex was purchased from a Swiss dealer for the Byzantine collection at Dumbarton Oaks in Washington, where it is preserved as "Ms. 3." Two other excised leaves are in the Benaki Museum in Athens (Benaki 66) and the State Tretyakov Gallery in Moscow (2580).

Since the Dumbarton Oaks manuscript includes a set of paschal tables for the years 1084 to 1101 (fol. 3v), the Cleveland leaf was likely completed in or shortly before 1084. The sophisticated style of the illuminations further suggests that the manuscript was produced in the Byzantine capital, Constantinople, where it must have served its owner as a book of private prayer and devotion. Exactly how and when the codex reached the Pantokrator Monastery on Mount Athos cannot be determined with certainty. It may have been the gift of a certain monk named John, who owned the book in the late 15th or early 16th century and added a pair of miniatures (now missing) with his own portrait in front of the New Testament portion of the manuscript.

The decoration of the Cleveland leaf, which originally opened the First Epistle of Peter on folio 254 of the Dumbarton Oaks manuscript, is dominated by a half-page miniature of St. Peter holding a scroll as a sign of his authorship. Dressed in a light blue tunic and brownish pallium, the apostle stands before a draped wall set against a golden ground. The bottom half of the leaf contains the epistle's title, written in gold ink, and the first 13 lines of text. Starting with the words "Πέτρος ἀπόστολος ἰεσοῦ χριστοῦ" (Peter, apostle of Jesus Christ), the text features a figural initial for the letter Π (pi), which is composed of representations of Christ and St. Peter supporting the letter's horizontal bar. Addressing the apostle with his outstretched right hand, a classical gesture of speech and teaching, Christ confers his authority upon Peter, whose receptiveness to the Lord's word is indicated by the slight inclination of his head and the open palm of his outstretched right hand. HAK

Purchase from the J. H. Wade Fund 1950.154

DIMENSIONS: 16.3 x 10.9 cm

BIBLIOGRAPHY: New York 1997, no. 54, 99–100; Princeton 1973, 104–5, no. 21. For the manuscript, see Kavrus-Hoffmann 1996, 296–302; Lowden 1988, 248–50; Der Nersessian 1965, 155–83; Lampros 1966, 1: 98, no. 1083. For other leaves from the same manuscript, see Lappa-Zizica/Rizou-Couroupou 1991 and Cutler 1983, 35–45.

Rosette Casket: Scenes from the Story of Adam and Eve

11TH–12TH CENTURY; MIDDLE BYZANTINE, CONSTANTINOPLE

IVORY AND WOOD

Gift of W. G. Mather, F. F. Prentiss, John L. Severance, J. H. Wade
1924.747

DIMENSIONS: 14.3 x 46.7 x 20.3 cm

INSCRIBED: on the cover: I(HCOY)C X(PICTO)C (Jesus Christ); AΔAM
(Adam); AΔAM YΠINOCAC EYA EΞHΛΘEN EK TIC ΠΛEBPA AYTON

(While Adam was asleep, Eve came out of his rib); KAH(N) ΦONEYH
TON ABEΛ (Cain murders Abel); on the long sides: AΔAM (Adam);
EYA (Eve); EYA (Eve); AΔAM (Adam); AΔAM ΠOY H (Adam where art
thou?); ΓABP(IHΛ) (Gabriel); AΔAM EΞEBΛIΘH (Adam was cast out);
AΔAM (Adam); AΔAM (Adam); on the short sides: EYA (Eve); AΔAM
(Adam); AΔAM (Adam)

Decorated with scenes from the Old Testament story of Adam and Eve and their children Cain and Abel, this Middle Byzantine ivory box belongs to a distinct group of objects known as "rosette caskets," the term deriving from the thin ivory strips with rosette medallions that serve as framing devices and decorative borders.

While the imagery on most Byzantine rosette caskets is secular in nature, often featuring scenes from classical mythology, heroic warriors in combat, or childlike *erotes* (cupids) as dancers and musicians, the Cleveland casket forms part of a group of related boxes with scenes from the Old Testament. The story of Adam and Eve starts on the lid with two ivory plaques depicting the Creation story. In the creation of Adam, God the Father is represented in the form of his prefigured son, Jesus Christ, whose half-length figure is identified as such by an inscription. In

the creation of Eve, only the hand of God is visible, reaching out from heaven. In contrast to the Creation scenes, which are laid out horizontally but placed vertically on the lid, the other two plaques represent a single scene that is narrated across the rosette strip between them. As the inscriptions suggest, the scenes represent Cain's slaying of Abel.

The story of Adam and Eve is taken up again on the front of the box in nine (originally ten) consecutive scenes that, at times, consist of more than one plaque. The narrative begins on the left with a plaque depicting the naked full-length figures of Adam and Eve facing each other. Eve picks fruit from a tree between them, and two of the tree's branches swing outward to cover their pudenda. The next two scenes are both narrated across two plaques. In the first Eve shares the forbidden fruit with her receptive mate on the opposite panel while the snake whispers into her ear. What follows is a scene in which God, once again shown in the prefigured form of Christ, questions the remorseful Adam with the words: "Where art thou?" The story continues on the lock side of the box with two plaques showing the seated Adam and Eve weeping over their transgression; the plaque on the back depicts the archangel Gabriel expelling the pair from Paradise. The following two plaques show Adam tilling the ground and harvesting grain. The last plaque on this side, which may have shown Eve spinning, is now lost, replaced with a wooden panel. Concluding the Creation story is a large single scene on the box's small side. It shows the first human pair at the forge, Eve blowing the bellows on the left, and Adam working a piece of iron with hammer and anvil on the right.

It has often been suggested that boxes such as this one were made to contain jewelry or small valuables and, considering their imagery, that they may have been given as wedding gifts. Unfortunately, such specific uses cannot be proven with any certainty. However, the assembly-line method of production, with mass-produced strips of rosette ornaments and standardized narrative panels carved from ivory (and sometimes bone), suggests that these boxes were made for a broad urban clientele rather than a small aristocratic elite. HAK

BIBLIOGRAPHY: Cutler 1984, 32–47; Baltimore 1947, 43, no. 118; Cleveland 1936, 18, no. 11; Goldschmidt/Weitzmann 1979A, 48–49, no. 67; Eastman 1927, 157–68; Milliken 1925A, 5–13; Graeven 1899, 297–315.

Reliquary Box: Scenes from the Life of John the Baptist

14TH CENTURY; LATE BYZANTINE, CONSTANTINOPLE

TEMPERA, GOLD, AND WOOD

With at least 36 churches dedicated to his name in the Byzantine capital Constantinople alone, John the Baptist, or John Prodromos (Forerunner) as he is known in the Orthodox world, was one of the most revered saints in the empire. John, who preached repentance in the Judean desert and baptized his followers in preparation of the coming of the Messiah, plays a pivotal role in the gospel accounts because he was the first to recognize Christ as the promised Savior, baptizing him in the River Jordan. John later denounced the adulterous relationship of King Herod Antipas with Herodias, his sister-in-law and mother of Salome, which led to John's imprisonment and eventually beheading.

This small painted wooden box with its sliding lid features, on the long sides, four scenes from the life of St. John, curiously arranged in reverse chronological order and alternating with ornamental panels. The martyrdom of St. John takes place in front of an elaborate architectural background, which probably identifies Machaerus, the fortress in which he was imprisoned. The Forerunner is seen twice, once before his martyrdom, looking out of a window in the fortress, and a second time, immediately after his beheading, still standing bound and upright before the executioner while his severed head lies on the ground. The attending figure behind the executioner, dressed in red, may

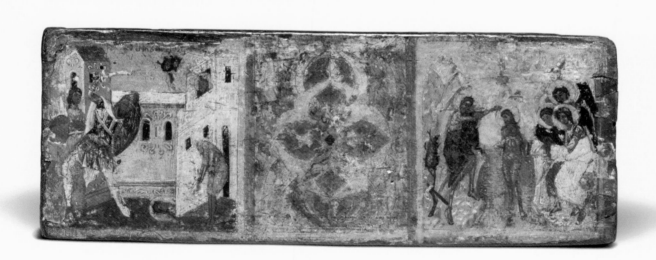

Celtic Head

ABOUT AD 100–300; ROMANO-BRITISH

SANDSTONE WITH TRACES OF RED PAINT

This stone head is a complete composition in itself; it was never attached to a torso. According to ancient literary sources, the Celts—who originally occupied most of northern Europe from Hungary to the British Isles—revered the human head, which represented the seat of human magical energy. Such stone heads were central to Celtic iconography and probably placed in religious shrines or grottos generally associated with springs, well heads, or natural landmarks for ritual veneration.

Although minimally carved and lacking classical naturalism, this head is imposing for its uniqueness and ethereal stare. Slightly larger than life-size, it was carved from a block of fine-grained sandstone with uneven surface coloration and has the lentoid eyes, long triangular nose, and simple slit mouth typical of many Celtic heads. The rough crosshatching indicates hair, and the ears may be equine in form. The terminus of the neck is slightly beveled, suggesting that it was originally inset into the masonry of a larger design. A triangular groove incised into the crown of the head may have been intended for ritual use. Depressions found on the crowns of several such Celtic heads suggest they were used to hold offerings or libations.

Recent scientific analysis has revealed traces of red paint, indicating that originally the entire surface of this head was painted. Such paint remnants have been discovered on other Celtic heads and suggest some unknown ritual purpose. Celtic stone heads have been found across Celtic Europe and date from the late Iron Age into the Roman occupation. They are especially abundant in the upland regions of northern England (the Pennines, the Peak District, and Cumbria) where this one was undoubtedly made by British Celts during the Roman era. Most of these heads have not been discovered in an archaeological context because in recent centuries they became part of the fabric of buildings—inset into stone walls or used as garden ornaments. Thus it is difficult to localize and date them with accuracy. SNF

Gift of Dr. and Mrs. Jacob Hirsch 1955.555

DIMENSIONS: 30 x 31 x 24 cm

BIBLIOGRAPHY: New York 2006B, 174–75, no. 70; Fliegel 1990, 82–103; Green 1986, 200–25; Jackson 1973, 2–3; Ross 1967, 61–126; Pulver 1919, 284.

28

Ten Ornamental Fibulae

ABOUT AD 100–300; GALLO-ROMAN OR ROMANO-BRITISH
BRONZE AND CHAMPLEVÉ ENAMEL

Fibulae functioned somewhat like modern safety pins. Since buttons were not used in antiquity, fibulae kept a cloak or garment closed and in place. Worn by both men and women, they were produced in a variety of sizes and shapes. This group of highly decorative fibulae, with their hidden pin gears, were used as garment clasps, much like the generally larger crossbow fibulae or penannular brooches. Fibulae such as those illustrated here are known today as plate brooches and survive in a variety of forms including discs and lozenges as well as zoomorphic and geometric patterns. Some have added knobs; others are pierced. The highly distinctive and colorful enamel work indicates that decoration could have been their main purpose.

The metal employed for these enameled objects was consistently bronze; silver and gold do not seem to have been used. The Romans practiced enameling (fusing a vitreous substance to a metallic base) on small objects, and the brightly colored ornament readily appealed to the peoples they conquered, with their tribal emphasis on personal adornment and horse trappings. The technique used for these fibulae is champlevé, in which small cells are cut or cast into the bronze in order to receive the vitreous paste. By the third century, enameled brooches like these were being made in abundance by the native peoples of Britain and Gaul, indicating that those parts of the empire were the primary areas of production. Plate brooches have also been found in Pannonia, Sarmatia, and the eastern Roman provinces, perhaps carried there by military personnel. Red was the primary color until the end of the first century when blue and yellow were added. A small number of fibulae have Celtic motifs—suggesting an antecedent for the tradition—but most surviving brooches are Roman provincial in style.

Enameled plate brooches derive from burial contexts and survive in excavated condition with bronze disease and pitted enamel. Notwithstanding such imperfections, these fibulae suggest an imaginative and vibrant native culture flourishing within the Roman provinces. SNF

Purchase from the J. H. Wade Fund 1930.230–39

DIMENSIONS: various sizes, from 1 x 2 cm to 5.3 x 5.3 cm

BIBLIOGRAPHY: Böhme-Schönberger 1997, 83–84; Trento 1997, 480–84; Hattatt 1994, 136–44; Butcher 1976, 42–51.

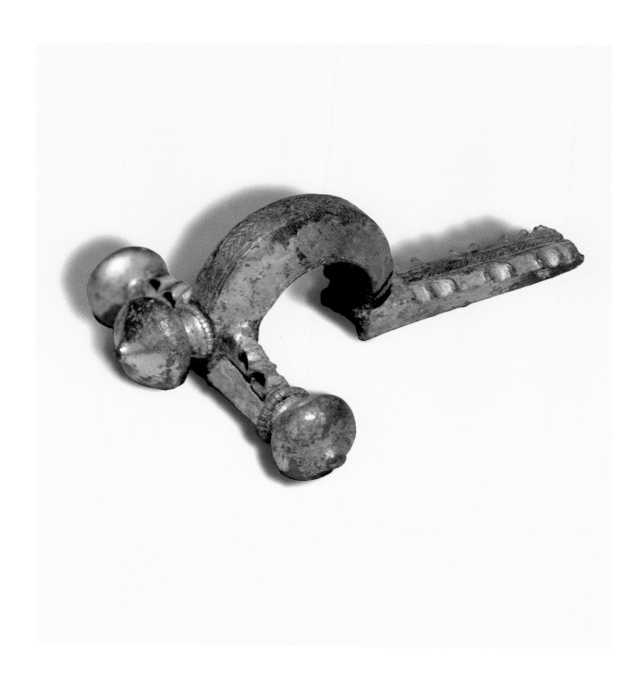

29

Crossbow Fibula

ABOUT AD 350–400; ROMANO-BRITISH OR GALLO-ROMAN

GILDED BRONZE, SILVER, AND NIELLO

Crossbow fibulae, called such because they resemble the weapon, were introduced by the Romans throughout the empire, and their use is documented from Britain to the Euphrates between the third and fifth centuries. Used as fasteners for clothing, they were commonly worn on the right shoulder as indicated by artistic evidence such as sculpture and mosaics and also by burial evidence. Some crossbow fibulae were made of silver, and some were so massive that they had to be constructed hollow, with openwork decoration, in order to retain their ostentation and yet not be too heavy.

Fibulae were often ornamented with gilding, inlays, or onion-shaped domes, as in this example. The decorative and technical features suggest that it may have been made in Roman-occupied Britain. With its onion terminals, running pattern of silver and *niello* chevrons, and molded volutes along the vertical foot, this crossbow fibula is among the more ornate examples and represents highly skilled workmanship. The mechanisms of crossbow fibulae can vary. In this example, the pin is attached at a slot cut through the back at the point where the vertical and horizontal elements converge, forming the hinge and representing a type called the T-shape or tubular-wing hinge. The pin extends down the length of the vertical foot and slips into a slit that runs the length of the foot.

The combination of decoration and mechanics of this fibula permits its dating to about AD 350–400 based on comparisons with nearly identical crossbow fibulae found throughout Britain. Typologically, it is made up of four distinct elements: the bow (the curved element); the vertical foot; the horizontal arm; and the three knobs or finials that appear at the three ends of the cross arms. The wings of the cross arm have no function; they suggest orientation as well as serving aesthetic purposes. SNF

Purchase from the J. H. Wade Fund 1930.227

DIMENSIONS: 10.2 x 7.1 cm

BIBLIOGRAPHY: Hattatt 1994, 118–25; Hattatt 1987, 3–10, 282–88; Baltimore 1947, no. 857.

30

Pair of Earrings

AD 400S; OSTROGOTHIC

GOLD WITH GARNETS

A Germanic people, the Goths invaded and settled in parts of the Roman Empire from about AD 200 to 500. They were a single nation or tribe, according to several sources dating up to the third century, when they split into Ostrogoths (East Goths) and Visigoths (West Goths). Both branches produced a highly decorative, vibrant art of personal adornment—a portable art that followed men and women to their graves. The Ostrogoths originated in South Russia and occupied Italy in 488, where they maintained a monarchy until 555. Their king, Theodoric the Great (r. 489–526), had been raised at the Byzantine court of Constantinople and sought to be seen as a Roman emperor. He made Ravenna his capital, imitated imperial coinage, and commissioned new buildings in the Byzantine style.

The design of these earrings derives from Late Roman jewelry, which had been adopted by Ostrogothic women during the fifth century. The garnet was a favored gemstone, and the hoops here end in multi-faceted (polyhedral) beads inlaid with thin pieces of the jewel, which contrast vividly with their gold surround. Granulated ornament also decorates the beads. Despite their efforts to imitate the classical culture of Late Roman antiquity, the Ostrogoths' greatest contribution to art was their retention of polychromed jewelry—rings, brooches, crosses, clasps—which they introduced into Italy from their South Russian homeland. Like this pair of earrings, such jewelry relied on the use of brightly colored stones set in gold cloisons, as well as filigree and geometric patterns. SNF

Gift of Dr. and Mrs. John R. McKay 1975.48.1–2

DIMENSIONS: 3.5 x 3.4 cm

BIBLIOGRAPHY: Florence 1989, no. 113; Dixon 1976, 68–70; Laszlo 1974; Backes/Dölling 1969; Hubert 1969; Bullough 1965, 158–74.

31

Eagle-shaped Fibulae

6TH CENTURY; FRANKISH

COPPER ALLOY WITH GILDING AND GARNET INSETS

Ornamentally distorted animal forms appear frequently in the art of the Migration Period. Although not a matched pair, these two eagle fibulae are similar in form and scale, and reflect the extensive taste for stylized bird forms in the jewelry of European peoples of the fourth through eighth centuries. While both brooches are cast and each bird is depicted in profile facing right, they vary in detail. The right wing of the larger fibula is folded vertically at its side, and its eye, wing, and tail are inlaid with red garnets. Repeated punch marks create details. The bird on the other brooch has an ovoid body with stylized feathers cast in parallel vertical grooves. Its left wing is folded laterally across its breast and its eye is an inset garnet. Although the pins are missing from the backs of both brooches, each fibula has the remains of a hinge-pivot.

Small-scale bird fibulae such as these dating to Frankish and Merovingian Europe have been found in an almost infinite variety in locations marked and mapped by Joachim Werner. (Little is known of the legendary Frankish king Merovech other than that he defeated the Huns and founded the dynasty that bears his name.) Eagle fibulae, produced in larger sizes in Visigothic and Ostrogothic Europe, were principally used to fasten an outer garment such as a cloak at both shoulders. Smaller varieties, commonly found in France and Germany, would have served as fasteners for lighter garments but their principal interest was sartorial. SNF

Gift of the John Huntington Art and Polytechnic Trust 1918.926 and 1918.928

DIMENSIONS: 2.6 x 1.3 and 2.9 x 1.3 cm

BIBLIOGRAPHY: for similar objects, see MacGregor 1997, 144–47, and Werner 1961, 44–47, 53–54, pl. 42–43.

32

Fibula

SECOND HALF OF 6TH CENTURY; FRANKISH, LORRAINE OR RHINELAND

SILVER WITH GLASS INLAYS

One of several west Germanic federations, the Franks entered the Roman Empire from today's central Germany and the southern Netherlands. They settled in northern Gaul and established a lasting realm, sometimes called Francia, in an area that eventually covered most of modern-day France, the Low Countries, and the western regions of Germany, forming the historic kernel of all these countries. The pagan king Clovis I defeated the Roman army, united all the Frankish tribes, and made Paris his base of operations. His conversion to Christianity in the late fifth century was a crucial event in the history of France and Europe.

Like other migratory tribes, the Franks were not attracted to the monumental arts of architecture and sculpture until they had long settled an area. By contrast, their graves were filled with weapons, tools, and jewelry, often magnificently decorated. Their art is almost exclusively one of personal adornment. Frankish jewelry consisted largely of a variety of buckles, brooches, pins, and fibulae such as the present example. These objects, which survive as grave goods, usually had the functional application of securing clothing. Because they were highly visible accessories in their own right, they often attracted decorative embellishment such as gilding, gemstones, and inlay decoration. Two styles dominate the history of "barbarian" art: the polychrome style, whose origins are found among the Goths of the Black Sea, later extending into Italy and Spain; and the animal style, characterized by animal motifs such as bird heads and griffins. This fibula is an example of the latter.

Fibulae were often made in pairs, one for each shoulder. This example ends with a stylized serpent head, and its surface is ornamented with chip carving, a technique probably learned from the Romans. Cut with a chisel, the channels and beds of this deeply incised pattern would have glistened in the sun. Often chip-carved decoration was not executed on the metal itself but on the mold from which the object was cast. This fibula was produced using that method. The glass inlays would have contrasted vividly with the silver when new. SNF

Andrew R. and Martha Holden Jennings Fund 1975.109

DIMENSIONS: 11 x 6 x 1.6 cm

BIBLIOGRAPHY: Salin 1950–52, 2: pl. A.

33

Belt Buckle

ABOUT 525–60; VISIGOTHIC, SPAIN

BRONZE WITH GARNETS, GLASS, MOTHER-OF-PEARL, GOLD FOIL, AND TRACES OF GILDING

This superb monumental belt buckle is made of a sheet of gold foil applied over bronze and inlaid with garnets, colored glass, and mother-of-pearl. The tongue of the buckle ends in a stylized animal head, its eyes inset with garnets. One end of the rectangular plate was originally attached with four small pins to a leather strap, with the tongue and loop at the other end. Such belts were thought to have been worn to fasten women's tunics; their mantles would have been secured with a pair of bow brooches or fibulae. Large rectangular belt buckles have been discovered in cemeteries across Visigothic Spain, and this one undoubtedly came from a woman's grave (men wore simple oval buckles with no plate). These buckles are strikingly uniform in shape yet endlessly varied in surface design, perhaps a sign that they expressed the personalities of their original owners. Finer examples have brilliant inlaid semi-precious stones and colored glass.

The Visigoths, known for their technical skills and taste for multi-tonal opulence, were the principal agents for the dissemination of polychrome jewelry. Such jewelry constituted important items of dress and was probably restricted to the social elite. This buckle is a classic example of the motifs and techniques the Goths brought to Spain from their fourth-century homeland in the Ukraine. The Visigothic kingdom with its capital at Toledo survived until the Muslim invasions in 711.

The technique involved fitting carefully cut pieces of polished garnet into an intricate grid of cloisons (compartments). The rectangular plate of this buckle contains a geometric pattern composed around a central stone. Within this fixed formula, the variations are infinite. Five round flat-topped garnets, each incised with a circle, occupy the center and four corners of the plaque. The outer borders and the branches of an X-shaped St. Andrew's cross are set with S-shaped stones. Gold foil behind the translucent stones increases their brilliance, while cabochon "eyes" transform the tongue of the buckle into a snake-like monster. Even the flat loop contains inlays, an unusual and rich feature. So densely inlaid with garnets is this buckle that it presents a virtual carpet of red.

Garnets were highly valued in Hellenistic and Roman art, but the Goths also appreciated them for their symbolic and apotropaic qualities. Monumental buckles such as this one would have been costly and time-consuming to produce because the garnets had to be split into thin slices and then cut into the desired shapes using templates and high-speed wheels. This craft was highly specialized and restricted to exclusive workshops. SNF

Purchase from the J. H. Wade Fund 2001.119

DIMENSIONS: 13.2 x 7.1 cm

BIBLIOGRAPHY: López 2000, 188–203; New York 1999, no. 55; San Marino 1995, 184, 307–25; Adams 1992, 121–24.

34

Pair of Fibulae

6TH–7TH CENTURY; ALEMANNIC

CAST SILVER, PARCEL GILT, WITH NIELLO

Design and ornamentation indicate that this pair of matched fibulae was produced by the Alemanni, a tribal confederation and old adversary of Rome that occupied the territories of modern Germany and Switzerland between the third and the seventh centuries. The basic form is a semicircular headplate with radiating knobs and a narrow subrectangular footplate. Made of cast silver, which was then chip carved, chased with abstract patterns, and gilded, each fibula has a ridge down the center that is embellished with a meandering dot and vine motif in niello. Typically a single fibula was worn on the right shoulder, with a matched pair occasionally fastening an outer cloak at both shoulders. Following changes to feminine costume, fibulae were no longer needed as garment fasteners and instead were suspended from a woman's belt as jewelry. They were thus prized as personal accessories; brooches like this pair are associated with women's graves.

The animal style, characterized by motifs such as bird heads and griffins, achieved its peak in Scandinavia, Germany, and Anglo-Saxon England after the fifth century. The beautifully shaped dragon heads forming the five termini of each brooch put this pair among the animal-style objects of Europe's migratory peoples. This type is often called a digitated fibula, because its termini give the illusion of fingers. These fibulae were likely made for the same female owner and derive from a single grave. They survive in excellent condition and are of very high artistic quality. SNF

Purchase from the J. H. Wade Fund 2000.119.1–2

DIMENSIONS: 10.5 x 6.5 cm each

BIBLIOGRAPHY: Martin 2000, 226–40; Fuchs 1997, 192–95, 352–63; Christlein 1991, 143–46.

Among the various Germanic peoples who settled in the northwestern fringes of the Late Roman Empire, a confederation of smaller tribes called the Franks, under the leadership of the Merovingian family, emerged as the most successful conglomerate. Following the decline and disintegration of Roman power in northern Gaul during the later fifth century, Clovis I defeated not only the son of the last Roman military commander in Gaul but also the neighboring tribes of the Thuringi, Alemanni, and Visigoths, thus consolidating Merovingian rule and Frankish power in central and eastern Gaul. More far-reaching than his military successes, at least in terms of its consequences for the cultural history of medieval Europe, was Clovis's decision to adopt Orthodox Christianity for himself and his people. Frankish power was consolidated and expanded under the Carolingian dynasty, named for Charlemagne (Charles the Great), who ruled over a vast territory first as king of the Franks, then as king of the Franks and Langobards (since 774), and finally as emperor, having been crowned by Pope Leo III in Rome on Christmas Day of the year 800. Charlemagne's idea of a revival of the Roman Empire under decidedly Christian auspices resulted in a wide range of political and religious reforms as well as a renaissance of the arts and culture of the Classical and Late Roman past. Northern artists, deeply rooted in the abstract traditions of their Celtic or Germanic ancestors, started to copy Classical and Early Christian models in architecture, sculpture, painting, and fine metalwork, thus adopting styles and techniques of the Graeco-Roman tradition and blending them with their own in a hitherto unprecedented manner. Charlemagne's vision of a Christian empire with unified religious and liturgical practices placed an immediate demand on the production of new, corrected editions of the Bible and liturgical texts, which had become corrupted after centuries of copying and miscopying. Given the centrality of the recovery of the "true" text of the Bible, the production of liturgical books with sumptuous covers thrived both in scriptoria associated with Charlemagne's court and in monasteries, founded all over the empire as beacons of prayer, learning, and devotion. The surge in the manufacture of fine metalwork and the revival of ivory carving during the Carolingian period can likewise be linked to Charlemagne's reform agenda, which created an increasing demand for sacred vessels and other furnishings to be used in the divine liturgy.

While Charlemagne's immediate successors continued to promote art and culture, repeated Viking attacks and political unrest during the late ninth and early tenth centuries resulted in a sharp decline of high-level artistic patronage and production. This situation began to change only with the emergence of a powerful new dynasty in Saxony, named "Ottonian" after Otto the Great, who succeeded his father Henry I as king of the Germans in 936 and was crowned emperor in Rome in 962, and his successors Otto II and Otto III. These Ottonian rulers not only followed their Carolingian predecessors in reviving the arts and culture of the Late Roman Empire, but helped advance the arts of their period to a degree of sophistication, artistic accomplishment, and technical refinement that could claim comparison with the highly refined products of contemporary Byzantine court culture. Members of the clergy—often themselves of imperial descent—also played an important role as patrons of art and architecture. One of the most notable among them was Bishop Bernward of Hildesheim, whose artistic patronage established that city as a major center for the production of illuminated manuscripts, precious metalwork, and bronze casting for centuries. As in the case of the famous Guelph Treasure, such initial commissions could develop into important collections of sacred objects tied to a specific saint, church, or institution that would continue to attract high-level artistic patronage and sacred gifts for generations.

The Guelph Treasure

Named after a Frankish aristocratic family, the Guelph Treasure is one of the largest and culturally most significant ecclesiastical treasures to survive from medieval Germany. While the treasure has been associated with the Guelph dynasty since the 12th century, its early history links it to another prominent German family, the Brunons, whose male members are attested as the counts of Saxony since the early 11th century. In 1030, Count Liudolf I and his wife, Gertrude, founded a collegiate church within the precinct of their castle in Brunswick (Braunschweig) and dedicated it to St. Blaise. This church was to serve as the burial place for the count and his family, and after his death it received several important relics and liturgical objects from his wife. The most distinguished among these donations are a portable altar and two reliquary crosses dedicated to the memory of her husband, all acquired by Cleveland in 1931 (see no. 36). Together with an arm reliquary of St. Blaise (Herzog Anton Ulrich-Museum, Brunswick), Gertrude's original gifts form the core of the ecclesiastical treasure of the church of St. Blaise, which became known as the Guelph Treasure only in the late 19th century.

The sacred treasure was augmented considerably a century later by Duke Henry the Proud, the first Guelph ruler of Saxony, and his son Henry the Lion, who not only rebuilt the church of St. Blaise, but also bequeathed to it various sacred relics brought back from his pilgrimage to Jerusalem in 1172–73. At least two arm reliquaries in the treasure, those containing the relics of saints Theodore and Innocentius, can be directly linked to Henry's patronage through inscriptions. Other objects of 12th-century origin, such as the famous portable altar of Eilbertus of Cologne and the so-called Dome Reliquary (both Kunstgewerbemuseum, Berlin, W 11 and W 15), or certain works of Byzantine craftsmanship can only tentatively be attributed to his benevolence. Some of these works could also have been given by Henry's son Otto IV, who in his will specified that all but one relic formerly in his and his father's possession be given to the church of St. Blaise.

It was not until the early 14th and 15th centuries that the treasure again received serious attention from members of the Guelph family, the chapter of St. Blaise, and local nobility. Among them, Duke Otto the Mild was one of the most distinguished patrons, to whom the plenary reliquaries in Berlin and Cleveland (no. 40) can be attributed on the basis of their dedicatory inscriptions and style.

By 1482, the first preserved inventory of the treasury of St. Blaise, now in the Niedersächsisches Staatsarchiv in Wolfenbüttel (VII, B Hs. 166), listed 1,220 relics of 286 saints contained in 138 reliquaries, which at the time were kept in a sacristy cabinet, or armarium. The number of relics increased once again with the dissolution and destruction of the church of St. Cyriacus in Brunswick in 1545, an event that led to the transfer of that church's treasure to St. Blaise.

A new chapter in the history of the treasure began in 1671, when the city of Brunswick was besieged and conquered by an alliance of Guelph armies. In exchange for his military support, Duke Johann Friedrich of Hannover, a Catholic cousin of the protestant Rudolph August, Duke of Brunswick-Lüneburg, had requested and was granted the treasure as payment. On 16 July 1671, it was transported to the chapel of the duke's castle in Hannover. There it remained—apart from a few war-related interludes—until 1862, when King George V of Hannover removed all objects from the chapel and placed them in the newly founded Königliches Welfenmuseum. After Prussia annexed the Kingdom of Hannover in 1866, the relic chamber became the private property of George V. As a consequence, the treasure was moved to Penzing castle in Austria in 1867 and, two years later, given on loan to the Österreichisches Museum für Kunst und Industrie in Vienna. From 1906 to 1918 it was once again at Penzing castle. After a brief sojourn in Switzerland, the treasure was moved to Cumberland castle in Gmunden (Austria) until plans for its sale emerged in 1927.

The treasure, which by then included 82 objects, was sold on 6 January 1930 to a consortium of German dealers for 8,000,000 Reichsmark (about $2,000,000 in 1930) and subsequently exhibited in Berlin and Frankfurt, where Cleveland's new director and decorative arts curator William Milliken saw it and reserved six pieces for his museum. The following year the treasure was shipped to the United States and shown in sales exhibitions in six cities: New York, Cleveland, Detroit, Philadelphia, Chicago, and San Francisco. Apart from the 38 objects sold to museums and private collectors in Europe and the United States—the Cleveland Museum of Art eventually bought nine (see nos. 35, 36, 38–40), more than any other institution in the United States—the rest of the treasure was shipped back to Europe and stored in Austria. At the end of 1935 the state of Prussia acquired the remaining 44 objects for the Kunstgewerbemuseum, at that time located in the Berlin castle. During the Second World War this portion of the Guelph Treasure was safeguarded in a bunker in Berlin. After the war, it was placed under the protection of the U.S. occupying forces and taken to the Central Collecting Point in Wiesbaden. In 1948, responsibility for the treasure was handed over to the newly created states of Hessen and Lower Saxony. The treasure became the property of the Stiftung Preussischer Kulturbesitz in 1957 but remained on display in Brunswick at Dankwarderode castle until the Kunstgewerbemuseum reopened in 1963 at Schloss Charlottenburg in Berlin (West). Since May 1985, the objects have been on view at the new Kunstgewerbemuseum at the Kulturforum in Berlin. HAK

The Cumberland Medallion

LATE 8TH CENTURY; FRANKISH, MIDDLE RHINE?

CLOISONNÉ ENAMEL, GOLD, AND COPPER

This medallion is one of the finest examples of early enameling to survive from the Carolingian period. Often referred to as the Cumberland Medallion, it is also the oldest object in the Guelph Treasure, the famous ecclesiastical treasure of the collegiate church and later cathedral of St. Blaise in Brunswick, Germany. Because the object is listed neither in the earliest surviving inventories of the treasury of St. Blaise nor in Gerhard Wolter Molanus's *Lipsanographia* (1697), when the medallion entered the treasure and what function it originally served remain uncertain.

Executed in the technique of cloisonné enamel, in which delicate strips of gold are soldered to a copper base to form a composition of *cloisons,* or cells, that are in turn filled with colored glass paste, fired, and polished, the Cumberland Medallion shows a schematic bust-length figure holding a rectangular object with claw-like hands. The cross-inscribed nimbus and the Greek letters *A* (alpha) and *ω* (omega) flanking the figure leave no doubt

that the medallion represents Christ, the "Alpha and Omega, the first and the last, the beginning and the end," according to the Apocalypse (22:13). The apocalyptic theme spelled out in these letters is further enhanced by the two schematic heads immediately below. Rather than wind gods or roaring lions, they should be interpreted as the trumpet-blowing angels heralding Christ's Second Coming at the end of time (Apocalypse 8:2–13, 9:1–21).

The composition as well as the color scheme, which features opaque enamel in blue, green, red, and white on a dark green ground, find their closest parallels in a number of Frankish decorative plaques and fibulae, suggesting that the Cumberland Medallion was made in a late eighth-century workshop in the western parts of present-day Germany, presumably somewhere in the Middle Rhine region. It has been suggested that the object may originally have served as a pendant. However, it is equally possible that the medallion formed part of the decorative program of a reliquary shrine or casket. HAK

Purchase from the J. H. Wade Fund 1930.504

DIMENSIONS: diam. 5.1 cm

BIBLIOGRAPHY: Hasseloff 1990, 84; De Winter 1985B, 13–14, pl. IV; Cleveland 1967, 12–13, 348, no. I-1; Aachen 1965, 100, no. 125; Baltimore 1947, 108, no. 522; Falke/Schmidt/Swarzenski 1930, 26, no. 2; Milliken 1930, 175–76; Neumann 1891, 314–16, no. 78.

Portable Altar of Countess Gertrude

ABOUT 1045; GERMAN, LOWER SAXONY

GOLD, CLOISONNÉ ENAMEL, RED PORPHYRY, GEMS, PEARLS, NIELLO, AND OAK

This portable altar, commissioned by Countess Gertrude of Brunswick (d. 1077), wife of the powerful Count Liudolf of the Brunon family, is not only one of the earliest, but also one of the most sumptuous objects in the Guelph Treasure. It forms part of a group of at least four precious liturgical objects ordered by the countess not long after her husband's death in 1038 and destined for the collegiate church of St. Blaise, which the couple had founded within the precinct of their castle a few years prior, in 1030, as their burial place. Gertrude's commission, which also included two gold crosses (inset) and an arm reliquary for a relic of St. Blaise (Herzog Anton Ulrich-Museum, Brunswick, MA 60), forms the core of the ecclesiastical treasure of St. Blaise, which, over the centuries, came to include more than 140 items, most of which contained sacred relics.

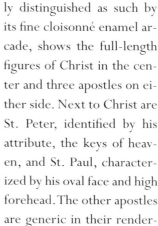

Like the golden crosses and arm reliquary of St. Blaise, which are identified by dedicatory inscriptions, Gertrude's altar has a lengthy inscription around its porphyry altar stone, recording the patron's name and pious intentions in metric verse. However, in decorating the altar and offering it to Christ, Gertrude not only hoped to secure for herself a place in heaven. Through the choice of materials, the quality of craftsmanship, and the iconographic program devised for the altar, she also made sure to spell out her more worldly ambitions, claims, and desires.

The altar's sumptuous ornament, which originally included no fewer than 184 pearls and

92 precious or semi-precious stones, has suffered significant losses over the centuries, but the figural and enamel decoration on the four sides is remarkably well preserved. Framed above and below by a profiled border with gold filigree and alternating gems and pearls, the main decoration consists of four continuous friezes of gold repoussé figures, each standing under an arch. The front panel, clearly distinguished as such by its fine cloisonné enamel arcade, shows the full-length figures of Christ in the center and three apostles on either side. Next to Christ are St. Peter, identified by his attribute, the keys of heaven, and St. Paul, characterized by his oval face and high forehead. The other apostles are generic in their rendering and thus cannot be identified easily. The back panel mirrors the arrangement on the front, with full-length representations of the other six apostles flanking the central figure of the Virgin, who has her hands raised in a gesture of prayer and intercession. Here, however, the arcades are embossed rather than enameled. Completing the figural decoration on the two side panels are four scepter-bearing angels in nielloed arcades flanking the central figure of St. Michael killing the dragon and a scene that can best be described as an adoration of the True Cross. Here, the nielloed arches are inscribed with the names of the figures on either side of the richly decorated enamel cross in the center: closest to the cross are Emperor Constantine and his mother, Helena, who are considered the founders of the cult of the True Cross in Jerusalem and

Constantinople. They are joined in their adoration by the Burgundian king Sigismund and the Ottonian empress Adelheid, wife of Otto I. If the choice of porphyry for the altar stone signaled Gertrude's imperial aspirations (porphyry had been considered an imperial color since classical antiquity and its use was restricted to the imperial family), the choice of historical figures in the adoration scene clearly underlines her political ambitions and claim of imperial lineage for the house of Brunon.

Following the prescriptions of the Seventh Ecumenical Council of Nicea of 787, according to which every consecrated altar was to contain sacred relics, the portable altar served both a liturgical and a reliquary function. Of the relics listed in the inventory of 1482, those of saints Bartholomew, Adelheid, Hermes, Gertrude, Marcian, Vincent, and others, are still preserved today. They were placed inside the precious container by means of a trap door still visible on the bottom. HAK

Gift of the John Huntington Art and Polytechnic Trust 1931.462

DIMENSIONS: 10.5 x 27.5 x 21 cm

INSCRIBED: around the porphyry stone on top: GERTRVDIS XPO [CHRISTO] FELIX/VT VIVAT IN IPSO/OBTVLIT HVNC LAPIDEM/ GEMMIS AVROQ[VE] NITENTEM (Gertrude offers to Christ, to live joyfully in him, this stone that glistens with gems and gold); on the

sides: SANCTA CRUX (Holy Cross); CONSTANTI[N]VS, S[AN]C[T]A HELENA; SIGISMVNDVS; S[AN]C[T]A ADALHEIT

BIBLIOGRAPHY: Peter 2001; Westermann-Angerhausen 1998, 51–76; Lasko 1994, 214; De Winter 1985B, 36–40; Gosebruch 1979, 9–42; Swarzenski 1967, pl. 36, 40; Milliken 1931, 23–26; Falke/Schmidt/ Swarzenski 1930, 105–6, no. 5; Neumann 1891, 129–35, no. 13.

❖ 37 ❖

Leaf from an Evangelary: The Nativity and St. Matthew

ABOUT 1190; GERMAN, HELMARSHAUSEN ABBEY

TEMPERA, GOLD, AND SILVER ON VELLUM

This magnificent leaf, profusely decorated on both sides, was excised from its parent codex, an evangelary in the Trier Cathedral library (MS 142/124/67), at an unknown date and preserved in a Westphalian castle before being acquired by the Cleveland Museum of Art. The leaf (fol. 2) and codex were illuminated in the famous scriptorium of Helmarshausen Abbey, a former Benedictine foundation (founded 999) located in the Weser Valley just north of Kassel in Lower Saxony. A major center of illumination, the abbey is also noteworthy for the metalworking activities of Roger of Helmarshausen, a monk there during the early part of the century. The earliest Helmarshausen manuscripts date to the first half of the 12th century. They belong to a group of four gospel books and evolve from the tradition of Ottonian manuscripts at Corvey and Echternach. These manuscripts also reveal the influence of Roger's work in metal and establish the Helmarshausen style. During the second half of the century, the scriptorium produced evangelaries and psalters for the abbey, other religious houses, and secular patrons. Among them are the esteemed *Gospels of Henry the Lion,* 1185–88 (Herzog August Bibliothek, Wolfenbüttel, Cod. Guelf. 105 Noviss. 2), one of the most richly decorated German manuscripts of the 12th century, as well as the manuscript from which this leaf came.

The Helmarshausen illuminators active in the service of Henry the Lion, Duke of Saxony and Bavaria, were among the most inventive of the 12th century. Their dynamic compositions typically feature floral, foliate, and geometric ornamentation painted with a rich palette of vivid blues, reds, and greens, and dominated by abundant use of gold and silver. The recto of the Cleveland leaf (the Nativity) includes two registers set within an elaborate border of palmettes, a format borrowed directly from the *Gospels of Henry the Lion.* The scene below features a reclining Virgin most likely borrowed from Byzantine models. The upper field contains allegorical figures, including King Solomon and the mystical bride at left and right, with personifications of Truth and Justice in the center. Each figure holds a scroll bearing a biblical text. The verso integrates the letter *L* [LIBER] enclosing the bust of St. Matthew within a meandering foliate motif. The text continues below in gold, forming the incipit to the Gospel of Matthew, "The Book of the Generation of Jesus Christ, the son of David, the Son of Abraham." The evangelist unfurls a scroll bearing a Latin inscription, "Christ is the true God and the true man."

Stylistically this leaf and its parent codex in Trier reflect strong English influences, perhaps the result of Henry's close ties to England. Obvious Byzantine elements exist such as the patterned fabrics of the reclining Virgin, the jagged draperies, and the physiognomy of the seated figure of Joseph to the right. Within the manuscript, the styles of three different Helmarshausen artists have been noted. Among them appears to be the monk Herimann, who was responsible for the major work in the *Gospels of Henry the Lion.* SNF

Purchase from the J. H. Wade Fund 1933.445.a–b

DIMENSIONS: 34.6 x 23.4 cm and 34.3 x 23.3 cm

BIBLIOGRAPHY: Ronig 1999, 19–20; Ronig 1992; Kötzsche 1989; De Winter 1985B, 110–14, pl. XXIII–XXIV; Swarzenski 1932, 263.

Arm Reliquary of the Apostles

ABOUT 1190; GERMAN, LOWER SAXONY
GILDED SILVER, CHAMPLEVÉ ENAMEL, AND OAK

Imitating a clothed lower arm with an outstretched right hand, this elaborately decorated reliquary from the Guelph Treasure belongs to a class of objects often referred to as body-part, shaped, or "speaking" reliquaries. Such reliquaries are generally believed to reveal their contents by taking the form of the body part from which the relic derived. Yet some arm reliquaries contain the remains of not just one, but several saints; others hold bones from different parts of a saint's body, or relics of an altogether different kind. While this reliquary indeed contains the ulna of an unidentified saint, the popularity of arm reliquaries must generally be considered a result of their usefulness as liturgical props, which allowed clergy to animate a saint's divine body during liturgical rites and processions so that the saint could, quite literally, bless, touch, and heal the faithful with his own hand.

First mentioned in the inventory of 1542, this arm reliquary is one of the earliest and finest of originally 11 in the St. Blaise treasury. It is commonly known as the Arm Reliquary of the Apostles for the 13 bust-length figures—Christ and the apostles—decorating the upper and lower borders of the elegant liturgical vestment in which it is "dressed." The hems of the beautifully draped upper garment, a chasuble or a dalmatic, are further decorated on one side with a floral border in dark and pale blue, turquoise, green, and yellow champlevé enamel. There is a similar border executed in repoussé on the other side. The undergarment, or alba, which is only partly visible at the wrist, consists of a series of tight ripples ending in a band of delicately stamped acanthus leaves.

Unfortunately, whose relic this elegant arm holds and when it entered the treasury of St. Blaise remain unknown. While two arm reliquaries are listed in the inventory of 1482 that have not yet been identified, namely those of St. Martin and St. Eustace, the iconographic program of the Arm Reliquary of the Apostles may indicate that it was not initially meant to serve as a container for the relic of a saint or martyr, but for that of an apostle. In fact, Henry the Lion, Duke of Saxony (1142–80) and Bavaria (1156–80), in whose reign the reliquary was likely manufactured, is known to have received important relics, including several apostle arms, as gifts from the Byzantine emperor Manuel I Komnenos (r. 1143–80) in Constantinople in 1173. Since Henry the Lion donated at least two arm reliquaries (those of St. Theodore and St. Innocence) to the church of St. Blaise, his patronage of the Arm Reliquary of the Apostles seems highly likely. If not originally destined for the treasury of St. Blaise, the arm reliquary must have entered it at some time between 1482 and 1542 from elsewhere. HAK

Gift of the John Huntington Art and Polytechnic Trust 1930.739

DIMENSIONS: 51 x 14 x 9.2 cm

BIBLIOGRAPHY: Brandt 1998; Braunschweig 1995, 247, no. D 60; Lasko 1994, 214; De Winter 1985B, 83–85, fig. 111 and pl. XIV–XVIII; Stuttgart 1977, 448–49, no. 578; New York 1970, 104–5, no. 110; Swarzenski 1967, 80, pl. 212; Swarzenski 1932; Falke/Schmidt/Swarzenski 1930, 47–48, no. 30; Milliken 1930, 165–67; Neumann 1891, 268–69, no. 47.

Ostensorium

ABOUT 1180–90 (PATEN), ABOUT 1350–1400 (MONSTRANCE); LOWER SAXONY, HILDESHEIM?
SILVER, GILDED SILVER, AND NIELLO (PATEN);
SILVER, GILDED SILVER, AND ROCK CRYSTAL (MONSTRANCE)

This sumptuous ostensorium is one of the most unusual reliquaries in the Guelph Treasure. Created in a goldsmith workshop in Lower Saxony during the second half of the 14th century, it was designed to facilitate the display and veneration of ten sacred relics. The artist responsible for its execution used elements of contemporary Gothic architecture in miniature to frame and display an elaborately decorated liturgical paten, the shallow disc or plate used for the elevation of the Eucharist during Mass.

The elegant six-lobed foot has an openwork quatrefoil frieze at its base, a gallery of six simple tracery windows divided by micro-architectural buttresses, and a node with lion-head bosses. Two graceful buttresses with turrets and spires flank the paten, which is surmounted by a triangular openwork gable with a rock crystal oculus that enshrines two pieces of wood arranged in the shape of a cross. A Latin inscription on an accompanying strip of parchment labels these fragments as particles of the "Wood of the Lord," thus identifying them as splinters from the so-called True Cross, the cross on which Christ was believed to have been crucified for the salvation of humankind.

The paten resembles an elaborate rose window in a Gothic facade. A finely executed representation of Christ enthroned on a rainbow and displaying his stigmata on outstretched hands decorates the recessed, eight-lobed center. Surrounding the figure of Christ are the symbols of the four evangelists and personifications of the four cardinal virtues, each carrying a scroll with an identifying inscription. Two nielloed inscriptions, one encircling the enthroned Christ and the other following the rim of the paten, allude to the mystery of the Eucharist and Christ's ultimate sacrifice on the cross. The style of the figural decoration suggests that the paten was made in the same late 12th-century workshop also responsible for the reliquary of St. Oswald in the cathedral treasury of Hildesheim. That the paten was included in an elaborate Gothic reliquary frame was likely the result of its alleged association with Bishop Bernward of Hildesheim (d. 1022), venerated in Lower Saxony and beyond following his canonization by Pope Celestin II in 1192/93. Its status as a relic is confirmed by an inscription on a strip of parchment visible through a protective layer of glass on the reliquary's reverse that identifies it as the work of the bishop himself. Also visible from this side are eight silk pouches arranged in a circle; according to their accompanying inscriptions, they contain the relics of saints John Chrysostom, Godehard, Nicholas, Auctor, Silvester, Servatius, Alexis, and Lawrence.

While neither the form nor the decoration of the paten supports the alleged association with Bernward, the object's inclusion in a reliquary ostensorium during the second half of the 14th century bears witness to a strong tradition that, during this period, linked this precious liturgical object to Hildesheim and its most important ecclesiastical patron. The fragments of the True Cross may have been included in the frame to reinforce this attribution, as it was well known that Bernward had received a small particle of this very relic from his protégé, Emperor Otto III. Interestingly, the earlier tradition seems to have become obscured by 1482, when the first inventory of the treasury of St. Blaise recorded the ostensorium as "a large monstrance, containing the paten made by St. Godehard," Bernward's sainted successor as the bishop of Hildesheim. HAK

Purchase from the J. H. Wade Fund with additional gift from Mrs. R. Henry Norweb 1930.505

DIMENSIONS: diam. 13.5 cm (paten), 34.5 x 15.9 x 14 cm (monstrance)

INSCRIBED: on the outer rim of the paten: + EST. CORPVS. IN. SE. PANIS. QVI. FRANGITVR. IN. ME: VIVET. IN ETERNVM. QVI. BENE. SVMIT. EVM. (+ The bread which is broken in me is the body [of Christ] itself. He who receives it in good faith shall live in eternity); surrounding the medallion with the enthroned Christ: + HVC. SPECTATE. VIRI. SIC. VOS MORIENDO. REDEMI (+ Behold, o men, I have thus redeemed you with my death); on the scrolls held by the four cardinal virtues: IVSTITITIA (Justice); PRVDENTIA (Prudence); FORTITVDO (Fortitude); TEMP[ER]ANTIA (Temperance)

BIBLIOGRAPHY: Hildesheim 2001, 145–47; Lasko 1994; Hildesheim 1993, 630–32, no. IX-28; De Winter 1985B, 84–86, fig. 109 and pl. XIII; Stuttgart 1977, 447–48, no. 577; Swarzenski 1967, 79, pl. 208; Falke/Schmidt/Swarzenski 1930, 156–57, no. 32; Milliken 1930, 167–68; Neumann 1891, 294–97, no. 65.

40

Book-shaped Reliquary

ABOUT 1000 (PLAQUE), ABOUT 1340 (FRAME); OTTONIAN, LORRAINE (PLAQUE)
AND GERMAN, LOWER SAXONY (FRAME)

IVORY, GILDED SILVER, PEARLS, RUBIES, EMERALDS, CRYSTALS, ONYX, CORNELIAN, AND OAK

This sumptuous object, which closely resembles a deluxe medieval book cover in both form and decoration, was most likely commissioned by Duke Otto the Mild of Saxony (r. 1318–44) from a goldsmith workshop in Brunswick, Germany, around 1340. Simulating the cover of a book, the object was in fact designed to be a reliquary for "four leaves of the four gospel texts [and] also relics of the eleven thousand virgins and four other saints," as specified in the earliest surviving inventory of the Guelph Treasure of 1482. These relics, none of which survives in situ today, were originally preserved in a cavity hollowed out of the wood core and covered by a delicately carved ivory plaque depicting events at the wedding at Cana (John 2:1–11).

Surrounded by an intricately carved floral border and divided into two registers by a wavy band of vegetal scrollwork, the story of Christ's first miracle is presented in three scenes. In the upper left, the Virgin informs Christ and his apostles of the lack of wine at the wedding banquet. On the right, the groom, his bride, and their guests sit behind a table, two servants offering them goblets. In the lower register, two attendants pour water into the first of six storage vessels while Christ addresses his mother and the bride.

Like the four intaglio gems and cameos that decorate the wood frame, the ivory plaque was not made to adorn the 14th-century reliquary but appropriated centuries after its manufacture in an

Ottonian workshop around the year 1000. While using such spolia (spoils) is frequent in the luxury arts from the Carolingian period on, it is rare to find proof of an artist's use and adaptation of a specific model, here a plaque by a Carolingian artist of the Metz School of 875 now in the collection of the British Museum in London (inset). Despite certain misunderstandings—the servants in the lower register, for instance, hold the streams of water rather than the rims of their amphorae—the Ottonian artist remained faithful to the iconography and compositional scheme of his Carolingian model, translating its figure style and spatial disposition into a decidedly Ottonian idiom that is more concerned with emphatic gestures and spatial clarity than depth of field and accuracy of perspective.

Whether or not the Ottonian ivory was perceived as a relic when it was placed at the heart of the book-shaped reliquary remains elusive. Its enormous size, however, clearly dictated the dimensions of the reliquary as a whole. The elaborate frame that surrounds it with pearls, cameos, and precious stones in radiating ivy leaf settings on a stippled ground indicates that no effort was spared to enhance the collection of prized relics in the treasury of Brunswick Cathedral, whose main patron saints—Blaise, John the Baptist, and Thomas Becket—are represented engraved in full figure within an elaborate architectural frame on the reliquary's back. HAK

Gift of the John Huntington Art and Polytechnic Trust 1930.741

DIMENSIONS: 17.8 x 14 cm (plaque), 31.6 x 24.4 x 7.5 cm (frame)

BIBLIOGRAPHY: Fritz 1998, 367–85; Little 1998, 77–92; Lasko 1994, 80, 118–19; De Winter 1985B, 118–21, fig. 149; Swarzenski 1967, 39, pl. 14; Cleveland 1963, 208, no. 53; Falke/Schmidt/Swarzenski 1930, 173–75, no. 43; Milliken 1930, 176–77; Goldschmidt 1914–26, 1: 46–47, no. 14; Neumann 1891, 232–36, no. 37.

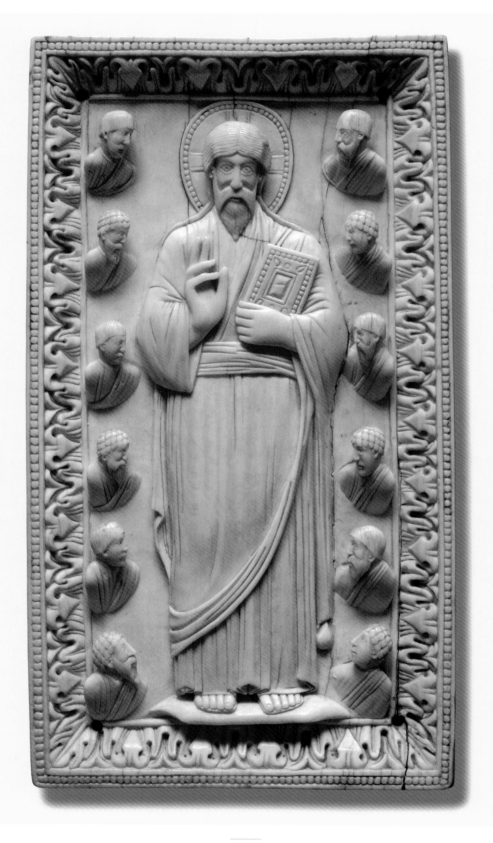

41

Plaque: Christ's Mission to the Apostles

ABOUT 970–80; OTTONIAN, MILAN

IVORY

Framed by a band of beaded pearls and an elabo-rate border of acanthus leaves, this exquisite ivo-ry plaque presents the full-length figure of Christ flanked by bust-length portraits of the apostles in vertical columns on either side. Christ is standing on a shallow mound that projects out of the pic-ture plane, holding a precious book in his left hand while raising his right in a gesture of speech and blessing. With his large eyes fixed on the be-holder and his mouth slightly open, he seems about to ad-dress the assembled crowd of disciples as well as the viewer with the words: "All power is given to me in heaven and in earth. Going therefore, teach ye all nations; baptizing them in the name of the Father, and of the Son, and of the Holy Ghost. Teaching them to observe all things what-soever I have commanded you" (Matt. 28:18–20). While there is no internal evidence to suggest that this scene is indeed an illustration of Christ's mis-sion to the apostles as recorded in the Gospel of Matthew, it is an identification that corresponds well to Christ's awe-inspiring presence and com-manding gaze.

The finely carved plaque may originally have formed the central decoration of an Ottonian book cover such as the one Christ carries. However, it is

equally likely to have formed part of a group of ivo-ries that served an entirely different purpose. What is more certain than the ivory's original function is the fact that it was carved by one of the leading artists in a tenth-century ivory workshop in the city of Milan in northern Italy. The same workshop was also responsible for a series of ivory plaques commissioned by Emperor Otto the Great (r. 936–73) for the cathedral of Magdeburg in Germany, founded in 968, and a number of related plaques. The artist responsible for the Cleveland ivory may in fact be the same individual who carved an ivory plaque representing Christ in Majesty now in the collection of the grand dukes of Luxem-bourg. While firmly rooted in a Western tradition of ivory carving that extends back through the Carolingian pe-riod to late antiquity, the artist seems also to have known contemporary Byzantine ivory carving, as suggested by an ivory plaque of the same subject in the Louvre (inset). While neither the name nor the nationality of artist and patron have come down to us, the high technical skill and artistic quality of this plaque suggest that it was executed by one of the most accomplished craftsmen of his era, and com-missioned by a high-ranking courtier or member of the clergy connected to Otto's court. HAK

Gift of the John Huntington Art and Polytechnic Trust 1967.65

DIMENSIONS: 18.2 x 9.9 x 1 cm

BIBLIOGRAPHY: Magdeburg 2001, 413–15, no. VI.14; New York 1997, 490, no. 324; Lasko 1994, 90; Little 1988, 94–95; Little 1977, 181–82; Wixom 1968, 273–89; Goldschmidt 1914–26, 2: 20, no. 18; Darcel 1877, 180–81.

42

Plaque: The Journey to Bethlehem

ABOUT 1100–1200; SOUTH ITALIAN, AMALFI

IVORY

Representing the Virgin Mary, Joseph, and one of his sons from a previous wife on their way to Bethlehem to be registered following the decree of Emperor Augustus, this fine ivory plaque combines the brief account given in the Gospel of Luke (2:1–5) with a more elaborate version of the same story in the apocryphal Infancy Gospel of James (Protogospel of James) (17:2): "And he [Joseph] saddled the she-ass, and set her [Mary] upon it, and his son led it and Joseph followed after." The intimate scene is set in front of an architectural background that blends Byzantine decorative elements with Islamic architectural motifs. Mary is shown seated sidesaddle on the back of the ass while the smaller figures of Joseph and his son walk in front of and behind the animal. The Virgin's importance as the Theotokos (God-bearer) who carries Christ in her womb is emphasized by her size and central position, by the architectural background, which underscores the tripartite figural composition in the foreground, and by the artist's careful use of gestures and attributes as framing devices. The walking sticks Joseph and his son carry, for instance, create an outer frame that is repeated in the parallel left hands of Joseph and Mary, which in turn direct the viewer's gaze toward the Virgin's womb as the composition's center.

Reflecting an indebtedness to Byzantine, Western, and Islamic traditions in terms of its iconography, compositional arrangement, and decorative motifs, the Cleveland ivory was the product of a workshop active in or around the city of Amalfi, near Naples, during the first decades of the 12th century. The subject matter, composition, and attributes further reveal that the artist responsible for the ivory's execution was inspired by two earlier plaques representing the journey to Bethlehem and the flight into Egypt, now preserved in the cathedral of Salerno (a few miles south of Amalfi). Carved around 1084, these earlier plaques form part of a large group of ivories that remained a strong source of inspiration not only for later artists in the Amalfi workshop, but also for others who went on to work for the rulers of Norman Sicily.

The Cleveland ivory is closely related in style and dimensions to a small group of other 12th-century ivory plaques also ornamented with New Testament scenes. All may have originally decorated a single piece of liturgical furniture such as a bishop's throne, altar frontal, or sanctuary door. HAK

Leonard C. Hanna Jr. Fund 1978.40

DIMENSIONS: 16.3 x 11 x 1 cm

BIBLIOGRAPHY: New York 1997, 492, no. 327; Bergman 1980, 135–36, no. 9; Wixom 1979A, 86–89; Fillitz 1967, 14, 19; Goldschmidt 1914–26, 4: 40, no. 130; Sprinz 1925, 3, no. 1; Lehner 1871, 80, no. 314. For the Protogospel of James, see James 1924, 45.

43

Boxwood Casket: Scenes from the Life of Christ

ABOUT 1050; ANGLO-SAXON, WEST MIDLANDS?
BOXWOOD, COPPER ALLOY, AND GLASS INLAYS

This very fine casket, carved from boxwood in the shape of a small house, is a rare, if not unique, example of high-quality woodcarving from Anglo-Saxon England. Thanks to the Liverpool collector Philip Nelson (1872–1953), the object survives today essentially intact with only one of its hinges and the lock missing. Having acquired the bottom half of the casket from a private owner in 1921, Nelson rejoined the casket with its lid when it was brought to his attention in 1937 as being in the possession of the convent of the Sacred Heart in Hammersmith (London).

The carved decoration occupies all sides of the casket and its lid, presenting a variety of scenes from the life of Christ. Much abbreviated in its iconographic formula, the principal face of the casket shows the Nativity reduced to the representation of the infant Jesus in the manger just below the lock. On either side is a group of three haloed figures who have thus far escaped convincing identification. It has been argued, however, that the group on the right may represent the communion of the apostles. The lid above shows the Crucifixion with the mourning Virgin, St. John, and other haloed figures. Flanking the cross above them, two flying angels complete the composition. On one short end Christ stands in a large baptismal font in the center, with John the Baptist on the left and an unidentified figure on the right. On the opposite end is the entry into Jerusalem, with Christ riding on an ass while two attendants spread their garments out before him. On the back is the Ascension: Christ, in a mandorla flanked by two flying angels, strides forward, pulled heavenward by the hand of God issuing from a cloud in the sky. On the lid the enthroned Christ is shown in majesty with two flying angels framing his mandorla.

Carved by an Anglo-Saxon artist whose confident technique and angular figure style reveal the work of a great master active in the West Midlands during the mid 11th century, the Christological subject matter indicates that the box was made for an ecclesiastical purpose, presumably to serve as a reliquary container. HAK

Purchase from the J. H. Wade Fund 1953.362

DIMENSIONS: 9 x 7.8 x 15.7 cm

BIBLIOGRAPHY: Rushton 2001, 44; London 1984, 125–26, no. 9; Wilson 1984, 193–94; Swarzenski 1967, 49, pl. 66; Talbot Rice 1952, 169; Nelson 1936, 91–100.

Luce nelis ueri nos illuftrare
GREGORI·

44

The Moralia in Job: Title Page

ABOUT 1142–78; ATTRIBUTED TO ABBOT FROWIN (SWISS, ENGELBERG MONASTERY)
TEMPERA ON VELLUM

The Benedictine abbey of Engelberg, in the Diocese of Constance, was founded in 1082. In the 12th century it maintained a flourishing scriptorium, especially during the abbacy of Frowin (1142–78). Renowned for his learning and intellectual abilities as well as his sanctity, Abbot Frowin established a school at his monastery emphasizing the study of theology and philosophy. He is known to have amassed an important library, and many of the books in it were attributed to Frowin's hand, both as a copyist and author. By the 17th century, Engelberg's library held some 20,000 volumes—both printed books and manuscripts—many of which were destroyed or lost during the following century by fire and the pillaging of Napoleonic troops. In spite of these losses, some 30 manuscripts attributed to Frowin are extant in the library there. They include a great bible in three volumes and a four-volume copy of the *Moralia in Job* (Engelberg Codex 20), to which this leaf belongs.

The *Moralia* is a massive work of scriptural exegesis in 35 books written by Gregory the Great, one of the four fathers of the Latin Church, and produced some years before he became pope in 590. Essentially a commentary on the biblical story of Job, it had great influence on the religious thinking of the Middle Ages. The text involves the question of why believer and nonbeliever should suffer alike. Deeply mystical and allegorical, it offered profound meaning to monks and those living the religious life.

This leaf has two scenes set within upper and lower registers and framed within a border of scrolling acanthus-like vines. The palette is muted and dominated by red and green. The upper scene presents the ubiquitous image of Job, a model of piety, seated on a rubbish heap. Having lost his material possessions, he suffers for his faith as his three friends mock and admonish him. The lower scene shows Gregory dictating to his scribe, the deacon Peter, symbolized by a scroll the two grasp. Gregory's words are inspired by the Holy Ghost who appears above in the form of a dove. A Latin text next to him reads, "May you illuminate us with the light of the Truth." This leaf was most likely the frontispiece to volume one of Engelberg Codex 20 as the set contained no other illuminations. The *Moralia* and the Cleveland leaf were described in a catalogue of the Engelberg manuscripts in 1787. The leaf must have been removed sometime afterward. Whether Frowin illuminated this leaf cannot be established with certainty, but that he was responsible for the Engelberg Codex as illuminator or scribe, or both, appears very plausible. SNF

Purchase from the J. H. Wade Fund 1955.74

DIMENSIONS: 27.3 x 19 cm

BIBLIOGRAPHY: Ganz 1960, 153, fig. 110; Milliken 1955B, 183–86; Schilling 1933, 117; Durrer 1901, 42, fig. 43.

45

Pendant: Virgin and Child

ABOUT 1160–70; CIRCLE OF GODEFROID DE HUY (MOSAN)

GILDED COPPER, CHAMPLEVÉ ENAMEL, AND VERNIS BRUN (REVERSE)

This exceedingly beautiful object, which may have served as a reliquary container, combines various metalworking techniques such as champlevé enamel, *vernis brun,* and repoussé. It was made by a master craftsman working in what is commonly called the Mosan region, which lies between the Meuse (Maas) and Rhine rivers in modern Belgium, where the existence of wealthy monasteries such as the powerful Benedictine abbey of Stavelot and readily available natural resources such as copper and tin from local mines created a fertile ground for the production of fine metalwork, especially champlevé enamels. While the identity of the master and exact location of the workshop responsible for the pendant's execution cannot be determined with certainty, it shares certain elements of style, technique, or iconography with a number of Mosan objects—the Stavelot Triptych (Pierpont Morgan Library, New York), the head reliquary of Alexander (Musée Royaux d'Art et d'Histoire, Brussels, 1033), and a cross reliquary (on loan to the Cloisters, New York, L1979.143).

Made to be suspended from a chain, the multilobed pendant is decorated on both sides. Figural representations in champlevé enamel occupy the principal face; an elaborate floral design in vernis brun covers the back (inset); and an embossed frieze of palmette leaves lines the border. The front is organized in three superimposed layers and along four principal axes: horizontal, vertical, and two diagonals. At the center of the composition is an almond-shaped enamel depicting the enthroned Virgin with the Christ child seated in her lap. The Virgin's status as Regina Coeli (Queen of Heaven) is emphasized by her diadem and scepter, which recalls the sprouting rod of Joseph as well as Old Testament types, namely the rod of Aaron and the root of Jesse. The enamel is placed within a diamond-shaped repoussé frame surrounded on its two diagonal axes by four semi-circular enamels representing humility, virginity, piety, and mercy in the guise of angelic figures, each holding a globe. Four other semi-circular lobes, each studded with cabochon gems and silver pearls, emerge from between the enamels on the vertical and horizontal axes. They form an additional frame for the central image of the Virgin and Child and the virtues associated with them. The refined quality of the figural enamels is matched by the beauty and precision of the vernis brun decoration on the reverse. The rhomboid field in the middle is filled with a scrolling vine made of four tendrils while four other vines cover the space between the lobes and the field in the center, a decoration that functions as a metaphor not only for the Virgin, but also for the salvific power of the relic that is presumed to be enclosed inside the pendant. HAK

Purchase from J. H. Wade Fund 1926.428

DIMENSIONS: 19.8 x 17 x 3.2 cm

INSCRIBED: around the central plaque: S[AN]C[T]A MARIA MATER D[OMI]NI (Saint Mary, Mother of the Lord); on the surrounding plaques (clockwise from upper left): HVMILITAS (humility); VIRGINITAS (virginity); PIETAS (piety); MISERICORDIA (mercy)

BIBLIOGRAPHY: Kroos 1985, 117, 130; Verdier 1975, 66–69; Kötzsche 1972, 211–13; Gauthier 1972, 138–39, 352, no. 96; Milliken 1927, 51–54; Milliken 1926A, 67–68; Migeon 1905, 20, 26.

46

Four Plaques: Seated Prophets

ABOUT 1170–80; GERMAN, LOWER SAXONY, HILDESHEIM
ENGRAVED AND GILDED COPPER, AND CHAMPLEVÉ ENAMEL

These champlevé enamel plaques with representations of the prophets Isaiah, Zacharias, Elisha, and Hosea seated on elaborate arcaded thrones are part of a group of nine surviving enamels that presumably formed part of the enamel decoration of a reliquary shrine. The other five are now dispersed among museums in Europe—in Dijon, Düsseldorf, and St. Petersburg—as well as a private collection in Switzerland. Whether the full prophet cycle originally consisted of 12 or 16 plaques is uncertain, but the direction of the prophets' gazes suggests a number of likely scenarios for their original presentation. In one such scenario they were arranged in four groups of three, decorating the sides of a cruciform reliquary with a central dome not unlike objects now preserved in the Kunstgewerbemuseum in Berlin (W 15) and the Victoria and Albert Museum in London (7650-1861). A second setting suggests that they were arranged in two groups of five and two groups of three as decorations for the long and short sides of a rectangular shrine such as a portable altar in the church of St. Servatius in Siegburg. In a third scenario they decorated the sides of a centralized domed structure like the 12-sided reliquary in the Hessisches Landesmuseum in Darmstadt (54.239).

The somewhat exaggerated and mannered style of both figures and draperies, and the use of fine metal pins throughout the dark blue enamel backgrounds with their white and green borders are among the likely indicators that the cycle of prophet plaques was manufactured in a goldsmith's workshop located in the city of Hildesheim in Lower Saxony. After Cologne, Hildesheim seems to have emerged as one of most important German centers for the production of champlevé enamels and other fine metalwork during the 12th century. Based on stylistic similarities between the prophet plaques and the so-called Reliquary of Henry II in Paris (Musée du Louvre, OA 49), which depicts the monk Welandus offering the reliquary to the sainted emperor, the workshop responsible for the execution of these related works has previously been referred to as the Welandus workshop. However, such a designation obscures the fact that a number of independent workshops were probably responsible for the execution of champlevé enamel works in Hildesheim. HAK

Purchase from the J. H. Wade Fund 1950.574.1–4

DIMENSIONS: 8.9 x 5.9 x 0.3 cm (largest)

INSCRIBED: on banderoles: ESAJAS PROPhETA (Prophet Isaiah); HELISEVS PROPhETA (Prophet Eliseus); ZACHAPIAS PROPhETA (Prophet Zacharias); OSEE PROPhETA (Prophet Hosea)

BIBLIOGRAPHY: Hildesheim 2001, 189–90, no. 4.22e; Brandt 1987, 65–71; De Winter 1985B, 82; Verdier 1974, 339–42; New York 1970, 177–79, no. 183; Swarzenski 1967, 75–76, pl. 440; Milliken 1951, 72–74; Migeon 1905, 17, 25–26; Spitzer 1890–93, 1: 98, no. 6.

47

Pyxis

ABOUT 1170–80; GERMAN, LOWER SAXONY, HILDESHEIM

ENGRAVED AND GILDED COPPER, CHAMPLEVÉ AND CLOISONNÉ ENAMEL, AND WOOD

This uniquely shaped wood *pyxis* (box) is decorated with ornamental and figural enamels in a technique that combines both champlevé and cloisonné elements. It was likely made in Hildesheim, a city in the region of Lower Saxony that emerged as one of the leading centers for the production of champlevé enamels during the second half of the 12th century. Composed of a rectangular central portion and two slightly narrower semicircular apses on each end, the pyxis has four enamel plaques with diaper motifs on the sides and a large enameled plaque on top mirroring its shape and serving as its cover.

The rectangular central portion of the cover plaque shows on a dark blue enameled background the Crucifixion with Ecclesia and Synagoga, the personified figures of the Christian Church and the Jewish faith, on either side. The mourning Virgin and St. John, who are traditionally represented below the cross (see nos. 80, 88, 103, and 106), are depicted here in a secondary position, the Virgin standing next to Ecclesia and John next to Synagoga. Following an established iconographic tradition, Ecclesia wears a crown and holds a cross-topped victory standard while collecting in a chalice the blood that gushes from Christ's side. The blindfolded Synagoga, whose diadem is falling to the ground, points with her right hand toward the crucified Christ and carries two of the instruments of

his Passion in her left—the lance that pierced his side and the reed with the sponge soaked in vinegar. Above the cross arms, two medallions show the personified figures of the Sun and Moon weeping over Christ's crucifixion. Rather than just illustrating the gospel text, the representation stresses the symbolic and sacramental dimensions of the Crucifixion. While Synagoga chooses not to recognize Jesus as the Savior of humankind and is complicit in his death, Ecclesia, his mystical bride, carries his victory banner and preserves the blood he spilled on the cross.

Adding a further dimension to the central scene, the semicircular fields framing the Crucifixion depict events from the Old Testament that have been interpreted to anticipate or prefigure events in the life of Christ. Here, God's sacrifice of Christ is paralleled with two sacrifices recorded in the book of Genesis, Abel's giving the "firstlings of his flock, and of their fat" (4:4–5) and Abraham's offering of Isaac (22:1–19). The significance of these scenes is further exemplified by the two accompanying inscriptions, which likewise relate the Old Testament sacrifices to the Crucifixion. Given the strong emphasis on the sacrificial nature of Christ's death on the cross, this enameled pyxis is likely to have served as a container for the consecrated host. HAK

Purchase from the J. H. Wade Fund and the Fanny Tewksbury King Collection by exchange 1949.431

DIMENSIONS: 5.4 x 21.3 x 9.3 cm

INSCRIBED: + H[A]EC DATA P[ER] IVSTV[M] [. . .]AT IN CRVCE VICTIMA CHR[ISTV]M (These offerings, made by the just, [signify?]

Christ as the sacrificial victim on the cross); + HOC ARIES P(RE)FERT Q[VO]D [. . .] D[EV]S HOSTIA P[ER]FERT (This ram prefigures what God [. . .] endures as a sacrificial victim)

BIBLIOGRAPHY: Hildesheim 2001, 194, no. 4.34; Brandt 1987, 38–39; De Winter 1985B, 79; Verdier 1974, 339–42; Milliken 1949, 166–70; Falke 1930, 272; Read 1926, 187–88.

48

Plaque: Condemnation and Martyrdom of St. Lawrence

ABOUT 1180; GERMAN, LOWER SAXONY, HILDESHEIM?
GILDED COPPER AND CHAMPLEVÉ ENAMEL

St. Lawrence was one of several deacons of the Roman Church who were martyred during the persecutions of Emperor Valerian (r. 253–60). A native of Spain, Lawrence was allegedly called to Rome by Pope Sixtus II (r. 257–58) and ordained by him as a deacon. Following an imperial edict commanding the apprehension and execution of Christian bishops, priests, and deacons, however, the pope and seven of his clergy (Lawrence among them) were martyred in Rome in early August 258. Later accounts of Lawrence's martyrdom relate a variety of details about his death that attest to his great popularity and veneration by the fourth and fifth centuries. According to these legendary and semi-legendary accounts, Lawrence had been put in charge of the treasures of the Church and was promised to be spared from execution if he delivered them to the Roman prefect. Seemingly agreeing to the prefect's offer, the saint assembled the sick, poor, and elderly of the Christian community of Rome, and presented them to the prefect as the true treasures of the Church, which in turn led to his condemnation and martyrdom by roasting on a gridiron.

This champlevé enamel plaque depicts the last two events in distinct but continuous scenes. On the left, Lawrence stands in front of a crowned and enthroned figure, which clearly represents the emperor as the person ultimately responsible for the saint's execution. Dressed in an alb and a richly decorated dalmatic, the traditional vestments of a deacon, Lawrence holds or receives a blank scroll from the emperor while being led away by an attendant. On the right, the naked saint is bound to a gridiron, and two torturers hold him down with long poles. Ready to receive the martyr's victorious soul into heaven, an angel appears from a cloud in the upper right corner.

While the Cleveland enamel's medieval provenance is unknown, a closely related plaque was discovered during construction work in the city of Halle, Germany, in 1978. The size, style, and subject matter of this second plaque, which shows Lawrence introducing the sick, poor, and elderly to the emperor, leave little doubt that the two plaques once formed part of a cycle that may have adorned a reliquary shrine of St. Lawrence in one of the city's churches. HAK

Purchase from the J. H. Wade Fund 1949.430

DIMENSIONS: 9.6 x 20.8 x 0.2 cm

INSCRIBED: on frame: + ECCE DEI MILES SVP[ER]AT LAVRENTIVS IGNES : + S[AN]C[TV]S LAVRENTIVS (+ Behold the soldier of god, Laurentius, defeats the fire. Saint Laurentius)

BIBLIOGRAPHY: Nickel 1988, 254–55; De Winter 1985B, 67; Milliken 1949, 167–70; Boston 1940, 74, no. 255. For the enamel plaque found in Halle, see Halle 2001, 230–33; Nickel 1988, 247–63; and Nickel 1986, 223–24.

49

Altar Cross with Stand

ABOUT 1140–50; GERMAN, LOWER SAXONY, HILDESHEIM?

CAST, GILDED, ENGRAVED, AND CHASED BRONZE

In addition to those *vasa sacra* (sacred vessels) necessary for the celebration of the Eucharist, namely chalice and paten, candlesticks and altar crosses, often made of cast bronze and gilded, were among the most common liturgical implements found on a medieval altar. From the 11th century onward, such altar crosses often featured elaborate bases as well as three-dimensional representations of the crucified Christ, thus visualizing the Crucifixion at the altar, where Christ's sacrifice was commemorated in sacramental terms by the priest celebrating the Eucharist.

Likely made in a goldsmith workshop in Lower Saxony, this mid 12th-century bronze cross, which still preserves its original stand, is a fine example of such an altar cross. On the front a simple inscription identifies Christ as the "King of the Jews" according to the gospels' account. The main focus of the cross is a delicately modeled corpus, cast in bronze and decorated using a fine chisel. Christ is dressed only in a loincloth, his arms outstretched horizontally and his feet resting on an elegant footstool pierced by a triple arcade. Rather than representing Christ as a crowned figure (see

no. 57), he is shown here without a crown, his eyes half-closed and his head inclined toward his right, suffering with great dignity and resolve. In contrast to the richly decorated front, the back of the cross is adorned with five engravings, representing medallions with symbols of the four evangelists, one at the end of each cross arm, and the sacrificial Agnus Dei (Lamb of God) in the center, a program commonly found on crosses of this period.

Perhaps the most elaborate part of the cross's decoration is its cast and chased three-sided stand, which features a lavish array of intertwining scrolls that emerge in symmetrical fashion from three paw-like legs. On each side, two birds are perched in the foliage, their bodies turned away from each other while their heads are intertwined with those of the next pair. Issuing organically from the point where the main branches of the scrolls merge are three downward-facing dragon heads, emphasizing the central axis of each of the stand's sides. The openwork knob above, into which the cross is set by means of a flange, is similarly decorated with an undulating scroll inhabited by three birds marching from left to right. HAK

Purchase from the J. H. Wade Fund 1944.320

DIMENSIONS: 43.4 x 22.5 x 8 cm

INSCRIBED: IHC[OVC] (= IESVS) NA[Z]AREN[VS] REX IVDEO[RVM] (Jesus from Nazareth, King of the Jews)

BIBLIOGRAPHY: De Winter 1985B, 94; Springer 1981, 134–36, no. 24; Ithaca 1968, 130–31, no. 43.

❖ 50 ❖

Lion Aquamanile

1200–1250; GERMAN, LOWER SAXONY, HILDESHEIM?

CAST, CHASED, AND PUNCHED COPPER ALLOY

Made as water vessels to be used for hand washing in both sacred and secular contexts, medieval *aquamanilia,* from the Latin *aqua* (water) and *manus* (hand), have a long ancestry connecting them to Islamic works of the eighth through eleventh centuries. Like the earlier Islamic objects, Western medieval aquamanilia are often zoomorphic in shape, taking the forms of a variety of animals and fantastic beasts such as lions, horses, birds, dogs, and dragons. Many of the surviving Western medieval aquamanilia—more than 350 are known, and they range in date from the 12th to 15th centuries—were produced in German lands. Major centers of production were located in the Mosan region (named for the Meuse River that flows through modern-day Belgium and the Netherlands), Lower Saxony, and, later in the Middle Ages, in the city of Nuremberg.

Like all other surviving medieval aquamanilia, this fine lion-shaped example with a dragon-tail handle was cast in copper alloy using the *cire perdue* (lost-wax) method. Because the object had to be cast hollow in order to serve its function as a water vessel, the initial wax model was built over a core and secured within the surrounding clay mold by a series of pins, some of which are still visible inside the object today. With its almond-shaped eyes, round ears, and stylized mane collar, the Cleveland aquamanile is one of a group of related lion-shaped vessels that were modeled on the monumental cast-bronze lion commissioned by Duke Henry the Lion for his residence in Brunswick, Germany, around 1166. These works also show close stylistic similarities with a baptismal font in the cathedral of Hildesheim, commissioned in bronze by a certain Wilbernus (attested as provost of the cathedral from 1216 to 1221); thus the workshop for the Cleveland aquamanile has likewise been located in Hildesheim, which had a long tradition of casting works in bronze going back to the time of Bishop Bernward, who commissioned his famous bronze door and triumphal column shortly after the first millennium. Whether the Cleveland aquamanile originally served in a secular or liturgical context cannot be determined. Because a number of lion and dragon aquamanilia are mentioned in a number of medieval church inventories, this vessel could have been used on the altar table of a church just as easily as at the dinner table of an aristocratic or upper-class medieval patron. HAK

Gift of Mrs. Chester D. Tripp in honor of Chester D. Tripp 1972.167

DIMENSIONS: 26.4 x 29 x 15 cm

BIBLIOGRAPHY: Mende 1998, 387–423; De Winter 1985B, 113–14; Gibbons/Ruhl 1974, 268–69; Wixom 1974A, 260–68; Wixom 1973, 253–60; May 1968, no. D 24. For related examples, see Mende 1998, figs. 22, 24, and 25; for medieval aquamanilia in general, see New York 2006A.

Two Bifolia from a Psalter: Scenes from the Life of Christ

1230–40; GERMAN, LOWER SAXONY (DIOCESE OF HILDESHEIM), BRAUNSCHWEIG?
TEMPERA AND GOLD ON VELLUM

This pair of bifolia consists of two sheets of vellum each folded in half to create four leaves. In the bound volume, they would have originally been inserted one inside the other to form part of a large psalter. Medieval manuscripts of the Psalms were used in liturgical as well as private devotional contexts and often contained ancillary texts such as a calendar, canticles, creeds, a litany of the saints, and prayers. In these bifolia, the miniatures decorating each leaf are subdivided into four panels and illustrate sequentially the life of Christ. The scenes extend from his infancy to events following the Resurrection. This particular format, along with the style, helps localize the psalter's place of production to northern Germany and the Diocese of Hildesheim. A vibrant tradition of psalter illustration emerged in northern Europe after the 11th century in which miniature cycles emphasized the life of David (author of the Psalms) juxtaposed with the life of Christ, as seen here. This association implied the connection of lineage, since Christ was the descendant of the house of David. It is possible that the parent volume also included a "David" cycle.

Several lines of evidence suggest these bifolia were illuminated in Lower Saxony and probably in Braunschweig. Foremost is the similarity of the miniatures' style to those of the Arenberg Psalter, a manuscript in the Bibliothèque Nationale in Paris (Cod. Nouv. Acq. Lat. 3102). Seven leaves from this psalter are now dispersed among public institutions. The Arenberg Psalter is thought to have been commissioned by Otto, Duke of Braunschweig, for the marriage of his daughter Helen to Landgraf Hermann II of Thuringia on 9 October 1239. Like the Arenberg Psalter and a core group of three other manuscripts all datable to the 1230s, the Cleveland bifolia belong to the Saxon-Thuringen school of illumination.

The decoration of this group is painted in the *Zackenstil* (jagged style) in which the drapery folds appear angular and frozen, a Germanic contribution to Gothic illumination of the 13th century. Byzantine sources are also evident in these leaves, providing further linkage to Lower Saxony where Byzantine influence was prevalent. Such influence may be noted especially in compositional details such as the frontal configuration of the seated Virgin and Child in the Adoration of the Magi in the first folio. This frontality undoubtedly derives from Byzantine sources such as ivories or icons. SNF

Purchase from the J. H. Wade Fund 1933.448.1–2

DIMENSIONS: 30.7 x 31 cm and 31 x 22.5 cm

BIBLIOGRAPHY: Milliken 1934, 36. For comparable objects, see Voelkle/Wieck 1992, no. 34, 118–21; Washington 1975, no. 33, 119–25; Klamt 1968, 155.

"It was as if the whole world had shaken herself and cast off her old age, and were clothing herself everywhere in a white garment of churches . . . the faithful rebuilt and bettered almost all the cathedral churches . . . monasteries . . . and smaller parish churches."[1] Thus wrote the monk Radulfus Glaber at the turn of the millennium, describing the church building then occurring in northern Europe on an unprecedented scale. This trend persisted for more than three centuries as the initial interest in stone structures witnessed by Glaber developed and evolved, giving rise to dramatic architectural achievements. Centuries later, art historians coined terms to characterize the two roughly successive architectural styles of these churches, which are also applied to the artworks adorning them and to the eras in which they were created: Romanesque and Gothic.

The term "Romanesque" was invented in the 19th century to describe the architectural style of the many monasteries built in the 11th and 12th centuries throughout Europe. It reflects the opinion that these massive, broad buildings with their semicircular arches, thick walls, and small windows resembled ancient Roman structures. Their geometric articulation of mass and space is also a hallmark of works made in other media throughout this period, particularly painting and sculpture.

In France, the Carolingian Empire's disintegration in the ninth century caused a period of turmoil. Already fragmented into weak kingdoms, the French lands were further compromised by continuous barbarian invasions during which the monasteries that had thrived as centers of intellectual, spiritual, and artistic life under Charlemagne were sacked and burnt. Many regarded the year 1000 with apprehension, believing the millennium would bring the end of the world. However, once this fateful year had passed, the rebuilding of the lost monasteries commenced.

These monasteries prospered. The greatest among them—the largest and grandest was the Benedictine abbey of Cluny in Burgundy—possessed wealth and power rivaling that of secular rulers. In the absence of a strong central government or urban centers, a feudal system had developed: aristocratic landowners oversaw vast estates supporting a chiefly agrarian economy. Enjoying the patronage of lay benefactors, many monasteries also became feudal landlords, amassing and managing large and profitable land holdings. Also enriching the monasteries were pilgrimage (the sacred journey to shrines housing saints' relics undertaken as an act of devotion or contrition or in search of cures for physical disabilities) and the Crusades (mass armed pilgrimages to the Holy Land aimed at expiating personal sin and winning salvation, as well as at extending the Church's power). Some monasteries were themselves great shrines to which the faithful flocked. But perhaps more important, many were situated along the routes to Rome, Jerusalem, and the west's most venerated shrine, Santiago de Compostela in northwest Spain, where the relics of St. James the Apostle allegedly dwell. These foundations benefited handsomely from the traffic and trade passing along the main arteries of commerce and communication.

This great wealth allowed monasteries to emerge as France's foremost centers of civilization and culture, and thus of the arts. Grand abbey churches and extensive monastic complexes accommodating the monks' needs and activities were constructed in the style now called Romanesque. Abbey churches required liturgical furnishings such as altar crosses (see no. 53), chalices, and monstrances. Many foundations also commissioned ornate reliquaries to house their most holy treasures (see nos. 54, 55). In an 1125 treatise, a monk named Theophilus offered detailed instructions for creating works of art in gold, silver, stones, enamel, glass, and ivory, among other costly materials, indicating the variety of such media used in fashioning church furnishings. Monasteries were also heavily decorated with stone sculpture whose narratives attempted to communicate the Christian message to the largely unlettered faithful who visited when on pilgrimage. Church portals were a major focus of enrichment, with the Last Judgment, the terrible but awesome event foretold for the end of time, as a favored theme. Column capitals throughout church interiors and cloisters were adorned with biblical scenes, incidents from saints' lives, allegories such as the signs of the zodiac and labors of the months, geometric and foliate patterning, and fantastic confections frequently including curious beasts real and imaginary (see no. 58). From monastic scriptoria, where books were copied, illustrated, and bound, came magnificent illuminated manuscripts (see nos. 59, 60).

All, however, were not pleased with this outpouring of creative activity. In 1127, Bernard of Clairvaux, a member of the ascetic Cistercian order of monks, railed against the excesses he perceived in the art of his period: "We see candelabra standing like massive trees of bronze, fashioned with the marvelous subtlety of art, their gems glowing no less brightly than with the lights they carry. What do you think is the purpose of such things? To gain the contrition of penitents or the admiration of spectators? Oh vanity of vanities, yet no more vain than insane!"[2]

From the mid 12th and throughout the 13th century, a dramatic new style replaced Romanesque as France's predominant architectural manner. In daring feats of masonry, architects deployed pointed arches, ribbed vaults, and flying buttresses at the service of creating light-filled churches, predominantly cathedrals, that soar triumphantly heavenward, embodying the image of the city of God, the heavenly Jerusalem described in the book of Revelation. First used in Italy during the Renaissance, the word "Gothic" associates this style, erroneously, with the barbarian Goths responsible for sacking the Roman Empire in the sixth century and allegedly plunging Europe into the Dark Ages. Sixteenth-century Italian critics, obsessed with the classical past, condemned the style's rejection of Greek and Roman forms in favor of an entirely unique idiom. In their own time, the term *opus modernum* (modern work) was used to describe these cathedrals, demonstrating a contemporary awareness of the style's originality. Although the Gothic style eventually spread throughout Europe, contemporaries also called it *opus francigenum* (French work), indicating its status as a hallmark of the newly unified kingdom of France.

Indeed, from the mid 12th century, the foundations of the French nation-state were secured. Successive generations of the Capetian dynasty extended and consolidated their territorial holdings, brought the feudal barons under their control, and instituted systematic taxation throughout their domains. They also established an increasingly powerful centralized government and judiciary at their capital in Paris, which quickly became Europe's intellectual capital thanks to the rise of its university with its renowned theological faculty.

Under the Capetian kings, the Gothic style flourished. In 1140, Abbot Suger, who served Louis VI and Louis VII as prime minister and regent, began the remodeling of his church, the royal abbey of Saint-Denis outside Paris, traditional burial place of the French kings. Saint-Denis is considered the first church built in the Gothic style. Philip II, along with Maurice de Sully, the bishop of Paris, began in 1163 building the vast Gothic cathedral of Notre-Dame, creating an unmistakable symbol of royal power at his capital's heart. Between 1241 and 1248, determined to transform Paris into a new Holy Land, Louis IX (St. Louis) built the Sainte-Chapelle. In this jewel-like chapel, which enshrines the relics Louis acquired on Crusade, the Gothic style may be seen at its most exquisite. Capetian Paris became an artistic center where many of the period's most spectacular illuminated manuscripts (see no. 64), ivory carvings, and goldsmith's works were made. And perhaps most remarkable, between 1180 and 1270 some 80 cathedrals in the Gothic style were built in France as a consequence of the Capetians' massive geographical and political expansion of their realm, combined with the ambitions of competitive bishops keen to establish their sees as sites of wealth and power.

A rich decorative profusion adorned these cathedrals (see no. 62). As with their Romanesque predecessors, sculpture played a prominent role. The church portal remained a focal point, although sculpture increasingly expanded across these buildings' facades, offering ever more nuanced, complex, and complete narratives of human progress from Creation to future salvation. Apocalyptic visions featured as before, but Marian themes also received unprecedented emphasis, reflecting the exponential growth of the cult of the Virgin in this period and the dedication of many cathedrals to her (see no. 63). Scenes from Christ's life and Passion, saints' lives, Old Testament stories, and allegorical narratives that had in the Romanesque era been confined to column capitals appear instead on church facades. The fantastic beasts of Romanesque capitals also migrated to exteriors, becoming the grotesque gargoyles through which water drained off the sides and roofs of churches. Also frequently depicted on cathedral facades were Old Testament kings and queens, the ancestors of Christ whose appearance glorified the institution of the monarchy, and thus the French kings. These stone monarchs often appear as full-length jamb statues, a formal innovation that originates in Gothic sculpture. Just as novel was the naturalism with which the human face was depicted, sculptors capturing personalities and moods as never before. Inside the cathedrals, stained glass windows provided the buildings with their characteristic sublime and spiritually transcendent luminosity while presenting various sacred narratives for the benefit of the illiterate faithful.

As in the Romanesque period, ecclesiastical foundations of the Gothic era built vast treasuries of liturgical objects fashioned from the most expensive materials. Abbot Suger, who was particularly zealous in this pursuit, justified the lavishness and expense of the works he commissioned by claiming that contemplating them induced flights of spirituality: "The loveliness of the gems has called me away from external cares, and worthy meditation, transporting me from material to immaterial things. . . . I seem to myself existing on some level, as it were, beyond our earthly one, neither completely in the slime of the earth nor completely in the purity of Heaven."[3] VB

1. Glaber 1981, 18.

2. Bernard 1971, 168–69.

3. Suger 1979, 62–65.

52

Medallion: Warrior Fighting a Dragon

ABOUT 1170–80; ANGLO-NORMAN, ENGLAND?

GILDED COPPER AND CHAMPLEVÉ ENAMEL

This gilded-copper medallion features a fine champlevé representation of a youthful warrior fighting a winged dragon. A scroll of acanthus leaves wraps around the figures; the young hero is depicted barefoot, dressed in a blue tunic with broad yellow collar and a studded belt. Wielding a sword with his right hand and carrying a large round shield with his left, the youth strides forward while the beast turns its head toward him, its snake-like tail curled up and its wings spread out.

Since there is no inscription accompanying the scene, the identity of the young hero remains unknown. The northern epic tradition boasts a number of valiant dragon slayers that may be associated with the representation: Siegfried killing the dragon Fafnir, for instance, or the Arthurian hero Tristan fighting the dragon of Ireland. Given the medallion's stylistic affinities with English manuscript illumination and technical indebtedness to Limoges enamel work of the later 12th century, an identification with Tristan seems especially compelling because Thomas of Britain's poem *Tristan,* possibly written for Eleanor of Aquitaine, gained popularity at the Plantagenet court of Henry II of England shortly before the medallion was created. As both Henry and Eleanor were important patrons of Limoges enamel work, the medallion was either the product of an Anglo-Norman enamel workshop active in England during the latter part of Henry's reign, or a French workshop using English models.

Now isolated from its context, it is difficult to determine what function the medallion was originally intended to serve. Given the mythological nature of its decoration, it was likely part of an object intended for secular use such as a wood coffret, a metalwork ciborium, or a *hanap* (cup). HAK

Purchase from the J. H. Wade Fund 1951.546

DIMENSIONS: diam. 6.5 cm

BIBLIOGRAPHY: Gauthier 1987, 121–22, no. 128.

53

The Spitzer Cross

ABOUT 1190; MASTER OF THE ROYAL PLANTAGENET WORKSHOP (FRENCH, LIMOGES)
ENGRAVED, STIPPLED, AND GILDED COPPER, AND CHAMPLEVÉ ENAMEL

The city of Limoges in southwestern France was famous for its fine metalwork and richly colored enamels during the Middle Ages. Known as *opus lemovicense* (Limoges work), enameled objects produced in Limoges workshops were highly prized by an international clientele of secular and ecclesiastical patrons and thus exported across medieval Europe. While Limoges objects such as book covers, candlesticks, croziers, and reliquaries have survived in great number and variety in church treasuries, museums, and private collections, only a few objects can rival the so-called Spitzer Cross in terms of its completeness, artistic quality, and condition.

Named after the Viennese art dealer and collector Baron Frédéric Spitzer, who owned it in the 19th century, the Spitzer Cross has justly been hailed as the finest Limoges enameled cross to survive from the medieval period. However, it is not a complete cross, but merely the front face, consisting of five champlevé enamel plaques. The main focus of the decoration is Christ's Crucifixion, placed within the boundaries of the larger cross form. Following a passage in the Gospel of John (19:26–27) in which Jesus entrusts his mother to the care of his beloved disciple John and vice versa, Christ is flanked at the terminal ends of the horizontal cross beam by the half-length figures of the Virgin Mary and St. John the Evangelist. Above the *titulus,* which is inscribed with Christ's abbreviated name, busts of two angels appear from the clouds; St. Peter stands below, holding a precious codex as well as the keys of paradise. The reverse of the cross, several enameled plaques of which survive in museums and private collections, originally showed the symbols of the four evangelists, one at the end of each cross arm, and presumably the image of a blessing Christ in the center.

The elegant figure of the crucified Christ exemplifies the refined quality of the enamel decoration. Dressed in a knee-length loincloth, knotted at the center, Christ's exposed body is rendered in white enamel with his stylized rib cage, abdomen, and the musculature of his arms and legs defined by graceful lines of gilded and stippled copper in reserve. The stark whiteness of his body contrasts not only with the gilded background of the cross itself, but also with the vibrant green, blue, and yellow enamel that defines the arbor vitae, or tree of life, on which Christ is suspended. His chalk-white torso, rose-colored complexion, and the fine lines that define his body connect the Spitzer Cross to a number of other fine enamels known to have been made for the monastery of Grandmont outside Limoges. In the later 12th century, this monastery enjoyed the patronage of King Henry II of England. During his lifetime and upon his death in 1189 he donated substantial funds that were, in turn, used to adorn the sanctuary of the church with costly reliquary shrines and liturgical objects produced in local workshops. While the name of the artist responsible for the execution of the Spitzer Cross is not known, his refined style is so characteristic of a number of highly prestigious, presumably royal commissions for the abbey of Grandmont that scholars have named him the Master of the Grandmont Altar or the Master of the Royal Plantagenet Workshop. HAK

Gift of J. H. Wade 1923.1051

DIMENSIONS: 67.4 x 41.9 cm

INSCRIBED: IHS [IHSVS] (Jesus); XPS [XPISTVS] (Christus)

BIBLIOGRAPHY: Gauthier 1987, no. 255, 209–12; New York 1970, 139–40, no. 144; Cleveland 1967, 105, 357–58, no. III-31; Souchal 1967, 21–71; Thoby 1953, 97–98, no. 14; Cleveland 1936, 19, no 13; Milliken 1924, 30–33; Spitzer 1890–93, 1: 102, no. 17.

❖ 54 ❖
Plaque from a Châsse for Relics of St. Thomas Becket

ABOUT 1220–25; FRENCH, LIMOGES

ENGRAVED AND GILDED COPPER, AND CHAMPLEVÉ ENAMEL

On 20 December 1170, four knights in the service of King Henry II entered Canterbury Cathedral and killed Archbishop Thomas Becket in front of one of the altars of his church. The circumstances of this brutal murder, presumably planned by the knights to gain favor with the king, who had been engaged in a fierce legal dispute with the archbishop, are well known through a number of contemporary accounts, which spread across much of western Europe the news of the archbishop's martyrdom and the subsequent miracles that occurred at his tomb. Canonized by Pope Alexander III on 21 February 1173—barely three years after his death—Thomas Becket soon became one of the most popular saints in England, France, and beyond, with throngs of pilgrims flocking first to his tomb and, after 1220, to his magnificent shrine in the new choir of Canterbury Cathedral.

The fast spread and popularity of the cult of Thomas Becket, particularly in England and France, is reflected in the large number of enamel châsses produced in Limoges workshops during the late 12th and early 13th centuries. At least 52 such châsses or parts thereof are known to have survived, and more than a dozen others are known from historical records. Among them is this fine enamel plaque, which once formed the principal face of a châsse that contained relics of Thomas Becket. Based on the style of the figures and their elegant appliqué heads, the enamel may have been made in the workshop of a certain Master Alpais, whose name is recorded on a magnificent ciborium in the Louvre (OA 49). Unusual about this plaque is its decoration with two scenes: the Crucifixion on the left and the martyrdom of Thomas Becket on the right. The latter scene represents Thomas standing behind a prepared altar as he receives a deadly blow from the first of two knights approaching him from the left. The blessing hand of God emerges from the sky above the altar as if to reaffirm the archbishop's saintly status. While both scenes follow standard iconographic formulas, their pairing on this plaque is a rare occurrence that, visually and symbolically, equates the martyrdom of Thomas Becket with the Passion of Christ. The roof of the châsse, from which this plaque derived, would most likely have shown the entombment of Thomas or the assumption of his soul to heaven. HAK

Purchase from the J. H. Wade Fund 1951.449

DIMENSIONS: 16.9 x 28.5 cm

BIBLIOGRAPHY: Caudron 1999, 60–61; Caudron 1993, 62; Cleveland 1967, 116–17, 359, no. III-36; Milliken 1952, 7–13; Migeon 1905, 19, 28; Troyes 1882, no. 1.

55

Châsse

ABOUT 1225–50; FRENCH, LIMOGES

REPOUSSÉ, ENGRAVED, STIPPLED, AND GILDED COPPER, CHAMPLEVÉ ENAMEL,

AND OAK CORE

This oblong châsse, produced in a 13th-century Limoges workshop, has a different scene on each face. The principal face is decorated with both full-length appliqué figures and engraved figures in reserve (meaning that they were left in gilded copper) with appliqué heads. The figures are set in front of a dark blue enameled background divided by a median band of turquoise and strewn with rosettes. The back and one end (the one with a figure in a door is a later replacement) show engraved figures in reserve on similar blue-and-turquoise enameled backgrounds strewn with rosettes and other motifs of various shapes and sizes. The châsse is crowned by an engraved crest with three superimposed crystal knobs that decorate the ends and center of the posts. At rhythmic intervals between the crest's twelve keyhole arches are four crystal cabochons, each mounted in a lozenge-shaped flat setting.

The châsse's tripartite design and iconographic program follow a common formula, with the Crucifixion and Christ in Majesty decorating the central fields of its principal face. The Crucifixion adheres to the standard iconography with the engraved figures of the Virgin and St. John next to the cross on either side and the personified figures of the Sun and Moon above. On the lid, the half-length figure of Christ is inscribed in an engraved circle with the symbols of the four evangelists in the spandrels. Christ emerges from a bank of clouds, holding a codex and blessing the beholder with his outstretched right hand. The Greek letters *A* (alpha) and *ω* (omega) describe him as "the first and the last, the beginning and the end" (Apocalypse 22:13). Flanking the central scene on both the front face and roof panel are two standing appliqué figures who may represent deacons or saintly figures of ecclesiastical rank. Each is placed underneath an arch supported by columns and half turrets emerging from the springing of the arches. The back of the châsse consists of two panels with identical decoration. The wings of the angels in each panel spread beyond the boundaries of the medallions in which they are inscribed. Only one of the end panels is preserved in its original state, decorated with the half-length figure of an imposing angel in reserve emerging from a bank of clouds. Here, the dark blue enameled background shows an even greater variety of enameled rosettes and other motifs of various shapes and sizes, all engraved, stippled, and gilded like those on the sides. HAK

Gift of S. Livingston Mather, Constance Mather Bishop, Phillip R. Mather, Katherine Hoyt Cross, and Katherine Mather McLean in accordance with the wishes of Samuel Mather 1940.347.a–b

DIMENSIONS: 24.7 x 24.2 x 10.4 cm

BIBLIOGRAPHY: Milliken 1941, 36–41.

56

Enthroned Virgin and Child

ABOUT 1225–50; FRENCH, LIMOGES

REPOUSSÉ, ENGRAVED, CHASED, AND GILDED COPPER, BLACK GLASS BEADS, AND LIGHT

TURQUOISE ENAMELED PEARLS

Produced in a Limoges workshop, most likely during the second quarter of the 13th century, this elegant relief of the enthroned Virgin and Child originally formed part of a larger ensemble. While its exact functional context remains elusive, similar appliqué figures were used to decorate precious altar frontals, devotional tabernacles, and elaborate reliquary chasses. Within its original context, the relief of the Virgin and Child would presumably have been applied to an enameled plaque, richly decorated with ornamental scrollwork on a blue enameled ground. As such, it may have served as the counterpart to a similar plaque with the figure of the enthroned Christ, as seen on the principal face of the chasse of Sainte-Viance (parish church of Sainte-Viance, Corrèze) or the outer wings of the tabernacle of Cherves (Metropolitan Museum of Art, New York, 17.190.735).

Despite their small size, the figures appear monumental in both form and conception. Seated on a cushionless throne, the Virgin is dressed in her traditional attire: a long-sleeved tunic girded above her waist, a long mantle wrapped around her knees and the left side of her body, and a shoulder-length veil that frames the elegant features of her face. The courtly nature of the Virgin's attire is emphasized by decorative bands studded with turquoise enameled pearls at the wrist of her proper right hand and below her left knee. Further accentuating the material preciousness of her garments is the engraved and stippled surface decoration at the hem of her mantle, which imitates fur lining. Raising in her right hand a golden sphere or globe, the symbol of Christ's rule over the cosmos, she gently supports the Christ child with her left. Echoing his mother's gesture, Jesus raises his right hand in blessing but carries a book in his left. Like his mother, he is represented as a crowned figure dressed in royal garb that consists of a long-sleeved tunic with a fur-lined mantle and bead-studded collar. The subtle parallelism in the depiction of the Virgin and Christ is more than mere coincidence. It stresses the close relationship between the mother and child and their joint rule over the heavenly kingdom. HAK

Purchase from the J. H. Wade Fund 1962.29

DIMENSIONS: 21.9 x 10.6 x 3.8 cm

BIBLIOGRAPHY: Taburet-Delahaye 1996, 36–37; New York 1970, 77–78, no. 83; Cleveland 1967, 148–51, 363, no. IV-17; *CMA Bulletin* 49 (1962): 228, no. 31.

57

Corpus from a Crucifix

ABOUT 1130–40; FRENCH, BURGUNDY, AUTUN?

POLYCHROMED WOOD

As the culminating event in Christ's life and, according to Christian belief, the ultimate sacrifice of God on behalf of humankind, the Crucifixion on Mount Golgotha was one of the most important themes in Western medieval and Byzantine art. From the fifth century on, pictorial representations of the Crucifixion became a standard feature of Christian art in all media except sculpture in the round, which had carried the stigma of idolatry since late antiquity. While Byzantine artists remained faithful to the Early Christian tradition and never explored three-dimensional religious sculpture as an artistic medium, Western medieval artists, especially those from north of the Alps, felt less bound by such ancient customs. Three-dimensional religious sculptures, including those of the crucified Christ, are known to have existed during the Carolingian period. Yet it was not until later, in the 10th and 11th centuries, that monumental crucifixes, carved from wood and painted, became a common feature of church decoration across Europe. Placed above the main altar of a church, these enormous crucifixes served to remind the viewer of Christ's sacrifice on the cross, which was re-enacted every time the Holy Eucha-

rist was celebrated on the altar below, and invited prayer and meditation on Christ's salvific deed.

This fragmentary corpus (body) of the crucified Christ, said to have come from the town of Clamecy (Nièvre), preserves traces of its original polychromy. It once formed part of a Romanesque crucifix made for a church in Burgundy, France. As was common during much of the 12th century, Christ is represented not as suffering, but as triumphant on the cross—eyes wide open and crowned head slightly inclined toward his right. While the figure is missing its arms, left foot, parts of its crown, and the supporting cross, the high quality of the carving and the serenity of the facial expression make it easy to forget the sculpture's fragmentary condition. The fine carving of Christ's face, his long wavy hair, perfectly groomed beard, and sagging torso as well as the rendering of his carefully draped and knotted *perizonium* (loincloth) call to mind works by the sculptor Gislebertus, whose name is recorded on the Last Judgment tympanum of the cathedral of Autun. This impressive sculpture was likely made in a workshop intimately familiar with Gislebertus's work. HAK

Leonard C. Hanna Jr. Fund 1980.1

DIMENSIONS: 111.1 X 20.2 X 7.8 cm

BIBLIOGRAPHY: Cahn 1999, 147–48, no. B.III.1; Solms 1995, 183–84, pl. 76–77; Verdier 1981, 66–74.

58

Engaged Capital: Daniel in the Lions' Den

ABOUT 1125–50; FRENCH, SAINT-AIGNAN-SUR-CHER (LOIR-ET-CHER)
LIMESTONE

This engaged limestone capital depicts the story of Daniel in the Lions' Den based on two accounts in the Old Testament book of Daniel (6:1–24 and 14:1–42). The latter (apochryphal) passage describes how, during the reign of Evilmerodach, son and successor of Nabuchodonosor of Babylon, Daniel was cast into a den with seven lions for six days because he had destroyed the idol and temple of the god Bel and defeated a dragon worshiped by the Babylonians.

Seated frontally on a throne that resembles a church with two windows and a pitched roof, Daniel is shown here as a bearded man dressed in tunic and mantle, the traditional garb of a prophet in medieval art. He holds a closed book in his right hand and raises his left in front of his chest in a gesture that implies prayer as well as judgment and prophesy. Framed by an architectural canopy above and a roped astragal below, Daniel is surrounded by seven ferocious lions, four on the left and three on the right; the face and wings of an angel appear, partly obscured by the turret of the canopy, above the lions on the right. Since the capital omits the prophet Habacuc, who according to the apocryphal account of the story was carried to Babylon by an angel to feed Daniel, this can only be the angel described in the canonical account of the story as

having been sent by God "to shut up the mouths of the lions" (Dan. 6:22). The capital thus represents a conflation of both the canonical and the apocryphal versions of the story of Daniel in the Lions' Den.

Together with other historiated capitals, this imposing work of Romanesque sculpture once decorated the nave of the church of Saint-Aignan-sur-Cher, a city near Tours in northwestern France. It was probably removed from that church during a restoration campaign in the 1870s or early 1880s and replaced by a copy. The capital's art historical significance lies not only in its impressive size, but also in the compositional clarity of its layout and the refinement of its sculptural details, for instance the treatment of the prophet's hair, beard, and finely delineated garments with their cascades of concentric drapery folds. Significant also are the iconographic choices made to represent the story of Daniel. Rather than depicting the prophet with his hands raised in an *orans* (praying) position, as is frequently encountered in Romanesque sculpture, he is represented here in a stately pose that closely recalls representations of Christ in Majesty at the Last Judgment. The capital thus stresses the theme of divine judgment and deliverance through the representation of Daniel as a Christ-like figure. HAK

Purchase from the J. H. Wade Fund 1962.247

DIMENSIONS: 72.4 x 68.6 x 36.2 cm

BIBLIOGRAPHY: Cahn 1999, 155–56, no. B.III.6; Scheifele 1994, 47–82; Wixom 1979A, 42–43; Rosenzweig 1976; Cleveland 1967, 68–69, 352–53, no. III-12; Green 1948, 10–11, 63–64, no. 1.7; *MIA Bulletin* 12 (1923): 1, 26–28.

quod opante agricola oportrat defructib; suise
dere; irnatum publici curiositaxte ne n tā uolen
tib; dm ~~demonstra~~sse uiderem. quā fastidienti
buf peludisse. EXPT argu mentum PRÆFATIO.

ria eni
helisabeth
exerit gra
tate eni q
rumi usc
adhuc ce
conuertet
tū inspu
parū inf
ru. parari
ad anglm
arcoi me
dū et ta
sui sū loq
erracen
Per qd nō
mepre sui
imutauon
sui aū non
usione u
tt ip mar
duet offici
erei concep
sib; quincg
respect aut

168

59

Fragment from a Bible: St. Luke

ABOUT 1100; FRENCH, BURGUNDY, CLUNY ABBEY

TEMPERA WITH GOLD AND SILVER ON VELLUM

This small fragment from a Latin bible preserves an important portion of the material legacy of the library of the abbey of Cluny, one of the wealthiest and justifiably famous monasteries in Europe. Cluny possessed a significant library of about 570 volumes in the 12th century, a huge number at the time, the majority of which are now lost. It was also the site of an important scriptorium and school of painting. The Cleveland fragment represents the tangible remains of a quarto bible, specifically the lower outside quarter of the page. Most likely used on a lectern, the bible was written in a two-column format in uncial letters. The remaining fragments of these two columns of text may be seen on both recto and verso of this cutting. The recto includes the end of the Gospel of Mark and the opening lines of St. Jerome's preface to the Gospel of Luke. On the verso appear the closing lines of Jerome's preface and a spectacular author portrait of St. Luke.

The miniature of Luke presents the basic ingredients of evangelist portraiture established centuries earlier in Byzantine art: he sits on a throne before a lectern holding a quill pen and writing into an open scroll. The remaining three evangelists would have been similarly treated. Byzantine gospel lectionaries typically included such classically draped portraits of the evangelists to introduce their respective gospels. These artistic conventions were adopted by artists in the Latin west through direct or indirect exposure to Byzantine models. Further evidence of an awareness of Byzantine manuscript painting may be seen in the specific treatment of Luke's hair and beard as well as the "damp fold" system of rendering his draperies. These stylistic and compositional elements are apparent in an 11th-century Byzantine miniature of St. Matthew (see no. 23), which provides an example of such possible antecedents, although how they were transmitted is uncertain. The Cluniac artist may have been exposed to Byzantine manuscripts carried to the west or come into contact with Byzantine painting through artistic centers in Italy, perhaps at Monte Cassino or in Rome. Crusader artists active in the Holy Land may also have played a role.

The St. Luke miniature attests to the magnificence of the bible from which it came. No other fragments from the same manuscript are currently known, though related examples of manuscript painting from Cluny by the same atelier and very likely the same hand are preserved. They include an illustrated lectionary (Bibliothèque Nationale, Paris, Cod. Nouv. Acq. Lat. 2446) and an excised miniature of the Ascension from the same codex (Musée National du Moyen Âge, Paris, Cl. 23757). Further, a group of frescoes painted in the same formal Byzantinizing style are preserved in the priory of Berzé-la-Ville, a Cluniac dependency. This evidence suggests the presence of a highly active atelier at Cluny toward the end of the 11th century and involving several artists. The Cleveland St. Luke provides an important link to a style of painting fostered by a great and very influential abbey. SNF

Purchase from the J. H. Wade Fund 1968.190

DIMENSIONS: 17.3 x 16.1 cm

BIBLIOGRAPHY: Huchard 2004, 13–15; Russo 2000, 57–87; New York 1997, 473, no. 311; Wixom 1969, 130–35; Cleveland 1967, 34–35, 349, no. II-7.

INCIPIT CAVSA PRIMA IN QVA DE SIMONIACIS AGI TVR

Qidam habens filiū
obtulit eū diuissimo ce
nobio. Exactus ab albate
z fratrib' decē libras sol
uit. ut filius suscipetur.
ipso tñ beneficio etatis
hoc ignorante. Creuit
puer: et p incrementa
tpr̄m & officioꝝ ad
urilem etate. et sacer
doti gradū puenit.
Exinde suffraganbus meritis in
epm eligitur. Interueniente obse
quio et paternis pcibus. data qq; pecunia cuida ex con
siliarijs archiepi. consecratur iste in antistitē. nescius
paterni obsequij: et oblate pecunie. Procedente ū tpr̄
innullos p pecuniam ordinauit. quibusdã ū gratis be

Causarū
iudicium.
goetium. ab
iusticia. ab
causa est r
hic inse gre
in dicendo
cum certaꝝ
narū int

p̄ p.
quens.
ã mor
cunitas
cie. ut
uedã u
u repre
n electi
es apli
soluen
nquen
tt am
conces
dē ad
phen
et ordi
matice
st. non
directo
seacen

60

Leaf from a Decretum

ABOUT 1160–65; FRENCH, BURGUNDY, PONTIGNY ABBEY

TEMPERA ON VELLUM

This beautifully decorated leaf was excised from a manuscript of the handbook of church law known as the "Concordia Discordantium Canonum" (Concord of Discordant Canons), more commonly known as the "Decretum." The text was written by Gratian, an Italian Camaldolese monk and ecclesiastical lawyer active in Bologna about 1130–40. Gratian intended his book as a basis for the teaching of canon law and applied the same method developed by the scholastic philosopher Peter Abelard for theological discourse: stating a proposition or posing a question and then applying contradictory canons supporting the different positions that are then resolved by a dictum supporting doctrine. The Decretum has two parts: the first introduces 101 *distinctiones* (distinctions) establishing the types, origins, and definitions of law as well as ecclesiastical government and discipline; the second presents 36 hypothetical *causae* (law cases) followed by questions and resolution. Gratian's Decretum became the standard textbook of European law schools during the 12th through 14th centuries. As such it was widely copied and commented upon.

The focus of the verso of this leaf is an elaborately decorated letter *Q* [*uidam habens filium obtulit*] with spiraling lotus petals introducing the first case. Beginning "A man having a son offered him to a very wealthy cloister," this case concerns the definition of simony (making profit from sacred things)

and the sanctions to be applied. It is preceded on the recto by the closing passages of the 101 distinctions and an elegant diagram in the form of a quadruple arcade deriving from established canon tables. The arcade encloses the letters of the Greek and Latin alphabets with numerical correspondences.

The style of the illumination and especially the script date this leaf to 1160–65 and associate it with the important Cistercian abbey of Pontigny in the Archdiocese of Sens in Burgundy. The style is traditionally referred to as the Channel school of illumination since it was current in both England and northern France during the second half of the 12th century. Vivid colors, spiraling tendrils, and interlace ornamentation are characteristic of this style. In November 1164, Thomas Becket, archbishop of Canterbury, took refuge at Pontigny as a result of his conflict with King Henry II. During his stay, Becket immersed himself in the study of church law, as evidenced by his later use of citations from the Decretum. This leaf could have been part of the manuscript he consulted. The Pontigny Decretum, the earliest known French copy of Gratian's text, was listed in several inventories before the French Revolution but dismembered after the monastery was suppressed during the revolution. Possible other fragments are in the Bibliothèque Municipale in Auxerre (Ms. 269) and the Victoria and Albert Museum in London (PDP 8985,B-F). SNF

Purchase from the J. H. Wade Fund 1954.598

DIMENSIONS: 44.8 x 32 cm

BIBLIOGRAPHY: Cahn 1975, 47–59; Melnikas 1975, 107–10, fig. 5; New York 1970, 242–43, no. 241; Cleveland 1967, 92–93, 356, no. III-24.

61

Pair of Angels

ABOUT 1250; FRENCH, VICINITY OF REIMS
WALNUT WITH TRACES OF GILDING AND POLYCHROMY

These two angels are clearly from the same ensemble. Despite their fragmentary condition, they embody the monumental style of 13th-century High Gothic cathedral sculpture in France. On another level, the two figures compare favorably with small-scale sculpture of the period in deluxe materials such as ivory associated with workshops in the French capital or northeastern France and the patronage of the court. These angels, at once delicate and powerful, represent the sculpture of the epoch with a particular eloquence. Each is carved from a block of walnut. Once brilliantly hued in gold and blue to suggest a rich brocade, their tunics now show only traces of paint; their heavy mantles were gilded on the exterior and red on the inside. Their cap-like coifs, articulated by parallel grooves and a fringe of tight curls, were also originally gilded. Finally, their sublime faces have been thought to portray tragic interest, anguish, or even deep psychological concern. The two figures when new would have made a luxuriant impression to the beholder.

The loss of the angels' hands, along with whatever attributes they held, makes contextualization difficult. Typically such angels, whether of wood, stone, ivory, or the painting medium, hold a variety of attributes: instruments of the Passion, chalices, candelabra, and censers, being the more common. Extant wood sculptures of angels dating to the 13th and 14th centuries have often been thought to have served as altar angels, which stood on columns surrounding an altar. The columns, in turn, supported curtain rods and curtains. Such arrangements appear frequently in panel paintings and manuscript miniatures. Yet these angels are not carved fully in the round. Their lower backs are flat and unfinished, suggesting that they were meant to be installed against a smooth surface but clearly intended for interior use. They may have filled the spandrels of a carved and painted wood ciborium suspended over an altar, or perhaps they flanked a large crucifix. Ultimately, their placement and function remains conjecture as the medieval liturgical furnishings of most French churches have not survived.

The style, localization, and dating of the two angels have been cogently argued by William Wixom; their physiognomies, especially the faces, relate to the sculptural program of the west facade at Reims Cathedral around 1230–45. Some scholars have considered an English origin, citing the 13th-century angels in the interior of Westminster Abbey. Such speculation has not been convincing primarily because the Cleveland angels are carved from walnut (in widespread use in France, but rare in English medieval sculpture). Antecedents for the angels are more reliably found in the Reims milieu. Since the chronology of the Reims sculptural program has more recently been revised, a date of 1250–65 now appears more tenable for the two figures. SNF

Leonard C. Hanna Jr. Fund 1966.360 and 1967.27

DIMENSIONS: 75 x 41.5 x 22.5 cm (left) and 78.5 x 37 x 23.8 cm (above)

BIBLIOGRAPHY: Kurmann 1987; Wixom 1974, 83–96; Sauerländer 1972; Cleveland 1967, 186–87, 366, no. V-9.

62

Apostle Head

ABOUT 1235–40; FRENCH, THÉROUANNE (PAS-DE-CALAIS)
OOLITIC LIMESTONE

This monumental stone head was discovered along with four others in the wall of a house in the town of Saint-Omer in 1923. The five heads eventually made their way to the art market by way of Belgium and London. The Cleveland Museum of Art acquired two (left and inset), and the others are now in the collections of the Museum of Fine Arts, Houston (80.148), the Victoria and Albert Museum in London (A.25-1979), and a private collection in New York. That all five form a cohesive, homogeneous group cannot be questioned. Each displays the same degree of weathering, especially on the front, while retaining the same details of modeling and style. Each has wavy hair and a curly beard, deeply carved and drilled by the same sculptor from the same stone. None of the five includes royal regalia, so they could not have belonged to a *galerie des rois* (gallery of kings) on the west facade of a French cathedral. Instead, they are now widely accepted as jamb figures representing apostles. Their condition and size supports this assumption. The fifth head (V&A) has been proposed to be a trumeau figure of Christ. All belong to the classic phase of High Gothic sculpture produced at the beginning of the 13th century at cathedrals such as Chartres, Sens, Laon, and elsewhere. Northern European cathedrals of this era traditionally embellished their portals with life-sized statues on the jambs flanking a door with a figure of Christ or the Virgin Mary occupying the trumeau column.

The heads have been associated with a Judgment group of similar scale and weathering from the destroyed cathedral of Thérouanne in northeastern France. Dedicated in 1134, little is known of the cathedral's form and decoration. The town was demolished by order of the Habsburg emperor Charles V of Spain following his failed siege of Metz. The cathedral was dismantled beginning 20 June 1553. Within six weeks it had been completely razed, with some 2,000 workers reportedly employed to this end. The Judgment group—Christ the Judge flanked by a kneeling Virgin and St. John—was installed in the nearby collegiate church of Saint-Omer in 1553. The heads subsequently discovered in the wall of the house in Saint-Omer must have been transferred at the same time.

Some scholars have argued that the ensemble and the five heads once formed the decorative program of the south portal at Thérouanne Cathedral. This assumption was based upon a perspective drawing, largely inaccurate, executed about 20 years before the cathedral was destroyed. A more recent supposition is that the extant sculptures were intended for a west doorway. Firm conclusions for the placement of these sculptures in the program at the cathedral remain elusive without documentary or archaeological evidence. Yet these heads remain fragments of highly important monumental jamb figures on a par with those from Notre-Dame de Paris discovered in 1977. SNF

Leonard C. Hanna Jr. Fund 1978.56.1

DIMENSIONS: 41.9 x 30.4 x 32.4 cm

BIBLIOGRAPHY: New York 2006B, 35–38, no. 8; Davezac 1983, 11–23; Williamson 1982, 219–20; Wixom 1979A, 97–100; Lille 1978, 19–21; Sauerländer 1972, 468.

63

Virgin and Child

ABOUT 1385–90; FRENCH, CENTRAL LOIRE VALLEY?
LIMESTONE WITH TRACES OF POLYCHROMY

The image of the Virgin and Child is one of the most ubiquitous subjects in Gothic European art, and the standing figure of the Virgin and Child is perhaps the most frequent subject for free-standing sculpture in France in the 14th and early 15th centuries. Such sculptures once occupied the side chapels of great cathedrals as well as parish churches, private chapels, and even roadside shrines. Throughout the Middle Ages, the aristocracy opened their purses to build churches in the Virgin's honor and commission paintings, statues, masses, and votive crowns for her shrines. Beginning in the 12th century, the Virgin became the focus of a vigorous and fertile grassroots piety. The devout recognized her unique position as intercessor with her son on behalf of sinners. As such she was accorded particular honor over and above that due the saints. While God is owed adoration and the saints veneration, Mary occupies the principal mediating position as a being belonging to both earth and heaven, clearly symbolized by this sculpture.

Carved from soft, chalky limestone, this sculpture was frequently painted throughout the centuries. Most of this paint is now gone. In its original configuration, however, the sculpture may have been left unpainted (not unlike its present appearance), with the exception of the flesh tones and the gilding of the hair and edges of the draperies. Both figures originally wore crowns, probably of metal.

A crown denotes the Virgin as Queen of Heaven and her white garments signify her virginity. The flower stalk scepter, now damaged, in her right hand would have held a lily or other long-stemmed flower. The Christ child clasps a bird symbolizing the human soul and his role as redeemer of humankind. The sculpture exudes the courtly elegance and delicate naturalistic detail associated with the International Gothic style, which pervaded courtly workshops toward the end of the 14th century.

The vibrant naturalism of the Virgin's face, her long flowing hair, and the deep, rich folds of drapery are characteristic of the work of itinerant artists from the Netherlands who found employment at the Valois courts of France in Paris, Berry, and Burgundy. Their native styles and attention to realistic detail fused with local French artistic traditions toward the end of the 14th century and took fertile root. The provenance of the Cleveland sculpture is unknown, but stylistic analysis suggests a credible relationship with similar sculptures made for churches and abbeys of the central Loire Valley, specifically from Loiret and Monceaux-le-Comte. The style of André Beauneveu has also been noted as an influence. Beauneveu came from Valenciennes and worked at the ducal court of Jean de Berry at Bourges in the Loire Valley, as well as in Hainault, Flanders, Paris, and Burgundy. His commissions were abundant and his influence widespread. SNF

Purchase from the J. H. Wade Fund 1962.28

DIMENSIONS: 135.3 x 41.3 x 30.5 cm

BIBLIOGRAPHY: Dijon/Cleveland 2004, 58–60; Paris 2004, 98–99; Scher 1992; Cleveland 1967, 230–31, 373, no. VI-8; Wixom 1963A, 14–22; Bober 1953, 741–53.

64

Miniature from a Psalter: The Deposition

ABOUT 1240–50; MASTER OF THE POTOCKI WORKSHOP (FRENCH, PARIS)

TEMPERA AND GOLD ON VELLUM

This detached miniature depicting the Deposition, blank on its verso, derives from a Parisian luxury psalter today known as the Potocki Psalter after its former owner, Stanislaw Kostka Potocki (1755–1821), a renowned Polish historian, art critic, and art collector. Much of his collection eventually entered Polish national institutions, with the psalter going to the National Library in Warsaw in 1933. Several miniatures that had been removed before then are now in public collections in the United States and Great Britain.

The illustrations of the Potocki Psalter are superb examples of Parisian Gothic painting at its most refined stage, with a strong emphasis on line and color. As a whole, they illustrate the new court style of King Louis IX in which tall figures assume sinuous postures and the drapery forms large broken folds about the body. These compositions are closely related in style to the frescoes executed between 1240 and 1248 at the Sainte-Chapelle in Paris. Both the miniatures in this psalter and the Sainte-Chapelle frescoes are the creations of a gifted, forward-looking group of painters among whom the Master of the Potocki Workshop undoubtedly played an important role. The psalter would have

been an important commission, and the Cleveland miniature clearly shows his genius.

A psalter, essentially a book of Psalms to which ancillary texts such as a calendar or litany of the saints were usually appended, was the principal book of private prayer for the lay person before books of hours became popular in the 14th century. Psalters were used in both liturgical and private devotional contexts, and the Psalms could be divided in various ways as use dictated. Representations of King David, author of the Psalms, are common. Prefatory cycles were often added, especially in deluxe volumes. The Cleveland miniature formed part of a Christological cycle of at least ten miniatures that would have been grouped at the beginning of the volume. Set against a burnished gold ground within an alternating blue and pink frame, this scene shows Christ's body being taken down from the cross by Joseph of Arimathea, a wealthy and respected man and secret follower of Christ who had obtained permission from Pilate to bury the body. The cross is flanked, as is traditional, by the Virgin and St. John the Evangelist. In the psalter, the Deposition would have come between the Crucifixion and the Three Marys at the Tomb. SNF

Mr. and Mrs. William H. Marlatt Fund 1985.80

DIMENSIONS: 15.4 x 10 cm

BIBLIOGRAPHY: Plonka-Balus 2005; Thoss 1978, 67; Branner 1971, 165–72; Branner 1968, 1–42; Sawicka 1938, 38–44, pl. IVa–b.

65

Two Miniatures from a Manuscript of the Apocalypse:
The Woman upon the Scarlet Beast and the War in Heaven

ABOUT 1295; FRENCH, LORRAINE

TEMPERA AND GOLD ON VELLUM

The final book of the New Testament, the Apocalypse (book of Revelation) is the visionary text of St. John the Evangelist, supposedly written while he was banished to the island of Patmos during the reign of Domitian (AD 81–96). John's cryptic and prophetic visions—forceful images of salvation, sin, and celestial retribution—are understood to have been received through divine providence. Manuscripts of the Apocalypse were much in vogue in 10th- and 11th-century Spain and 13th-century England and France perhaps because fears about the antichrist and the end of the world were rising at that time. The Apocalypse provided a visual and graphic medley of terror, awe, numerology, and majesty. Since the text was often incomprehensible, these manuscripts were frequently accompanied by commentaries and elaborate picture cycles that provide some of the most intense, if bizarre, Christian art of the Middle Ages. Such Apocalypses, with their monsters, demons, vengeful riders, and colorful women, would have also readily appealed to a literate and secular audience steeped in the knightly adventures of Arthurian romances.

This pair of cuttings from a late 13th-century Apocalypse, each a double-sided miniature, conforms to this Anglo-French tradition, expressing through symbolic language images of sin and its re-sulting punishment as well as salvation and victory. The parent manuscript was dismembered around 1795 and pasted into an album sold to Daniel Burckhardt-Wildt (d. 1819), a Basel merchant. The original manuscript contained six full-page miniatures illustrating an Ars Moriendi (manual on the art of dying) that was appended to the Apocalypse proper. Another 88 half-page miniatures contained apocalyptic scenes. An abridged commentary by Berengaudus preceded the text of St. John beneath each half-page miniature. The 77 known miniatures from the Burckhardt-Wildt Apocalypse, including the two cuttings here, were sold at auction in 1983, dispersing them among numerous public institutions and private collections.

These miniatures are splendid examples of 13th-century miniature painting and of Apocalypse illustration in particular. Though judged to be English at the time of their sale in 1983, they relate stylistically to a group of manuscripts illuminated in the Lorraine region of eastern France in the decades around 1300. Lorraine had a well-established cultural tradition, but by the 13th century English models were very popular in this region. Thus the decoration of the Burckhardt-Wildt Apocalypse may ultimately depend on English prototypes. SNF

Mr. and Mrs. William H. Marlatt Fund 1983.73.1.a and John L. Severance Fund 1983.73.2.b

DIMENSIONS: 10.2 x 14.7 cm and 12 x 14.2 cm

BIBLIOGRAPHY: Cambridge 2005, 112–15, no. 40–41; De Winter 1983B, 396–417; Morgan 1982–83, 162–69; Ivanchenko/Henderson 1980, 97–106; Henderson 1970, 22–31.

❖ A Splendid Patronage: Valois Burgundy ❖

After the investiture of Philip the Bold as duke of Burgundy in 1364, the duchy of Burgundy became a branch of the French royal house of Valois. The fourth and last duke of Burgundy of the Valois line, Charles the Bold, died on the battlefield in 1477 leaving no male issue. Thus, the legendary dynasty came to an abrupt end. Yet the history of Valois Burgundy has assumed the mystique of sublime ostentation and aesthetic refinement. The dukes commanded vast financial resources, and their collective reigns chronicle the rise and fall of one of the most sophisticated courts in Europe.

During the heyday of the Valois, the cosmopolitan city of Paris was the major center for the visual arts in northern Europe, largely because of the activities of the royal court and its attendant aristocrats. Paris attracted artists from the Netherlands, Germany, Italy, and elsewhere who wished to apprentice in the capital or hoped to earn their livelihood in this vibrant and creative milieu. It was in Paris that the Burgundian dukes and many others acquired their luxury objects—enamels, jewelry, goldsmith works, and manuscripts. In the years around 1400, France also experienced troubles: the madness of King Charles VI, the Great Schism with its antipopes, the return of the plague, the civil war between the Burgundians and the Armagnacs, the French defeat at Agincourt, and the English occupation. Throughout this difficult period, Paris remained a hub of artistic activity. Philip the Bold commissioned luxury objects there, and his three older brothers—King Charles V and the dukes Louis I d'Anjou and Jean de Berry—were also keen patrons of the arts.

The wealth of the house of Burgundy stemmed from matrimony. On 19 June 1369, Philip the Bold, the youngest son of King John II (John the Good), married Margaret de Mâle, the only child of Louis II de Mâle, Count of Flanders, in Ghent in an impressive display of splendor. Through his wife, Philip inherited a vast group of lands made up of five earldoms: Nevers, Franche-Comté, Artois, Rethel, and Flanders. Flanders, with its commercial wealth, was unquestionably the most attractive. This inheritance provided Burgundy with two large blocks of territory extending from the Swiss and German borders in the east to the North Sea and including parts of modern France, Belgium, and Holland. Philip and his successors further consolidated their power and wealth through marriage. In 1378 he planned a union with the house of Austria, a project that, in 1392, resulted in the marriage of his daughter Catherine of Burgundy to Duke Leopold IV of Habsburg. In 1385, following bitter negotiations with Aubert of Bavaria, regent for the counts of Hainaut, Holland, and Zealand, Philip's eldest son, John, Count of Nevers (John the Fearless), married Margaret of Bavaria and William of Bavaria married John's sister Margaret of Burgundy. Subsequently, in 1401, another of the duke's daughters, Marie, married Amédée VIII, Count of Savoy. The following year Anthony of Burgundy, Philip's second son, wed Jeanne of Luxembourg, daughter of the Count of Saint-Pol.

His Flemish legacy allowed Philip the Bold to reorganize the institutions in his principalities. Subsequently, the income drawn from Flanders and the royal treasury soared enormously, easily reaching 500,000 livres a year. These monies came from different sources including property and gifts from the king, but the tax revenues allowed the dukes to commission art, architecture, and music on a lavish scale.

The dukes' devotional needs and political ambitions, with the requisite pomp and ceremony, produced a brilliant patronage in whose service painters, sculptors, and goldsmiths could exercise their talents to the full. The first two dukes embraced the arts as a means of enhancing their status and displaying their taste. Their sophisticated court became a model for emulation across Europe. The works they commissioned, especially sculpture, inspired the development of the Burgundian court style, with its love of volume, space, and realistic detail. Philip the Bold and then John the Fearless constructed an elaborate complex at their capital in Dijon. Eventually, it was supplemented by dozens of residences scattered throughout Burgundy and the Netherlands, including two Parisian townhouses.

To embellish their residences the Burgundian dukes assembled the largest collection of tapestries of their day, with Philip and his wife owning more than one hundred. The tapestries were rolled up and traveled with them as part of their baggage. These allegorical or historical scenes easily functioned as portable propaganda or princely metaphors and became essential to the success of princely ceremonies. Unfortunately, no tapestries from the period of the first two dukes are known.

Philip and Margaret also purchased large and costly gemstones and commissioned jewels known as fermaux, elaborate brooches fashioned from enameled gold with additional pearls and gems. Extraordinary gold vessels and votive shrines, exquisitely wrought in translucent or ronde bosse enamel, were exchanged as gifts. Most of these purchases were made not in the dukes' domains but in Paris, which was at the time a major manufacturing and trading center for metalwork and other sumptuary arts. The city was a principal European center for goldsmithing throughout the 14th century largely because of the originality of the large numbers of artisans working there, the high quality of work being produced, and the patronage of the French court.

Like other noblemen of his era, Philip the Bold commissioned precious objects as gifts for weddings, to celebrate the New Year, or for ceremonial entry into a town. His patronage played a significant role in innovations that appeared in the 1400s, such as the fashion for enameled gold jewelry. In 1352 the accounts of John II mention for the first time gold jewels with red and white enamel. Fifteen years later, in 1367, there is a reference to a white-enamel decoration for a gold belt made for Philip the Bold's youngest son. At the beginning of the reign of Charles VI in 1380, Philip (who was then the king's guardian) was a major force behind the fashion for white-enameled jewels decorated with animals, angels, or gentlewomen. The records show that he gave a great number of jewels as gifts in the years 1382–93. Duchess Margaret also owned an impressive collection, which was minutely described in the inventories prepared at her death in 1405.

By about 1400 a large number of books of hours (private devotional books for the lay person) were being written and illuminated in Paris. Probably for the first time books were being produced in quantity for sale. The city was the undisputed center of the publishing trade, but not all its scribes and illuminators were native to the French capital; some came from the north. The principal business for most must have been books of hours, although secular texts such as hunting treatises and classical texts were also popular. Records indicate that the bookshops in Paris were also associated with the university book trade and many were located in the vicinity of the Cathedral of Notre-Dame.

The ducal libraries were among the most significant private collections of illuminated codices. Philip the Bold's library included some 200 volumes. Two book lists made shortly after his death in 1404 describe the collection of the duke and duchess. By the death of Charles the Bold, the ducal library had expanded to 1,500 volumes—the largest private collection in Europe outside of the papal library in the Vatican. It contained manuscripts illuminated by the Limbourg brothers, Loyset Liédet, Jean Tavernier, the Boucicaut Master, Girart de Roussillon, Willem Vrelant, Simon Marmion (see no. 82), and the Master of Mary of Burgundy.

Burgundian court artists often supplied ducal religious foundations and private chapels with sculpture, panel paintings, altarpieces (both carved and painted), liturgical vessels, and illuminated manuscripts. The central focus of Philip the Bold's patronage was the Carthusian monastery of Champmol and the ducal tombs that once occupied its choir (see nos. 73, 74). The founding of the Chartreuse de Champmol, and its embellishment, was foremost among Philip's grand artistic projects. The complex located on the outskirts of Dijon featured some of the finest examples of Burgundian court sculpture produced by Claus Sluter and his nephew Claus de Werve as well as Antoine le Moitourier and Jean de la Huerta. Altarpieces and private devotional panels and diptychs were commissioned for the church and monks' cells from painters Jean de Beaumetz (see no. 70), Henri Bellechose, Melchior Broederlam, and Jean Malouel —all of whom served as court painters.

The artistic and political emphasis of the later dukes Philip the Good and Charles the Bold gradually turned from their capital at Dijon to the Netherlands, where they ruled the towns of Ypres, Bruges, and Ghent. Their patronage extended largely to major painters and other artists and illuminators of the so-called Northern Renaissance. The visual realism that became the hallmark of Netherlandish art exerted a strong influence on artists in all the northern lands, and the wealth of the Burgundian state, along with the artistic interests of its dukes and their marked preference for Netherlandish artists, created the nexus for the diffusion of Netherlandish art.

Some of the most significant innovations in panel painting that flourished in the Netherlands of the 1430s had been anticipated decades earlier at the Valois courts. The patronage of the first two Burgundian dukes and the Netherlandish artists prominent in the construction and furnishing of the Chartreuse de Champmol saw their continued legacy in the next generations and the painting of Robert Campin and the van Eycks.

The Valois dukes of Burgundy remain fundamental to any discussion of European art or history during the late 14th and 15th centuries. Indeed, Valois Burgundy has become synonymous with refinement, sophistication, and opulence, and no study of the visual arts for this period is complete without considering the role of Burgundy. The court served as a cultural and artistic trend-setter. The dukes embodied prevalent contemporary values: magnificence in appearance, ceremony, and surroundings; chivalry inspired by Greco-Roman antiquity; and power manifested through ingenious ensembles of luxury arts. Their splendid deployment of goldsmithwork, tapestries, manuscripts, music, and pageantry elevated the dukes beyond their titular status to rival kings. SNF

66

Mirror Case

ABOUT 1325–50; FRENCH, PARIS

IVORY

During the 14th century, ivory was valued by courtly patrons as the most exquisite material for indicating the human form, or for suggesting in miniature the marble or limestone sculptures found in the portals of Europe's Gothic cathedrals. The quantity and availability of this material is suggested by the large number of surviving boxes, combs, hunting horns, knife handles, and other objects. Such items were produced for a secular clientele steeped in romantic literature and with an appetite for luxury objects. Mirror backs like this one survive in large numbers; typical decorative subjects are amorous encounters and chivalrous behavior. This mirror case originally had four corner terminals in the shape of Chimeras (monsters), now lost, which are often preserved on other examples. The hole at the top was drilled for suspension at an unknown time. There are no indications of polychromy or gilding, but other examples often have traces of both.

The Cleveland mirror case shows a man and woman engaged in a game of chess. The setting appears to be the interior of a tent. The male figure grasps the tent pole with his left hand as he moves a chess piece on the board. He wears a hooded flowing gown revealing his lower legs and feet; his companion's gown is even longer, obscuring her feet, and she wears a wimple on her head. The man's coiffure is typical of those seen in sculpture and manuscript miniatures of the early 14th century. Both figures have faint smiles. The woman gestures to the game board with her right hand while holding a captured piece in her left. The courtly gestures of the pair—the tipped heads and crossed knees—are standard mannerisms found in many media of the period. Paris was the center for luxury ivories during the 14th century, and this mirror case belongs to a group of at least 15 Parisian ivory mirror backs that survive with the same scene, though the details are sometimes different. The Cleveland case is one of the finest of this group.

Chess, a popular game at the time, could represent both love and war in medieval iconography. It was an indoor battle comparable to tournaments, and the contest is mentioned in many romances of the period. For this reason, modern scholars have sought to identify the subject. Among the several possible scenarios is the game between Huon of Bordeaux, the hero of a *chanson de geste* (a type of popular French medieval epic), and Yvarin, the daughter of a Saracen admiral. The stakes were high: if Huon lost, he was to be decapitated; if he won, he was to gain the lady's favors and a sum of money. Alternatives sometimes suggested are the romantic pairs Tristan and Iseult or Lancelot and Guinevere. Without precise attributes or inscriptions the identities of the figures are difficult to know with certainty. Doubtless the subject derives from a specific literary source, and the clientele that favored this subject would have understood the connection. SNF

Purchase from the J. H. Wade Fund 1940.1200

DIMENSIONS: diam. 10 cm, depth 1 cm

BIBLIOGRAPHY: Detroit 1997, 232–33, no. 58; Randall 1993, 123–24, no. 184; Cleveland 1967, 206–7, 369, no. V-18; Cheney 1941, 124–25; Longhurst 1926, 26–63.

67

Panels from a Casket

ABOUT 1330–50; FRENCH, LORRAINE?

IVORY

Among the most lavish products of French ivory ateliers of the 14th century were large caskets typically carved on top and sides with elaborate scenes drawn from courtly romances. At least seven complete caskets survive, as well as fragments from about a dozen others. Some caskets feature events from a single story, but the vast majority illustrate scenes drawn from bestiaries or as many as 11 different Arthurian romances. The Cleveland panels (front, lid, and back) are from one of these composite caskets.

Large ivory caskets were usually reinforced with silver mounts and a lock, and probably used to store valuables such as jewelry, seals, or documents. Caskets with scenes relating to romantic love may have originally been gifts between a man and a woman. Clearly their visual interest must have superseded their purpose. The expense of the materials and labor as well as the decoration clearly indicate that such caskets were produced for an aristocratic and literate clientele well-versed in the tales of romance and chivalry then circulating in manuscript form.

The largest Cleveland panel, the lid, depicts a tournament, the most splendid and romantic of knightly activities during the 14th century and after. The most common variant was the joust, seen here. Above, a gallery of nobles witnesses the moment just before the knights, wearing mail and armor, collide. The three-pointed heads on the lances indicate that the event is a "joust of peace," in which specially blunted weapons were used to avoid injury. These colorful events were showcases for male prowess and female favors. To the right of the jousting scene is a favorite allegory of chivalric love: knights assaulting the fortress of love. Two knights climb ladders and one below prepares a basket of roses to be launched in a catapult, while the two ladies above prepare to throw roses, symbols of surrender, on their assailants below. The castle would have been understood as woman and the attack as courtship. The scene at left shows the aftermath: a knight rides away with a lady on his horse while another, above, caresses a lady's face.

The front panel illustrates the fountain of youth, the capture of the unicorn, and an elephant and castle with lovers toward whom the god of love points his arrow. The back panel shows Sir Gawain slaying a lion and Lancelot, the lover of Guinevere, crossing the sword bridge. These images suggesting chivalry, fertility, virginity, and idealized courtly love likely derive from manuscripts including the *Roman de la Rose,* Richard de Fournival's *Bestiaire d'Amour,* and the poems of Chrétien de Troyes. Such texts were often found within the libraries of the aristocracy, so the casket's symbolic images would have been readily understood.

Where the Cleveland panels were produced is uncertain. Scholars have rejected Paris as the location of the atelier on the basis of style, the arrangement of the subjects, and compositional variations; the favored attribution is to Lorraine in eastern France or possibly even the Lower Rhineland. Yet all other surviving caskets and fragments are accepted as Parisian, or at least from the Île-de-France, making a conclusive attribution difficult. SNF

John L. Severance Fund 1978.39.a–c

DIMENSIONS: 9.8 x 25.9 x 1 cm (front), 13 x 26.2 x 1 cm (lid), 9.7 x 25.9 x 0.8 cm (back)

BIBLIOGRAPHY: Detroit 1997, 63–79, 240–48; Wixom 1979A, 110–26; Cleveland 1967, 208–9, 370, no. V-20; Koechlin 1924, 2: 449–54, nos. 1281–87; Dalton 1904, 299–309.

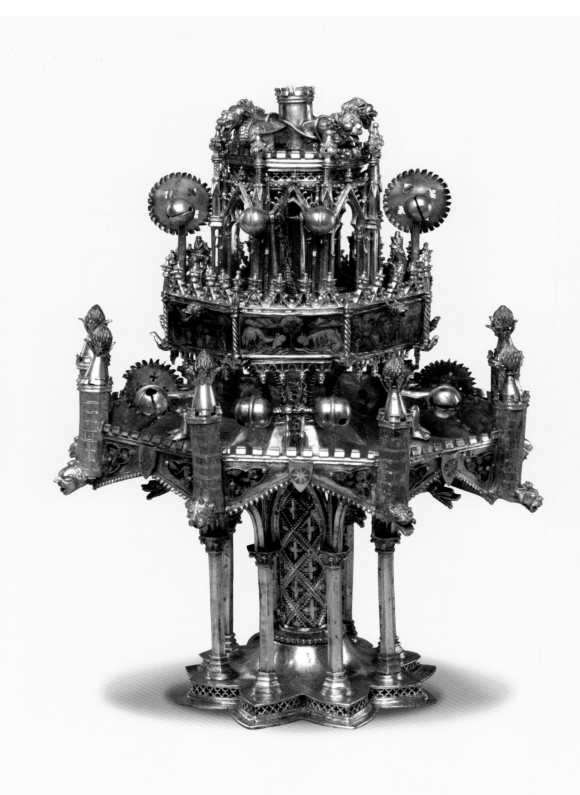

68

Table Fountain

ABOUT 1320–40; FRENCH, PARIS

GILDED SILVER WITH TRANSLUCENT ENAMEL

Documentary and pictorial sources exist indicating that mechanical contrivances, some spouting water or wine, for startling and entertaining guests, once existed in the Byzantine and Muslim worlds. Such devices—amusements for emperors, kings, viziers, and aristocrats—impressed contemporaries through sheer technical ingenuity. Eventually, they are known in the Latin West during the later Middle Ages. References to such objects in surviving documents, particularly in the household inventories of royalty and the higher aristocracy, suggest that automata once existed in substantial numbers. This was particularly true at the courts of the Valois during the late 14th and 15th centuries. The 1363 inventory of Charles V mentions two fountains, while that of his brother Louis I d'Anjou (1368) lists an astonishing 38 fountains. The paucity of such objects today may be explained by the inherent fragility of their mechanisms. Presumably some automata were constructed for temporary use and linked to a great ceremonial or social event. Others must have been destroyed in order to recycle their precious metals as fashions changed or to finance more pressing needs. While automata were constructed in a wide range of forms and sizes, using diverse materials and for varying functions, a core sub-group in the Latin West appears to be what are now commonly called table fountains.

Cleveland's table fountain is the most complete example known to have survived from the Middle Ages. Indeed, it appears to be a singular example of a genre of object now understood principally through documentary sources. Smaller fragments of similar fountains are preserved in Antwerp (Museum Mayer van den Bergh, 462) and Santiago de Compostela (Museo de Arte Sacro, Monastery of San Pelayo de Antealtares). The Cleveland fountain is extraordinary both for its very survival and for its ingenious conception as an architectural automaton. It was designed as a fanciful but completely functional mechanism. In addition to serving as an extravagant work of art to be admired for the beauty of its craftsmanship, it was clearly a feat of technical ingenuity intended to entertain guests through the motion of cascading water and the accompanying sound of ringing bells.

The fountain is a three-tiered assembly of individual sections of cut and bent sheet metal. Architectural elements—a crenellated terrace, Gothic columns, arches, and spandrels—are combined with cast and chased figures to which have been affixed a series of enameled plaques representing drolleries, some of which play musical instruments. Water wheels and bells were added to capture motion and sound. The entire assembly is an exquisite piece of Gothic architecture in miniature. Originally, the fountain would have stood in a large catch basin, a fact supported by inventory references. Water, pumped through a central tube, would have emerged at the top through a series of nozzles (shaped as animals and drolleries) creating water jets that, in turn, forced the rotation of the water wheels and rang the tiny bells. The water would have gradually cascaded from one level to the next through gargoyle heads, only to refill the catch basin once again for yet another cycle.

The table fountain most likely did not serve as a centerpiece for the banquet table as has been alleged by early literature on the object. The majority of these devices operated hydraulically. They were designed to pump and circulate water (in some cases perfumed), typically operating moving parts in the process. Their functionality required semi-permanent plumbing fittings to a cistern or reservoir that

could be hand-pumped or gravity fed. It is plausible that such objects were placed on special stands or used on tables other than those intended for banqueting. Inventories do not refer to these objects as "table" fountains, and contemporary miniatures of banqueting scenes do not depict such objects. They are generally associated with rose water. It seems more likely that secondary to their interest as objects of entertainment, they were intended to serve as room scenters. They were probably mounted on tripods or small side tables.

Elements of the design of the Cleveland table fountain compare favorably with surviving examples of Parisian goldsmithing and enameling datable to the first third of the 14th century. When considered in tandem with the stylistic evidence of the fountain's architecture, these comparanda argue in favor of an earlier dating for the fountain than that traditionally espoused. The evidence likewise tends to support the view that the table fountain must be a Parisian and not a provincial production. A distinctive trend in French Gothic decorative arts is to maintain complex links with contemporary architecture, through direct inspiration, imitation, or adaptation. The Parisian goldsmiths in particular seem to have shown a keen interest for this type of metalwork.

The original patron and context of the fountain remain unknown. What must be stated unequivocally is that the Cleveland table fountain, given its generally excellent condition and its status as one of a kind, remains an example of medieval secular goldsmithing of exceptional importance. SNF

Purchase from the J. H. Wade Fund 1924.859

DIMENSIONS: 33.8 x 25.4 x 26 cm

BIBLIOGRAPHY: Dijon/Cleveland 2004, 87, no. 26; Fliegel 2002B, 6–49; Paris 1981, no. 191; Cleveland 1967, 250–51, 376, no. VI-18; Baltimore 1962, no. 126; Milliken 1925, 36–39.

The Annunciation

1380S; NETHERLANDISH OR POSSIBLY FRENCH

TEMPERA AND OIL WITH GOLD ON PANEL

This small but opulent panel depicting the Annunciation was made for private devotional use. While the left side has a tooled gesso edge, the right side does not, suggesting that the panel was once joined to another alike in size, creating a diptych. Given the angle of the Virgin and her throne, the missing panel probably did not include an image of the donor; another biblical scene, such as the Crucifixion, may have been portrayed.

This panel's refined and ornate style represents the unified courtly aesthetic that emerged when artists began to travel throughout Europe in the late 14th and 15th centuries working in the service of royal and aristocratic patrons. However, like many other paintings created in the International Gothic style, such as the Wilton Diptych (National Gallery, London, NG4451), the convergence of various national styles in the Cleveland panel confuses its precise date and attribution. Indeed, over the course of the last century scholars have proposed dates for the painting spanning the entire second half of the 14th century and ascribed it to painters in France, Bohemia, the Netherlands, Italy, and Germany.

Diane Scillia's recent assertion that the panel was made to celebrate the marriage of John the Fearless of Burgundy and Margaret of Bavaria in 1385 was repeated in the exhibition catalogue *Art from the Court of Burgundy*. However, the iconographic and heraldic basis of these arguments does not conclusively support this position. More convincing is Gerhard Schmidt's discussion of the work along with a diptych portraying the Adoration of the Magi and the Crucifixion in the Museo del Bargello in Florence, long thought to have been painted by the same artist. Schmidt contended that the Bargello and Cleveland panels combine the Gothic traditions of mid 14th-century Paris with those of Sienese painters working in Avignon in the service of the popes, and that the impact of the panels' style can be traced through French, Bohemian, and Flemish works from the late 1350s onward. Schmidt concluded that the Cleveland and Bargello works must have come from northern France, and not later than about 1355–60. More recently Bodo Brinkmann and Stephan Kemperdick developed this premise by comparing the two works with paintings by Nuremburg masters working about 1350–60, suggesting that their French or Franco-Flemish author may have worked at some point in Germany.

On the panel's richly gilded and tooled reverse are the arms of the house of Hainault quartered with those of Bavaria. Hainault, Holland, and Zeeland became part of the holdings of Bavaria in 1345 when Countess Margaret of Hainault, wife of the Holy Roman Emperor Ludwig IV of Bavaria, inherited the territory following the death of her brother Count William IV of Hainault. After this date the arms of Hainault and Bavaria were regularly shown quartered. While this coat of arms is surely that of the work's patron—likely a member of the united dynasties of Hainault and Bavaria—his or her precise identity remains unknown. VB

Mr. and Mrs. William H. Marlatt Fund 1954.393

DIMENSIONS: 35.2 x 26.4 cm

INSCRIBED: on the angel's banderole: "aue gracia plena dominus tecum" (Hail Mary, full of grace, the Lord is with you); on the angel's halo: "Sanctus Gabriel Archangelus" (The Holy Archangel Gabriel); on the Virgin's halo: "Ecce Ancilla Domini fiat mihi secundum verbum tuum"

(Behold the handmaiden of the Lord; be it unto me according to thy word)

BIBLIOGRAPHY: Dijon/Cleveland 2004, 66–67, no. 18; Brinkmann/Kemperdick 2002, 40–42, 49–52; Scillia 1995, 345–56; Schmidt 1975, 47–63; *CMA European Paintings* 1974, 21–24, no. 8; Frinta 1965, 261–65; Francis 1955, 215–19; Robb 1936, 490.

❖ *70* ❖

The Crucifixion with a Carthusian Monk

1389–95; JEAN DE BEAUMETZ (FRENCH, ABOUT 1335–96)

TEMPERA AND GOLD ON PANEL

In 1376, Jean de Beaumetz became official court painter to Philip the Bold, Duke of Burgundy. Among the many projects Beaumetz undertook on behalf of his patron was the decoration of the Chartreuse de Champmol in Dijon, the Carthusian monastery the duke founded in 1383 and designated as the burial place of his dynasty. Between 1389 and 1395, Beaumetz and his workshop created 24 panel paintings destined for the cells of the chartreuse's monks. Only two survive: this painting and another in the Louvre (RF 1967-3).

Renowned for their pious austerity, Carthusian monks spent much of their lives in prayer and study within the isolated confines of their cells. This panel would have been such a cell's only ornament, and a powerful stimulus to the solitary devotional practices that played a central role in each monk's earthly existence. An image of the Crucifixion, the panel reflects and promotes the order's fervent devotion to the Passion. In the emotive expressions and gestures of those who mourn Christ—John the Evangelist tearfully wringing his hands to the right of the cross and the Virgin Mary swooning in the arms of two lamenting holy women to the left—the panel portrays compassionate experiences of Christ's suffering. This element of the work is closely related to Carthusian spiritual texts, which encouraged the monks in their meditations to suffer and grieve as if they were present at the Crucifixion. Indeed, at the feet of the crucified Christ, a Carthusian monk kneels in prayer, his arms crossed over his chest in the gesture these texts deemed appropriate to the contemplation of the Passion. Engaged in the kind of meditations the texts promoted, this figure is a model of supplication for the monk to whom the panel belonged, inspiring him to assume both the physical and spiritual attitude of his pictured brethren in his own devotions. The decorative foliate blossoms punched throughout the panel's golden ground represent Christ's redemptive sacrifice in death as the source of eternal life and also, perhaps, the spiritual flowering that might result from the monk's intent and daily contemplation of this most important devotional theme. VB

Leonard C. Hanna Jr. Fund 1964.454

DIMENSIONS: 56.6 x 45.7 cm

BIBLIOGRAPHY: Dijon/Cleveland 2004, 202, no. 71a; Hedeman 1995, 191–203; De Winter 1987, 405–49; De Winter 1977, 217–37; Francis 1966, 329–38; Troescher 1966, 1: 37–59; Sterling 1955, 57–81.

71

The Archangel Gabriel from an Annunciation Group

ABOUT 1350–70; FRENCH, PARIS?

ALABASTER WITH TRACES OF POLYCHROMY AND GILDING

This exceptionally beautiful genuflecting angel depicts Gabriel at the moment of the Annunciation to the Virgin Mary. The statuette was separated before 1900 from the accompanying figure of the Virgin, now preserved in the Louvre (RF 1661). Together they very likely formed part of a retable (inset). The two figures belonged to the parish church at Javernant (Aube), although they were probably made for the Benedictine abbey of Moutier-la-Celle, whose abbot was the lord of Javernant, or perhaps for the abbey of Notre-Dame-du-Pré, whose church was specifically dedicated to the Annunciation. The sculptures were probably transferred to the church at Javernant during the upheavals of the French Revolution.

The Cleveland angel and the Virgin now in Paris are distinguished by their refined modeling and courtly elegance. The treatment of the angel's hair, the contrapposto stance of the Virgin, and the draperies of both figures have been compared with Parisian ivories of the same period. Their place of production, however, has been much discussed. Formerly believed to have been carved in the region of Aube because of the figures' established provenance, more recent scholarship favors a workshop in the French capital based on their re-fined courtly appearance. The two may also prove to be the work of a Parisian sculptor working in the provinces. The angel, far better preserved than the figure of the Virgin, retains much of its original gilding and paint delineating the feathers of the wing, the hair, the hem of the drapery, and the words on the vellum banderole: "Ave Maria, Gratia Plena" (Hail Mary, Full of Grace). The disparate state of preservation between the two statuettes may have been a factor in their separation at the end of the 19th century after passing through the collections of barons Nathaniel de Rothschild and Alphonse de Rothschild.

Marian cycles were extremely popular in the Christian devotional iconography of the later Middle Ages, especially in painting, manuscript illumination, and sculpture. The Cleveland and Paris statuettes were clearly not intended to function in isolation. Instead they surely would have derived from a multi-scene retable, perhaps illustrating the infancy of Christ. Though both figures are technically carved in the round, they lack mass or volume (the angel is only 10.5 cm thick). They would more likely have served as relief sculptures and were probably placed within a shallow architectural recess or frame. SNF

Purchase from the J. H. Wade Fund 1954.387

DIMENSIONS: 56.5 x 26 x 10.5 cm

BIBLIOGRAPHY: Paris 1981, 113, no. 60; Baron 1973, 329–36; Cleveland 1967, 210–11, 370, no. V-21.

Enthroned Virgin and Christ Child

EARLY 1400S; FRANCO-NETHERLANDISH
LIMESTONE WITH POLYCHROMY AND GILDING

Certain aspects of this small devotional sculpture suggest its date and place of origin, and link it to a tradition of seated Virgins familiar in Netherlandish art of around 1400 that is also associated with the Valois courts in Paris, Dijon, and Bourges. These features include the exposed strands of wavy hair framing the Virgin's face, her high forehead and rounded chin, the draping of her mantle across her lap and over her left arm to partially cover the child, and the exposed portion of the foot beneath her robes—a detail that has been observed in sculptures by Claus de Werve. Though diminutive in scale, this enthroned Virgin and Child is surely among the most beautiful to survive from the early 15th century. The abundant draperies are deeply undercut, in keeping with the tendencies of Netherlandish and Burgundian sculptors of the period. The sculpture survives with most of its original polychromy, and the cabochons in the Virgin's gilded-copper crown remain intact. Remnants of the original fabric patterns may be seen on her pillow-seat and bodice, the delicacy of which suggests that the sculpture was meant to be experienced up close. The effects of plasticity, surface, and color merge to create an impact that is both sculptural and pictorial.

The theme of the Christ child who writes into an open book or onto a vellum banderole became prevalent during the third quarter of the 14th century and clearly had great appeal among both ecclesiastical and aristocratic clients because examples exist in many media. It undoubtedly refers to the educating and nurturing role of the mother in teaching the child, but also to the position of future adult Christ as author and teacher. This popular votive subject grew out of the widespread cult of the Virgin at the time.

The scale of the work and the fact that its back is uncarved suggest that it was made for an alcove or niche. Such diminutive sculptures would have been appropriate in the intimate setting of a small chapel or oratory. The sculpture would have been viewed frontally and perhaps from slightly below, its three-dimensionality emphasized in such a setting by the ever-changing light filtering through the chapel windows. The shadows and play of light would have created a luminous effect against the deep drapery folds and sumptuous polychromy. SNF

John L. Severance Fund 1970.13

DIMENSIONS: 44.8 x 31.5 x 15 cm

BIBLIOGRAPHY: Dijon/Cleveland 2004, 338–39, no. 131; Forsyth 1986, 52, fig. 15; Paris 1981, 163–65, no. 116; Wixom 1970A, 287–302.

Three Mourners from the Tomb of Philip the Bold

1406–10; CLAUS DE WERVE

(NETHERLANDISH, ACTIVE IN BURGUNDY, 1396–1439)

ALABASTER

The Chartreuse de Champmol, a Carthusian monastery just outside Dijon, was founded by Duke Philip and Duchess Margaret as the mausoleum for the Burgundian dukes; construction began in 1385. Philip died suddenly in Halle, near Brussels, on 27 April 1404, and the duchess arranged a funerary cortege to return his remains to the duchy's capital, Dijon. The clergy led the procession, followed by the casket, covered with a golden funeral cloth; next came the family and the duke's successor, John

the Fearless; finally, the torch bearers, the officers of the court, the nobility, and representatives of the cities under Philip's rule. All wore black mourning clothes, with each mourner's rank distinguishable only by the comparative richness of the fabric.

The tomb of Philip the Bold is celebrated as one of the most sumptuous and innovative tombs of the Middle Ages. The design consisted of two large slabs of black marble, with the upper slab supporting a prominent effigy of the duke lying in state, flanked by angels. Between the slabs was an intricate open arcade filled with 41 alabaster *pleurants* (figures of mourners). Although court sculptor Jean de Marville undertook the design and initial

construction of the tomb, responsibility passed to Claus Sluter after Marville's death in 1389. Upon Sluter's death in 1406, his nephew Claus de Werve completed the project in 1410.

The small, realistically carved statuettes have evoked a sense of awe and mystery as well as curiosity and admiration throughout most of their history. No two are alike. Not only do they retain minute realistic details of costume, some are almost portrait-like, their features and expressions suggesting actual individuals. The faces of others are fully or partially obscured by their hoods. The mourners were strategically placed around the tomb to suggest the funeral procession that accompanied the duke's remains to the Chartreuse de Champmol. While their garments and cowls suggest monastic garb, the majority of the statuettes represent secular mourners of the ducal court, not clergy. The pleurants were never fully polychromed, instead a few details of costume or accessory such as the bishop's crosier or the clasps of a breviary were gilded.

Many subsequent tombs—most notably that of John the Fearless—imitated the design. Philip's tomb was destroyed during the French Revolution; only the mourners and other fragments remain. The reconstructed tombs are today preserved in the Musée des Beaux-Arts in Dijon (CA1416 and CA1417). The three mourners here, plus another from the tomb of John the Fearless (see no. 74), were separated from the other pleurants during the aftermath of the French Revolution and passed through numerous private collections in France and the United States before their acquisition by the Cleveland Museum of Art. SNF

Purchase from the J. H. Wade Fund 1940.128 and Bequest of Leonard C. Hanna Jr. 1958.66–67

DIMENSIONS: 41.7 x 16.6 x 11.7 cm (left), 41.1 x 17.6 x 11 cm (center), 41 x 12.7 x 15 cm (right)

BIBLIOGRAPHY: Dijon/Cleveland 2004, 222–35, nos. 80–83; Fliegel 2004, 142–51; Morand 1991, 365–69; De Winter 1987, 412–23; Cleveland 1967, 256–57, no. VI-21; Quarré 1971; David 1951, 56–60, 107–12.

74

Mourner from the Tomb of John the Fearless

1443–45; JEAN DE LA HUERTA (SPANISH, ACTIVE IN BURGUNDY, 1443–57)

ALABASTER

John the Fearless, eldest son of Philip the Bold, became the second Valois Duke of Burgundy upon his father's death in 1404. When his father's tomb was installed in 1410 at the Chartreuse de Champmol near Dijon, John requested that he be interred at Champmol in "a tombstone similar to my late father's." Before work began, however, the duke was assassinated in 1419. In 1443, Philip the Good, third Duke of Burgundy, finally commissioned Jean de La Huerta, a sculptor from Spain, to construct his father's tomb. Following the wishes of both John and his son Philip, La Huerta's design was just slightly more elaborate than Claus Sluter's tomb for Philip the Bold, with the exception of the arcade architecture. For the tomb of John the Fearless, La Huerta responded to the more elaborate or "flamboyant" version of Gothic architecture currently in vogue by creating more complex and ornate arcades to contain the figures of mourners. The tomb was put in place at Champmol in 1470—more than 50 years after John's death—and no other tombs of comparable magnificence were built for the subsequent Valois dukes. Like the tomb of Philip the Bold, that of John the Fearless was severely vandalized in 1793 during the French Revolution.

The emotional power, psychological variety, and the beautiful use of enveloping drapery to describe the form beneath demonstrate La Huerta's close reliance on Claus Sluter's mourners from the tomb of Philip the Bold. Source documents confirm that La Huerta completed the greatest number of mourners for John's tomb before Antoine Le Moiturier assumed the commission in 1461. The attribution of this mourner to La Heurta is largely based on its adherence to tenets of his style.

Cleveland's mourner is noteworthy not only for its rich history, but also its exquisite quality and striking realism. Like all the mourners from John's tomb, it is masterfully carved with faithful attention to details of costume, facial features, expression, and gesture. Further, each mourner is meant to convey the essence of grief, anguish, and contemplation in a unique way. The arrangement of the mourners around the tomb, following that of Philip the Bold, would have suggested the atmosphere of a cloister. Light moving across the architecture of the arcade would have penetrated into the spatial recessions of the tomb and accentuated each statuette, creating an ethereal setting charged with deep spirituality, mysticism, and emotion. SNF

Purchase from the J. H. Wade Fund 1940.129

DIMENSIONS: 41 x 20.3 x 12.4 cm

BIBLIOGRAPHY: Dijon/Cleveland 2004, 251–55, nos. 92–94; De Winter 1987, 436–42; Quarré 1978, 99–102; Quarré 1972; Cleveland 1967, 304–5, 383, no. VII-6.

75

Kneeling Carthusian Monks

ABOUT 1400; FRENCH, BURGUNDY?

MARBLE

A Carthusian monk's most recognizable attribute was his full-length white hooded habit whose front and back panels were connected with a distinctive tab. Their garments thus identify these kneeling figures as members of the Order of St. Bruno. The statuettes were carved from marble with a soft lyricism that is distinctive from the Netherlandish monumentality of Claus Sluter and André Beauneveu, and there is no evidence that they were originally polychromed.

The Carthusian order, founded by St. Bruno in 1084, was committed to contemplation through silence, prayer, poverty, and penance, with each monk spending most of his time in a solitary cell. Monks gathered for the offices of matins and vespers as well as to celebrate the Mass; the other offices were recited privately in their cells. Only on feast days did the whole community say the office together in the choir and silently eat their strict vegetarian meal together in the refectory.

These two statuettes were intended not as portraits but as idealized representations of the perpetual devotion each monk assumed. The order was particularly dedicated to the Passion of Christ, and typically a small votive panel of this scene, usually including a monk, hung in individual cells for private veneration (see no. 70). These statuettes were clearly designed as figures flanking a central, now missing, object, possibly a crucified Christ or perhaps a larger Calvary group. Alternatively, a stand-

ing Virgin and Child may have once occupied the void between the two monks. They are not carved completely in the round; their backs are flat, suggesting that the figures were intended to be placed against a wall or within a niche, or perhaps incorporated into an altarpiece.

While the association of statuettes with a Carthusian monastery seems apparent, scholars have speculated about both its location and the actual setting for the figures. The pair may have come from the destroyed Chartreuse de Paris, from a single cell or perhaps two separate cells. Yet the recent provenance of the sculptures that passed through the collection of Carlo Micheli (d. 1895), the statuettes' earliest identified owner in modern times, has led to another supposition. In the inventory of the Micheli Collection (no. 137), the two Cleveland monks are described as being part of a small altarpiece featuring a standing Virgin in marble within an openwork pinnacle. The Micheli inventory asserts that the ensemble originated at Champmol, as does a supporting photograph of the group while in the Micheli Collection, now in the archives of the department of sculpture at the Louvre. That the individual elements of the ensemble may have been associated in modern times cannot be discounted. Although far from definitive, a scenario placing the two monks at the Chartreuse de Champmol has recently gained wider acceptance among scholars. SNF

John L. Severance Fund 1966.112–13

DIMENSIONS: 25.7 x 14.1 x 6.8 cm (left), 24.2 x 14.7 x 7.6 cm (right)

BIBLIOGRAPHY: Dijon/Cleveland 2004, 256–57, no. 96; De Winter 1987, 449 n. 36; Paris 1981, 142, no. 92; Cleveland 1967, 234–35, 374, no. VI-10; Wixom 1966, 349–55; de Coo 1965, 351.

Twelve Medallions

ABOUT 1400; FRENCH, PARIS

ENAMELED GOLD, PRECIOUS STONES, AND PEARLS

These medallions, which have loops on the backs, must have originally been sewn on a garment or, more likely, a woman's headpiece. In spite of the modern chain to which they are now attached, such medallions are unique items of feminine apparel dating to the decades around 1400. During the reign of Charles VI (1380–1422), Parisian goldsmiths and jewelers developed a new form of enameling known as *émail en ronde bosse* (encrusted enamel). This new technique involved the application of an enamel coat, most frequently in white or crimson, to the irregular surfaces of figures or objects "in the round" or in very high relief. These small-scale sculptural compositions are typically made of gold or silver and the new enameling technique resulted in a sumptuous object of great refinement. Paris was the center of ronde bosse enameling, providing the court and nobility across Europe with deluxe votive objects, jewelry, or personal accessories.

Miniatures from illuminated manuscripts depict similar medallions and would have been well known at the Valois courts. Each medallion is crafted with gold curling ivy leaves with veining, clustered pearls on prongs, green and red translucent enamels, encrusted enamel in white, and semi-precious stones. Though bearing an overall stylistic affinity to one another, each medallion is distinctive. The central medallion with an enameled "white lady"

is a superb example of the new Parisian technique and the obvious centerpiece of the group.

The origin of the ensemble is unknown. Traditionally, the medallions have been related to the jewels of Margaret of Brabant, wife of Louis de Mâle, Count of Flanders, who is said to have offered them to the Virgin of Louvain. There has been no clear confirmation of this idea. However, descriptions of similar jewels appear frequently in the account books and household inventories of the period. Philip the Bold and his wife, Margaret of Flanders, are known to have presented such jewels as gifts to family and friends and even on occasion to favored servants. The large central medallion features a young lady in a white dress with a gold coiffure, green diadem, black eyes, and red lips. Such white lady medallions are described in inventories of the period and two similar medallions survive today in Essen and Vienna. Burgundian account books state that Mary, daughter of Philip the Bold, presented her husband, the Duke of Savoy, with a "golden clasp with a white lady." A headpiece bearing enameled jewels, including one with a white lady, was delivered to Queen Isabeau of Bavaria in 1398 by Jean Clerbourc. While such descriptions are both tempting and suggestive, they at most provide a vivid context against which the Cleveland medallions should be seen. SNF

Purchase from the J. H. Wade Fund 1947.507

DIMENSIONS: 4.7 x 4.2 cm (central medallion)

BIBLIOGRAPHY: Paris 2004, 164, no. 86; Taburet-Delahaye 2002; Cleveland 1967, 252–53, 376, no. VI-19; Detroit 1960, no. 128; Müller/Steingräber 1954, 76, no. 26, fig. 66.

Kneeling Prophet from the Reliquary Châsse of Saint-Germain

1409; FRENCH, PARIS

GILDED BRONZE

This figure of a prophet, and another preserved in the Louvre in Paris (OA 5917), are the only known surviving fragments of the Reliquary Châsse of Saint-Germain. Architectural in form and fashioned from silver and gold with precious stones, the reliquary was designed to hold the body of the saint. An engraving made in 1724 (inset), about 70 years before the reliquary was destroyed, reveals that it resembled an elegant Gothic church with flying buttresses and that six gilt-bronze figures stood in an arcade on one side. It was housed in the ancient Benedictine abbey of Saint-Germain-des-Prés and was the monastery's great treasure through the French Revolution, when it was destroyed.

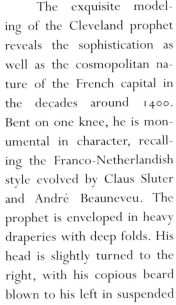

For nine centuries during times of war and plague, the relics of St. Germain, a sixth-century bishop of Paris, were carried through the streets of Paris in ritual procession. In the early 1400s Guillaume, abbot of Saint-Germain-des-Prés, commissioned a new, more elaborate, reliquary to replace the 9th-century original. A contract dated 18 February 1409 (Archives Nationales, Paris) gives the names of the commissioned artists, three Parisian goldsmiths: Jean de Clichy, Gautier du Four, and Guillaume Boey. It stipulates that the reliquary was to be 86.5 cm long. The gold and jewels from the earlier reliquary, which had been given by King Odo, were to be reused in the new one. A receipt dated 20 August 1409 reveals that the three goldsmiths received the necessary precious materials from the abbot to fabricate the reliquary: 101 sapphires, 140 emeralds, 25 amethysts, 220 pearls, and other precious stones. Seventeenth-century engravings show the reliquary carried in procession. In 1792 it was sent to the mint in Paris to be melted down for its precious metals. It yielded 6 kg of gold, 46 kg of gilt silver, about 3 kg of silver, and hundreds of precious stones. The destruction of this splendid reliquary was a serious loss for the study of medieval goldsmith work.

The exquisite modeling of the Cleveland prophet reveals the sophistication as well as the cosmopolitan nature of the French capital in the decades around 1400. Bent on one knee, he is monumental in character, recalling the Franco-Netherlandish style evolved by Claus Sluter and André Beauneveu. The prophet is enveloped in heavy draperies with deep folds. His head is slightly turned to the right, with his copious beard blown to his left in suspended movement. His hands gesture forward to grasp a curvilinear banderole, now missing. These features have invited comparison to the prophets on the celebrated Well of Moses in the cloister of the Chartreuse de Champmol completed by Sluter for Philip the Bold between 1395 and 1404. While this monument unlikely had any direct influence on the Parisian goldsmiths responsible for the reliquary, the Cleveland and Louvre prophets do reflect the elegance, refined sophistication, and interest in naturalism pervasive in courtly ateliers in Paris. The activity of Netherlandish artists in the capital at this time may have provided additional artistic currents. SNF

Leonard C. Hanna Jr. Bequest 1964.360

DIMENSIONS: 13.8 x 9.3 x 8.7 cm

BIBLIOGRAPHY: Paris 2004, 310–11, no. 190 C-D; Ultee 1981, fig. 11; Cleveland 1975, no. 3; Egbert 1970, 359–63; Cleveland 1967, 254–55, 376, no. VI-20.

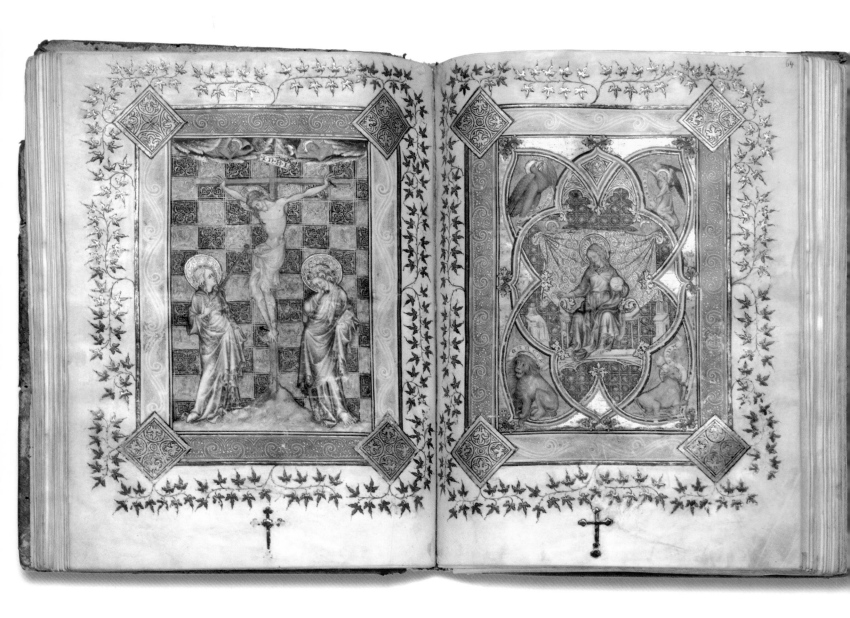

78

The Gotha Missal

ABOUT 1370–72; FRENCH, PARIS

TEMPERA AND GOLD ON VELLUM, 164 FOLIOS

This manuscript acquired its name from its 18th-century owners, the German dukes of Gotha. The volume's decoration falls stylistically within a large corpus of manuscripts produced in Paris for Charles V or contemporaneous aristocratic manuscripts. The calendar and use of the missal is Parisian and contains a cycle of 23 small miniatures, plus two facing full-page miniatures marking the introduction to the Canon of the Mass—a Crucifixion and a Christ in Majesty (fols. 63v–64), traditional subjects for this part of a missal. The page layout and border decoration are also decisively Parisian. The meandering ivy vines prevalent in the borders were by the 1370s a distinctive hallmark of Parisian manuscript painting.

Discussions about the authorship of the miniatures have varied considerably. The two full-page and 21 small miniatures appear to be the work of the Boqueteaux Master. The salient features of his style include distinctive mushroom-like trees. The figures are painted mostly in the grisaille technique (shades of gray), which is characteristic of a number of manuscripts made for Charles V and which some scholars believe indicate the king's taste in book decoration. The missal's grisaille figures are set against colored backgrounds to achieve contrasting effects and sharp tonalities. The overall effect is clearly one of sumptuousness and refinement.

The Boqueteaux Master was a popular artist at the court of Charles V, and apparently a number of book illuminators working around Paris shared his style. It is now known that this style was not ex-clusively connected with a single master or workshop, but fairly common in Paris at mid century. This "master" may actually have been several artists who were influenced by one chief source, perhaps Jean Bondol of Bruges, whose name is recorded in an inscription for the frontispiece of the *Bible Historiale of Charles V* (Meermanno-Westreenianum, The Hague, Ms. 10 B 23, f. 1).

Two small miniatures at the beginning of the volume, clearly by another hand, were added later, probably at the beginning of the 15th century: a Man of Sorrows and a Resurrection (fol. 1). Here also opinions about authorship have varied. Recent study relates these two miniatures to the oeuvre of an illuminator known as the Maître du livre des Femmes nobles et renommées de Philippe le Hardi, active about 1402–4. Works by this master include a *Golden Legend* (Ms. Fr. 242); a *Bible Historiale* (Ms. Fr. 159) mentioned in the inventory of Jean de Berry in 1402; and Hayton de Courcy's *Fleur des histoires de terre d'Orient* (Ms. Fr. 12201), one of three copies acquired by Philip the Bold. All are currently in the Bibliothèque Nationale, Paris.

While the original commission of the *Gotha Missal* is unclear, it has been argued that the volume was made for Charles V. This argument, not without merit, is largely based on the involvement of the Boqueteaux Master, an artist(s) often used by this king, in the book's decoration. Even without royal portraits and a colophon, the book's magnificent decoration would indicate that it was made for a Valois prince, if not for the king himself. SNF

Mr. and Mrs. William H. Marlatt Fund 1962.287

DIMENSIONS: 28.3 x 20.6 x 4.8 cm

BIBLIOGRAPHY: Dijon/Cleveland 2004, 79, no. 23; De Winter 1985A, 185, fig. 101, and 211; Cleveland 1967, 220–21, 371–72, no. VI-3; Wixom 1963C, 158–73; Kraus 1962, 32–39.

79

The Hours of Charles the Noble

ABOUT 1404; FRENCH, PARIS

TEMPERA AND GOLD ON VELLUM, 328 FOLIOS

This extensively decorated book was highly prized by its owner, Charles III, King of Navarre, a French-born prince who had his coat of arms painted on 20 folios. He likely acquired this volume in 1404 on one of his many visits to Paris. The center of the European book trade, Paris was also a vital point of convergence for painters, weavers, sculptors, and goldsmiths from all over Europe, who were attracted by the city's prestige, patronage, and wealth.

The period of Charles's reign almost exactly parallels an important interchange of creative ideas in the visual arts, and this manuscript represents one of the most remarkable fusions of French and Italian taste in book illumination. With the exception of a few blank leaves at the end, every single page has striking, individual decoration in the borders; large historiated initials appear on 82 folios; and 24 folios have large miniatures with involved borders. The contents of the volume are typical of deluxe French books of hours. In addition to the calendar, the gospels, office of the Virgin, litanies, and office of the dead are to be found an hours of the Holy Spirit and an hours of the cross. The decoration of this manuscript has been attributed to as many as six illuminators, the majority of whom were foreigners, suggesting the cosmopolitan character and eclectic taste of the French capital at the time. Though largely conforming to Parisian standards, some of the criteria of French book illumination were softened for this volume, such as the construction of *rinceaux* (bar borders) and the use of acanthus leaves and putti for marginal decoration on some folios.

Most of the book's major miniatures are the work of the Brussels Initials Master, an Italian il-luminator who had worked in Bologna and Padua but was active in Paris between 1400 and 1410. Known to have decorated at least one manuscript for Duke Jean de Berry around 1402, the Brussels Initials Master planned the decorative program of *The Hours of Charles the Noble*. Some scholars believe his principal assistant was another Italian, a Florentine known from his signature on folio 200 verso as "Zecho" or "Zebo da Firenze." The palettes of the two artists differ greatly. Zecho's marginal decorations—humorous, eccentric, or plainly secular—are filled with bright pinks, greens, and orange. The Brussels Initials Master used a deeper palette with greenish flesh tones characteristic of his Emilian roots. His miniatures are distinguished by their Italianate buildings with porticos, domes, and loggias. Missing are the linear French Gothic systems of architecture more typically found in Parisian manuscripts of the period.

The second master, credited with only five miniatures, is the Egerton Master, a Netherlandish artist probably from the Artois-Flanders area. He was largely responsible for the miniatures of the hours of the cross; his use of color and space, as well as the physiognomies of his figures, creates an atmospheric perspective very different from the Italianate systems used by the Brussels Initials Master. Contributions by an additional Netherlandish artist and two minor French illuminators have been noted by some scholars. How such disparate artists came together in the French capital to collaborate on a deluxe volume is unknown. The result is an unexpected blending of their different approaches, a harmonious fusion of heterogeneous pictorial traditions. SNF

Mr. and Mrs. William H. Marlatt Fund 1964.40

DIMENSIONS: 20.3 X 15.7 X 7 cm

BIBLIOGRAPHY: Paris 2004, no. 169 A, 274; De Winter 1983A, 338–44, 350, no. 38; De Winter 1981A, 42–59; Thomas 1979, 50, 191; Winternitz 1965, 84–91; Wixom 1965, 50–83.

80

Leaf from a Missal: The Crucifixion

1435–40; MASTER OF OTTO VAN MOERDRECHT (THE NETHERLANDS, AUGUSTINIAN
CLOISTER OF AGNIETENBERG, ACTIVE ABOUT 1420–55)
TEMPERA AND GOLD ON VELLUM

This splendid leaf, with its border of lamenting angels, once illustrated a missal, the indispensable service book for the priest at the altar. Such scenes formed the traditional subject to the frontispiece of the Canon of the Mass, the most solemn part of the service in which the Eucharistic bread and wine were transformed into the body and blood of Christ. The Cleveland miniature appears on the leaf's verso; it would have faced, on the recto, the opening words of the Canon, "Te igitur clementissime pater" (We humbly pray and beseech Thee, most merciful father), which would have been read silently by the priest.

The miniature is one of the most exceptional and ambitious Crucifixion compositions to be found in a Dutch missal prior to the end of the 15th century. It is remarkable for its receding landscape revealing Jerusalem in the distance against a golden horizon, unprecedented in a Dutch missal. It is also exceptional for its many figures at the foot of the cross. The figure of the dead Christ is flanked by the two thieves. Beneath are two separate groups of witnesses. On Christ's right appear the sympathetic mourners including the swooning figure of the Virgin supported by St. John and the Three Marys. On his left appear the executioners: a group of Romans on horseback who curiously seem to pay little attention to the crucified men above. A banderole emanating from the mouth of one of the soldiers proclaims "Vere Filius Dei Erat Iste" (Truly he was the son of God), as related in both Matthew (27:54) and Mark (15:39). This highly unusual depiction of the Romans was apparently copied from a now-lost painting by Jan van Eyck, known through copies in Budapest, Braunschweig, and elsewhere.

The miniature has long been attributed to the Master of Otto van Moerdrecht. This miniaturist derives his name from his illuminations in the Old Testament commentary of Nicholas of Lyra which Otto van Moerdrecht, a canon of Utrecht Cathedral, gave to the nearby Carthusian monastery of Nieuwlicht in 1424. He very likely worked in an urban workshop in Utrecht rather than in a cloister. Recent scholarship has shown the broad distribution of the "Moerdrecht style" in several Dutch centers between the 1420s and 1450s. Rather than a single itinerant Dutch artist, it now seems that the style was disseminated among a half dozen or so artists of slightly differing generations and abilities. Key features include a bright palette of contrasting red, orange, and blue tones. The designs are bold, but the figures often appear flat, the garments with parallel sweeping folds. The heads are often egg-shaped with narrow, slit eyes. Numerous manuscripts including bibles, liturgical books, and books of hours illuminated by the Master of Otto van Moerdrecht have survived. The stylistic relationship of the Cleveland miniature to those in the Thomas à Kempis Bible (now in Hessische Landes- und Hochschulbibliothek, Darmstadt, Ms. 324), originally made for the Augustinian cloister of Agnietenberg, near Zwolle, has prompted scholars to argue that it too was produced for the same cloister. SNF

Mr. and Mrs. William H. Marlatt Fund 1959.254

DIMENSIONS: 33.6 x 25.5 cm

BIBLIOGRAPHY: Brinkmann 1996, 20: 740–41; Utrecht 1990, 75–78, 82–83, no. 23; Gumbert 1974, 129–31, 181–85; Wixom 1963, 58–64.

81

Miniature from a Speculum Historiale: Claudius Designates Nero as His Successor

ABOUT 1447–60; MASTER OF JOUVENEL DES URSINS

(FRENCH, PROBABLY ACTIVE IN ANGERS AND TOURS)

TEMPERA AND GOLD ON VELLUM

This miniature, along with five others, was separated around 1790 from a sumptuous illustrated copy of the *Speculum Historiale* written by the 13th-century Dominican friar Vincent de Beauvais. The parent manuscript is preserved in the Biblioteca Nacional in Lisbon (Ms. Il. 126). Vincent undertook a systematic and comprehensive treatment of all branches of human knowledge under the patronage of Louis IX. His colossal four-part study was entitled *Speculum Majus* (The Great Mirror). *Speculum Historiale* (The Mirror of History), a history of the world from Adam down to Vincent's time in 31 books, is part three. Vincent's original work was much in demand and numerous copies were produced after his lifetime, including later printed versions.

The Cleveland miniature belongs to a deluxe copy possibly made for René d'Anjou, titular king of Jerusalem and a major patron of art and books in mid 15th-century France. This miniature, which likely derives from chapter 11 (the history of the Romans) of the *Speculum Historiale,* represents Emperor Claudius designating the line of succession to his stepson, Nero. Such sumptuously illustrated histories and chronicles were avidly sought by royalty and aristocrats in France and the Burgundian Netherlands during the 15th century for their rendering of portrait-like features (the group of courtiers respectfully watching from the left), deep interior spaces (here an imperial throne room), the contrasting play of light, and the use of perspective. While the scene is meant to represent an event from antiquity, the setting, as was customary, is a contemporary one that would have been familiar to 15th-century eyes.

The painter is a talented, if anonymous, master well-versed in the style of Jean Fouquet and named after Guillaume Jouvenel des Ursins, chancellor of France from 1447 to 1472, for whom he illuminated a copy of the *Mare Historiarum* by Giovanni Colonna (Bibliothèque Nationale, Paris, Ms. Lat. 4915). Typical of the Jouvenel Master is the dense composition with luminous and intense colors. He is adept at painting landscapes and architectural details, and his figures, with abundant draperies, have a monumental quality. His origins and career remain largely unknown, and while scholars have debated his identity, there is no consensus. All available evidence suggests that the Jouvenel Master was active in western France in the region between Angers and Tours. The Cleveland miniature is inexplicably unfinished along the right and bottom where the underdrawing can clearly be seen in the column, capital, and floor tiles. SNF

The John L. Severance Fund 1987.4

DIMENSIONS: 12.8 x 9.7 cm

BIBLIOGRAPHY: Reynaud 1992, 50–57; König 1982; Paris 1955; Porcher 1955, 117–24.

Leaf from a Breviary: The Martyrdom of St. Denis

ABOUT 1467–70; SIMON MARMION (FRENCH, VALENCIENNES, 1420S–89)

TEMPERA AND GOLD ON VELLUM

This miniature and another now in the Metropolitan Museum of Art (1975.1.2477) appear to be the only extant leaves from a profusely decorated breviary commissioned by the third Duke of Burgundy, Philip the Good, in 1467. Unfinished at his death that year, the manuscript was completed before 1470 for Philip's son, Charles the Bold, and Charles's wife, Margaret of York. The commission is fully documented; the original manuscript comprised more than 600 leaves, 95 full-page miniatures, and several thousand small initials. Illuminated on thin, almost translucent vellum typical of luxury manuscripts, the Cleveland leaf focuses on St. Denis, one of the patron saints of France. It would have introduced the devotions to this saint in the Sanctorale section of the now-lost breviary. The series of vignettes in the margins depicting episodes in Denis's life surround a full-page scene with an arched top revealing how he died. These compositional elements illustrate Simon Marmion's role as an innovator in page layout and marginal illustration and serve as an antecedent to the manuscripts of the Ghent-Bruges school, which he influenced.

The iconography of this devotional miniature is unusual. The verso shows the beginning of the office for the feast of saints Denis, Eleutherius, and Rusticus, which falls on 9 October. On the recto, the scene at the top right depicts Denis in Rome with St. Paul, restoring the sight of a blind man. The other scenes in the border show Denis being baptized; in his bishop's miter kneeling before Pope Clement I, who according to legend sent the three missionaries to Gaul; and the three saints taking communion after their imprisonment at the order of the Roman prefect in Paris. In the center scene they have been beheaded; miraculously, Denis stands holding his severed head.

Simon Marmion was one of the most esteemed miniaturists and panel painters of his generation. He is credited with surviving panels and manuscripts produced for his primary clients, the Burgundian dukes and members of their courts. The Cleveland miniature and its sister leaf, the *Holy Virgins Received by Christ,* are painted in pale tonalities dominated by hues of white, gray, blue, and liquid gold, which is consistent with Marmion's favored palette during the final two decades of his career. The miniature compares in both style and palette with the *Visions of Tondal,* a manuscript dating to the early 1470s (J. Paul Getty Museum, Los Angeles, Ms. 30). Other features echo those in the *St. Bertin Altarpiece* (National Gallery, London, NG 1302, 1303; Gemäldegalerie, Berlin, 1645, 1645a), painted by Marmion between 1454 and 1459 for Guillaume Fillastre, abbot of the abbey of St. Bertin at Saint-Omer. SNF

John L. Severance Fund 2005.55

DIMENSIONS: 15.2 x 11.2 cm

BIBLIOGRAPHY: Los Angeles 2003, 105–6, no. 10; Hindman 1997, 60–72; Hindman 1992, 223–32.

The Hours of Queen Isabella the Catholic

ABOUT 1500–1505; MASTER OF THE FIRST PRAYERBOOK OF MAXIMILIAN AND OTHERS

(FLANDERS, BRUGES AND GHENT)

TEMPERA AND GOLD ON VELLUM, 279 FOLIOS

One of the masterpieces of Flemish manuscript painting, this deluxe book was intended not for a cleric but for a lay person—Isabella the Catholic, Queen of Spain (1451–1504). Isabella's coat of arms and personal motto embellish the frontispiece, establishing her ownership of the volume. That the queen commissioned the book is unlikely, but the escutcheons in the miniature for the Mass of the Dead suggest a female patron, perhaps a Flemish noblewoman. It was likely presented to the queen as a gift, though the circumstances of this transfer are undocumented. A lover of Flemish art, Isabella is known to have treasured her many devotional books, which were largely kept in her private library at the palace in Madrid where they would have been available for use in her private chapel. The Cleveland volume is extensively decorated with a rich cycle of miniatures illustrating its various offices and texts: 40 full-page and 10 half-page miniatures, 24 calendar roundels, and elaborate trompe l'oeil borders throughout the book.

This book of hours was illuminated by a circle of at least six highly organized and distinctly talented manuscript painters active in Ghent and Bruges in the final decades of the 15th century. The principal illuminator was the Master of the First Prayerbook of Maximilian, an anonymous artist named after a manuscript in the National Library in Vienna, whose identity has been the subject of much scholarly debate. Despite being based largely on circumstantial and stylistic evidence, current scholarship identifies him with the documented miniaturist Alexander Bening (d. 1519). Related by marriage to the painter Hugo van der Goes, Bening is known to have entered the painter's guild in Ghent in 1469 and to have belonged to the confraternity of book trade in Bruges. Little else is known about his career. It must be assumed, however, that he regularly worked in close association with other miniaturists and panel painters, such as Rogier van der Weyden, Hugo van der Goes, and Gerard David, whose compositions are often adapted or replicated in Bening's miniatures. Bening is responsible for more than half of the volume's miniatures; other painters include the Master of the Prayerbooks of around 1500, Gerard David, and the Master of James IV of Scotland.

The Ghent-Bruges school represents the culmination of Flemish book painting. Its main features were rich colors, decorative and illusionistic effects, a love of landscape, and a strong sense of visual narrative. Manuscripts produced by this circle of artists are renowned for the decoration of their borders, which typically feature a rich variety of realistically painted flowers, scrolling acanthus leaves, birds, and butterflies. This distinctive innovation in border decoration emphasized realistic motifs that cast shadows into colored grounds to create a trompe l'oeil effect. *The Hours of Queen Isabella* is an example of luxury manuscript production at its waning moment, when the new technical process of movable type and woodblock printing was about to change the face of the book as it had been known for a thousand years. SNF

Leonard C. Hanna Jr. Fund 1963.256

DIMENSIONS: 23.5 x 17.3 x 4.8 cm

BIBLIOGRAPHY: Los Angeles 2003, 358–61 no. 105; Krieger 2000, 215–33; Smeyers 1998, 478; Washington 1991, 34, 155–56; De Winter 1981B, 342–427.

❖ Toward a Northern Renaissance: Late Medieval Germany ❖

Unlike in France, where the Gothic style had emerged, flourished, and matured over the course of the late 12th and early 13th centuries, the territories of the Holy Roman Empire remained resistant to the new trends in French art and architecture. Especially in the Rhineland, the monumental grandeur of the Ottonian and Romanesque tradition dominated local tastes well into the 13th century. While Gothic forms and motifs had begun infiltrating German art and architecture sporadically during the first decades of the 13th century, it was not until the second half of the century that architects and sculptors in Strasbourg, Cologne, and elsewhere began to adopt French Gothic aesthetic ideals and principles, and fuse them with local practices and traditions. The rise of the great mendicant orders in the towns and cities of southern Germany resulted in the development and dissemination of a new church type that served the orders' growing need for large but modest congregational spaces; it also brought about changes in religious attitudes among those who listened to the friars' sermons and followed their spiritual guidance. The mystical writings of theologians of the time such as Master Eckhart and Henry Suso gave rise to new forms of affective piety and a growing desire for devotional images that could inspire the beholder's meditation as well as identification with the protagonists of the story of Christ's Passion. Artists—both painters and sculptors—responded to the emerging demand by exploring new religious themes such as the Virgin mourning her dead son (see no. 93), Christ and St. John at the Last Supper (see no. 84), and related themes such as the Man of Sorrows that helped facilitate private devotion and prayer.

As in previous centuries, the emperor and his court as well as members of the nobility and the clergy remained the most important patrons of the arts and architecture during the High and Late Gothic periods. In Prague, Emperor Charles IV and his successors employed some of the most accomplished architects, painters, and sculptors from across Europe, transforming the Bohemian city into an imperial capital that attempted to emulate both Paris and Constantinople as a center of the arts, culture, and learning. In addition, the economic boom experienced by many German cities during the 13th and 14th centuries created a new class of patrons that consisted of merchants and burghers, as well as guilds and confraternities, who looked for opportunities to display their wealth, piety, and pride by furnishing churches and private chapels with cycles of stained-glass windows, devotional sculptures, or painted altarpieces commissioned from the most accomplished artists of the period. Inspired by Byzantine and Italian traditions, panel painting started to gain widespread currency in German lands during the second half of the 14th century, with Prague, Nuremberg, and Cologne as leading centers of production. By the beginning of the 15th century, artists working in this medium served the needs of a growing number of clients, both individual and institutional, executing small-scale devotional panels and epitaphs as well as large-scale altarpieces in a manner often called the International Gothic, based on its popularity across much of western Europe, or Soft Style, based on the refined elegance and suppleness that characterizes the representation of figures and flowing draperies. While many influential artists of the Late Gothic period such as the Master of Heiligenkreuz (see no. 87) and the Master of the Schlägl Altarpiece (see no. 88) remain anonymous, others such as Master Theoderic (who was employed by Emperor Charles IV to decorate his relic chapel at Karlstein castle in the 1360s), Conrad von Soest (who disseminated the international style in Westphalia a generation later), and Konrad Witz (who was active in the Upper Rhine region and settled in Basel in 1434) left traces in the historical and financial records of their time and can be identified on the basis of their signed work.

By the middle of the 15th century, the Upper Rhine region, with Strasbourg and Basel as its most prosperous urban and artistic centers, was an area in which many local and foreign artists such as the painter and engraver Martin Schongauer, the sculptor Nicolaus Gerhaert von Leiden, and the Master E.S. worked, flourished, and exerted a profound impact on the artistic production of their time. Later in the century, the rise of humanism and the development of the printing industry attracted such highly influential figures as Hans Holbein and Erasmus of Rotterdam, whose work also greatly influenced the course of European art and cultural history.

Farther east in Swabia and Franconia, the flourishing cities of Ulm, Würzburg, and Nuremberg likewise reared their local talent and attracted foreign masters, among them Hans Multscher and Michel Erhart in Ulm, Veit Stoss (see no. 92) and Albrecht Dürer in Nuremberg, and Tilman Riemenschneider (see nos. 90, 91) in Würzburg. Firmly rooted in the Late Gothic tradition of their native Germany, the inventive genius of these masters and the refined quality of their works mark the end of an era as much as the beginning of a new age, aptly called the Northern Renaissance. HAK

84

St. John Resting on the Bosom of Christ

ABOUT 1300–1320; GERMAN, SWABIA, LAKE CONSTANCE REGION

POLYCHROMED AND GILDED OAK

This sculptural group—Christ and St. John the Evangelist, dressed in golden garments and sitting next to each other on a bench—was based on the Gospel of John (13:23), which states that during the Last Supper one of Christ's disciples, namely "whom Jesus loved," was reclining on his bosom. With his eyes closed, a soft smile on his face, and his head leaning against Christ's shoulder, John seems asleep at the side of the Savior, who sits upright with his eyes directed toward the viewer. The intimate connection between Jesus and his beloved apostle culminates in the Savior's tender embrace and the gentle touch of their right hands over his lap.

One of the finest examples of its kind to survive from medieval Germany, the Cleveland group belongs to a class of religious images commonly called *Andachtsbilder* (devotional images), which appeared in considerable numbers in southern and southwestern Germany during the later 13th and 14th centuries. Intended to stimulate private devotion, help the beholder contemplate the story of Christ's Passion, and encourage affective piety through identification with its main protagonists, many of these devotional images depict episodes from the biblical narrative of the Passion and, in some cases, even embellish those stories based on apocryphal accounts. Responding to contempo-rary trends in German mysticism, particularly the writings of a number of prominent theologians and mystics such as Bernard of Clairvaux, Thomas Aquinas, Meister Eckhart, and Henry Suso, many of these devotional images fulfilled their intended function in convents of the Benedictine, Cistercian, and Dominican orders, where they were placed on secondary altars of the main church or in side cha-pels to encourage mystical exercises, prayer, and meditation.

Unlike the "Vesperbild" or "Pietà," a devo-tional theme that enjoyed great popularity in many parts of late medieval Europe, sculptural groups depicting Christ and St. John were far more local-ized in their distribution, with most known exam-ples coming from the region of Swabia, especially the area around Lake Constance in southwestern Germany. The great appeal of these sculptures, es-pecially among female patrons, may be explained by the fact that John, who in sermons and biblical commentaries was often identified as the bride-groom of the marriage at Cana and the bride of the Song of Songs, presents himself as an ideal model for female self-identification, and that the group itself, through its bridal overtones, embodies the mystical union of the soul with God, which lies at the heart of the viewer's devotional desire. HAK

Purchase from the J. H. Wade Fund 1928.753

DIMENSIONS: 92.7 x 64.5 x 28.8 cm

BIBLIOGRAPHY: Gillerman 2001, 326, no. 240; Jirousek 2001; Freiburg 1978, 42–43; Wentzel 1961; Milliken 1929; Pinder 1924–29, 1: 94–95, pl. VI; Oppenheim 1911, no. 117.

Nmedio eccle sie ap

ruit os e uis et imple

uit e um dominus

spiritu sapi entie et

in tel lectus sto

85

Leaf from a Gradual: Historiated Initial I with Scenes from the Life of St. Augustine

ABOUT 1330; WILLEHALM MASTER AND THE YOUNGER GRADUAL MASTER
(GERMAN, COLOGNE)
TEMPERA AND GOLD ON VELLUM

This imposing leaf comes from the three-volume Wettinger Gradual preserved in the Canton Library in Aarau, Switzerland (Ms. Wett. Fm 1-3). The focus of the decoration here is a single massive initial *I* constructed with four compartments featuring scenes from the life of St. Augustine, one of the four fathers of the Christian Church. The compartments read (from top to bottom): Augustine teaching before his conversion; the dream of Augustine's mother; Augustine's baptism; and Augustine teaching monks from his rule. The monk in the lower margin holds a banderole that reads: "Pray for us, blessed Father Augustine." The initial would have introduced the feast of St. Augustine (28 August) in the Sanctorale. The text reads: "In medio Ecclesiae aperuit os eius" (And in the midst of the church she shall open his mouth), introducing the Introit of that Mass. The prominence of this initial within the gradual and the depiction of an Augustinian canon in the lower marginal extender indicate that the manuscript was originally produced for a community of Augustinians. The identity of this institution has not been ascertained.

The illuminators were much influenced by Parisian manuscript decoration, especially the painter Jean Pucelle; they have added tendril extenders that support birds and animals, and below, an Augustinian monk in prayer. The composition is made opulent through the liberal use of burnished gold. Recent research has shown that volume one was completed by an older artist known as the Willehalm Master, named after a codex of Wolfram von Eschenbach's *Willehalm* (Hessische Landesbibliothek, Kassel, Ms. 2 poet et roman I). Volumes two and three of the Wettinger Gradual were a collaborative effort involving both the Willehalm Master, who provided much of the underdrawing, including that of the Cleveland initial, and another anonymous artist, the Second Master of the Wettinger Gradual, who applied the color. He has more recently been renamed the Younger Gradual Master. Though nothing is known of their lives or careers, the styles of both artists relate to manuscript and especially panel painting in Cologne. After Paris and London, Cologne was Europe's most populous city north of the Alps in the 14th century. A vibrant trading port on the Rhine, it was also a prosperous center of important schools of painting and sculpture. The Cleveland leaf, and the parent codex from which it came, probably belonged originally to a religious foundation within the city's environs. SNF

Mr. and Mrs. William H. Marlatt Fund 1949.203

DIMENSIONS: 57.9 x 38.3 cm

BIBLIOGRAPHY: Holladay 1995, 67–91; Wixom 1972, 96–99; Mollwo 1944.

86

Bifolium from an Antiphonary: Historiated Initial O with the Nativity

ABOUT 1405; BOHEMIAN, PRAGUE

TEMPERA AND GOLD ON VELLUM

This splendid bifolium and at least 16 other leaves once formed part of an important antiphonary produced for an unidentified Benedictine monastery in Bohemia. Given the deluxe nature of the illuminations, the original abbey and this commission must have been significant. The parent manuscript was acquired by a dealer shortly after World War I from the Seitenstetten Abbey in Lower Austria.

The Cleveland bifolium, an important example of Bohemian painting during the opening years of the 15th century, was produced in one of the great court centers of Europe, the city of Prague, by a circle of manuscript painters steeped in the "Beautiful Style" of the aristocratic courts of central Europe. The recent discovery of a description of the original manuscript while still intact, written by Josef Neuwirth in 1886, has made it possible to identify the Cleveland leaf as folio 58 out of a total of 296 leaves.

A majestic initial *O* containing a scene of the Nativity dominates the decoration of the leaf. A subsidiary scene in the background shows the annunciation to the shepherds. The angel's banderole reads "annuntio vobis" (I announce to you). The initial itself is placed within a square frame outside of which a single Benedictine monk observes the sacred event. His banderole declares "ora pro nobis ad d[o]m[in]u[m]" (Pray for us to the Lord). The initial introduces the Latin chants for the first vespers of Christmas day: "O iuda et iherusalem" (Oh Judea and Jerusalem). Framing the text on three sides are luxurious marginal extenders of scroll-ing acanthus leaves. Within the upper margin, two prophets emerge from the lush foliated tendrils to observe the scene just below. In this way, the antecedents and foretelling of the birth of Christ in the Old Testament are established visually.

The jewel-like colors, vivid imagery, variegated patterns, and luxuriously foliated borders are typical in manuscripts produced in Prague around 1400. The Cleveland leaf is painted in a brilliant palette including emerald green, deep red, lapis blue, and salmon pink. Heavily burnished and tooled gold was used within the frame of the miniature and for the haloes. The main miniature presents a picturesque naturalism in its grass and rocky terrain and the wattled wall and thatch of the stable. The figure of Mary, with dazzling lapis blue gown and golden hair, dominates the scene. Recent examination of other leaves suggests that several painters were employed on the project, which was not unusual. The individual style of the most prominent illuminator has not been definitively identified in other manuscripts. Clearly familiar with the work of several notable contemporaries including the Master of the Golden Bull and the Noah Master (named respectively after manuscripts now in Vienna and Antwerp), he apparently adapted their drapery styles and facial types. Within the gilding in the lower right of the miniature has been discovered a previously undetected punchmark in the form of a single-headed eagle, which may be the hallmark of an atelier, though its precise significance has yet to be determined. SNF

Andrew R. and Martha Holden Jennings Fund 1976.100

DIMENSIONS: 55.8 x 38.9 cm

BIBLIOGRAPHY: New York 2005, 269–74, no. 116; Schmidt 2005, 1: 337–40, 343, 347–49; figs. 1, 2, 5–7, 10–13; Wixom 1977, 311–25; Washington 1975, 152–59.

The Death of the Virgin

ABOUT 1400–1410; MASTER OF HEILIGENKREUZ

(AUSTRIAN, POSSIBLY BOHEMIAN, ACTIVE EARLY 15TH CENTURY)

TEMPERA AND OIL WITH GOLD ON PANEL

According to the legend of the Death of the Virgin first told in New Testament apocrypha, in her later days, the mother of God wished to see her son and was visited in her sorrow by an angel announcing her impending death. At her request, the apostles were summoned from the far corners of the Earth. She blessed them and prayed with them, and then laid herself down on her bed and prepared herself for death. When she expired, God received her soul and, accompanied by angels, carried it aloft to heaven.

This panel painting captures that narrative's main features. The Virgin reclines on a bed draped with a brocaded coverlet. Ten of the apostles are arranged in bas-relief just behind, performing funerary rites: one puffs air into a censer, two hold lit candles. At the center, Peter, prominent and solemn in his white papal robes and triple tiara, carries an aspergil (sprinkling device) and an aspersorium (vessel containing holy water) while reading from a book of prayers for the dead. In the foreground two apostles sit reading on a cushioned bench, one using a pair of eyeglasses, perhaps the earliest depiction of this invention in the visual arts. Above, choirs of angels delicately and unusually engraved on the panel's gold background wave banners and play musical instruments, rejoicing in the ascent of the Almighty and the child-like soul of the crowned Virgin into blue empyrean realms brimming with angels.

Until the early 20th century, the *Death of the Virgin* was joined to another panel, now at the National Gallery of Art in Washington, depicting the death of St. Clare (inset). Clare was the companion of St. Francis of Assisi and founder of the Poor Clares, an order of Franciscan nuns. This diptych was probably made for a Clarissan convent in central Europe. Given the common theme, the exemplary deaths of holy women, the panels may have been used in funerary or commemorative services honoring the nuns.

A skillful and highly individual practitioner of the refined International Gothic style characteristic of late medieval courts, the Master of Heiligenkreuz takes his name from a diptych once belonging to the Cistercian abbey of Heiligenkreuz in southeastern Austria (now Kunsthistorisches Museum, Vienna, 6523, 6524). Indeed, both the Cleveland and Washington panels—with their grave but dignified tone, extensive use of rich colors, wealth of highly creative surface embellishments, attenuated, willowy bodies with long, spidery fingers, and elaborate depictions of jewels, brocades, and other costly objects—bring the ideals entertained by late medieval courtly culture to vibrant life. VB

Gift of the Friends of The Cleveland Museum of Art in memory of John Long Severance 1936.496

DIMENSIONS: 71 x 54 cm

BIBLIOGRAPHY: Oberhaidacher 1998, 501–17; Hand/Mansfield 1993, 127–32; Eisler 1977, 232–36; *CMA European Paintings* 1974, 4–5, no. 2; Francis 1936, 153–56; Stange 1934–60, 11:4.

The Passion of Christ

ABOUT 1440S; MASTER OF THE SCHLÄGL ALTARPIECE (GERMAN, ACTIVE 1400S)

OIL AND GOLD ON PANEL

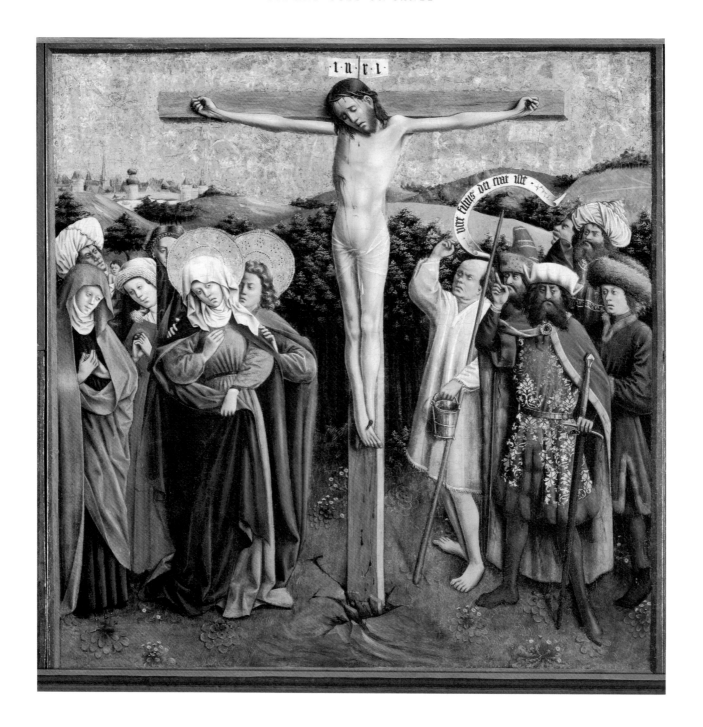

"You must direct your attention to these scenes of the Passion, as if you were actually present at the Cross, and watch the Crucifixion of our Lord with affection, diligence, love, and perseverance." Such are the instructions offered by St. Bonaventure's "Meditations on the Life of Christ," the most popular of the many vivid late medieval devotional manuals that sought to inspire a fervent and mystical brand of piety among the faithful. By providing ample and thorough visual stimulus to relive in meditation the prolonged and abundant grief and torments attending their Savior's Passion, an altarpiece like this one would have afforded its beholders an opportunity to heed the words of such texts.

Just as Christ's death on the cross constitutes the climax of the Passion narrative, so the representation of the Crucifixion dominates the center of this altarpiece, flanked by smaller scenes depicting events leading up to the Passion and its aftermath. To the left, Christ prays in the Garden of Gethsemane while three apostles sleep, the soldiers who will arrest him breaching the garden's fence; a blindfolded Christ is mocked; Christ appears before and is condemned by Pontius Pilate; and bound to a column, Christ endures flagellation. To the right, Christ is crowned with thorns; Christ carries the cross to Golgotha; and Christ falls to the ground, breaking beneath the weight of the cross. The eighth scene depicts a moment following the Crucifixion: the Lamentation over Christ's dead body. Every scene

abounds with carefully delineated details, each deliberately emphasizing the manifold torments Christ endured on behalf of humankind, and, indeed, of the viewer. It is likely that further scenes depicting events following the Crucifixion—possibly the Resurrection, Ascension, Pentecost, Ecce Homo, and Last Judgment—once elaborated and completed this already extensive cycle.

In the 1870s, a Munich painter by the name of Müller gave this altarpiece to the Premonstratensian abbey of Schlägl near Linz (Upper Austria). Both the altarpiece and the master who created it take their name from that foundation, where the painting remained for little more than a half-century before making its way to America. Although it probably came from a religious institution in the Westphalian region of Germany, its precise original location is unknown.

When the painting was acquired by the museum in 1951, the scenes were displayed as a unified rectangle. In its current presentation, the nine extant panels and four modern beige panels—standing in for hypothetically missing scenes—form an impressively large folding triptych comprising a central rectangle of five scenes over which two square wings of four scenes each close. This recent reorganization of the work in keeping with contemporary Westphalian altarpiece design attempts to return the panels to the format in which they may originally have been viewed. VB

Mr. and Mrs. William H. Marlatt Fund 1951.453

DIMENSIONS: 84.9 x 312.3 x 8.3 cm (framed reconstructed altarpiece)

BIBLIOGRAPHY: *CMA European Paintings* 1974, 31–33, no. 11; Musper 1970, 49–50; Francis 1952, 213–15; Stange 1934–60, 3: 216; Tietze 1913, 173–181, 187. For "Meditations on the Life of Christ," see Bonaventure 1961.

89

A Bridal Couple

15TH CENTURY; SOUTH GERMAN
OIL ON PANEL

In a verdant wood, a pair of lovers gaze smilingly into each other's eyes, the young man's arm wrapped around his lady's waist in a chaste embrace. Young, handsome, healthy, and wealthy, this couple enviably epitomizes the medieval courtly ideal of love. The circlets crowning their heads would have been placed there at the conclusion of the marriage rite, betokening an antique custom taken up again in the 15th century. The girl's unbound hair is that of a bride, an allusion to her purity. Dense with prickly leaves and delicate flowers reminiscent of a millefleur tapestry ground, the blossoming bower encircling the pair promises the fecundity of their marriage bond. The flowers themselves— roses, cherry and white currant blossoms, buttercups, clover, dandelions, lilies of the valley, cowslip, moneywort, and valerian—all denote love, those of fruit-bearing plants also alluding to the fruits their marriage will bear if those plants are properly cultivated. The couple's brightly colored garments, the man's in particular being at the height of aristocratic fashions of their day, are cut from the same cloth, each color in the lady's gown finding its mate in the youth's tunic and tights. They literally wear their feelings on their

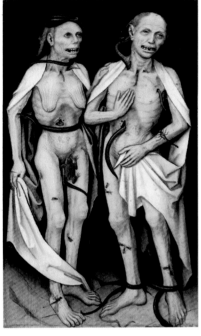

sleeves: the identical brown foliated damask of their left sleeves was a symbol in chivalric culture that announced to all who saw them that the pair belonged to each another. As the youth presents to his bride a small blue flower like that tucked into his circlet, probably wild chicory, a symbol of love thought to be rich with magical power, the two become one body.

Until the early 20th century, the *Bridal Couple* and the *Rotting Pair* (inset) were joined, each work occupying one side of a double-sided panel. In the *Rotting Pair,* the young lovers have turned into corpses, their naked flesh decaying on their exposed bones, their pretty faces shriveled into grimacing near-skulls, and their bodies swarming with snakes, toads, scorpions, and other vermin. Their fine clothing is no more, replaced with the sackcloth shrouds of the dead, and their lovely grove is now a desolate wasteland. Together forming a memento mori, an admonishment to beholders to reflect upon their own mortality, this fascinatingly disturbing and even repellent reminder of the vanity of all things illustrates the taste for macabre imagery prevalent in the later Middle Ages, particularly in northern Europe. VB

Delia E. Holden and L. E. Holden Funds 1932.179

DIMENSIONS: 62.3 x 36.5 cm

BIBLIOGRAPHY: Camille 1998, 159–62; Gotha 1998, 168–69, no. 83; Meadow 1992, 212–16; Hutchison 1958, 58–64; Francis 1943, 343–54; Stange 1934–60, 8: 8–9; Francis 1932, 127–31.

90

St. Jerome and the Lion

ABOUT 1495; TILMAN RIEMENSCHNEIDER (GERMAN, WÜRZBURG, ABOUT 1460–1531)
ALABASTER

Said to have come from the Benedictine abbey church of St. Peter in Erfurt, Germany, this small-scale alabaster statue depicts the Early Christian theologian, saint, and church father Jerome as he removes a thorn from the paw of a lion. The legendary account of Jerome's kindness toward a lion was well known by the 15th century through the *Legenda Aurea* (*Golden Legend*), the collection of saints' lives and legendary accounts compiled by the 13th-century chronicler and later archbishop of Genoa Jacobus de Voragine, as well as through a great number of painted representations that helped popularize the subject in northern Europe.

Likely inspired by representations based on paintings by the Netherlandish artist Rogier van der Weyden, Tilman Riemenschneider's St. Jerome is seated on a bench that is fully carved but visible only from the side and back. Gently holding the lion's front leg with his left hand, the saint extracts the thorn using a small knife or stylus. The lion sits, tail between its legs, looking anxiously to the side and toward the viewer. Following the common iconography of the scene, Jerome is dressed in the traditional robes of a Roman cardinal, with the cowl draped over his tonsured head and the broad-brimmed hat placed on his right leg as if to steady his arm for the impending surgical procedure.

While the sculpture appears unpainted today, traces of polychromy and gilding at the base, on the saint's face, robe, and hat, as well as on the lion's mane and other places suggest that it was once colored and gilded. The only areas left unpainted would have been the saint's hair, the fur lining of his mantle, and the bench on which he sits. Faults in the alabaster, now prominently visible on Jerome's forehead and the lion's snout and back, would thus have been rendered invisible. Drill holes in the hat further indicate that cords and tassels of fabric, typical of a cardinal's hat, would once have decorated the sculpture. Whether the statue was originally commissioned as the centerpiece for an altar in a private chapel or created to be appreciated for its artistic value in the study of a canon or a scholar associated with the university at Erfurt remains unknown. Its alleged provenance from a church there and Jerome's popularity as a patron saint of humanists and scholars make either scenario likely. That Riemenschneider is known to have worked in Erfurt earlier in his career and that a second alabaster statue depicting the Annunciation (Musée du Louvre, Paris, RF 1384) is said to have come from the same church indicate that Riemenschneider's St. Jerome was either part of a larger commission or one of several commissions. The choice of alabaster as a material certainly indicates local tastes and sensibilities, as alabaster was quarried just outside the city of Erfurt and likely shipped to the artist's studio in Würzburg for manufacture. Made in the early to mid 1490s, Riemenschneider's St. Jerome is not only one of the artist's more important early sculptures, it is also his only work in alabaster in a collection in the United States. HAK

Purchase from the J. H. Wade Fund 1946.82

DIMENSIONS: 37.8 x 28.1 x 15.9 cm

BIBLIOGRAPHY: Gillerman 2001, 333–35, no. 244; Kalden-Rosenfeld 2001, 125–26, no. 6; Washington 1999, 199–202, no. 11; Jopek 1988, 90–93, 154–56; Würzburg 1981, 263–66, no. 57; Bier 1951; Milliken 1946B; Gerstenberg 1941; Schmitt/Swarzenski 1921, 29, no. 143; Swarzenski 1921, 169, 189; Förster 1856, 24.

91

St. Lawrence

ABOUT 1502; TILMAN RIEMENSCHNEIDER (GERMAN, WÜRZBURG, ABOUT 1460–1531)

POLYCHROMED AND GILDED LINDENWOOD

Carved from a single block of lindenwood, this exquisite statue of St. Lawrence, a deacon and martyr of the Early Christian period (see no. 48), was made by Tilman Riemenschneider, one of the most outstanding artistic personalities in late medieval Germany. Born in the city of Heiligenstadt in Thuringia, he is believed to have received his early training in the city of Erfurt before traveling on as a journeyman to the Upper Rhine region and to Ulm in Swabia, where he apprenticed with Michel Erhart, a leading sculptor of the period. Riemenschneider settled in the city of Würzburg in Franconia, where he established a prolific workshop that produced numerous sculptures for altarpieces, tombstones, and epitaphs for high-ranking civic and ecclesiastical patrons of the region.

Together with a sculpture of St. Stephen (see p. 24) and two female saints preserved in the Historisches Museum in Frankfurt (X 2758, X 2759), this statue once formed part of an altarpiece that likely came from the Dominican nunnery at Rothenburg in Franconia. While the church itself was demolished in 1813, surviving records indicate that Riemenschneider received payments for his work there in 1507 and 1510, a fact that accords well with the differences in style that distinguish the two Cleveland statues. While Stephen's facial type and drapery style find their closest parallels in statues of around 1508 to 1510, Lawrence's body contour and drapery style have been compared to works created earlier, shortly after 1500. The martyr is dressed in typical deacon's garments, namely a long-sleeved alb and a fringed dalmatic. He raises an open book to his chest with his right hand and holds the handle of a gridiron, the instrument of his martyrdom, in his left. The elegant inverted S-curve of his body is further emphasized by the lifted dalmatic, which, caught underneath the book, crumples in a series of angular folds below his waist. The motif of the lifted dalmatic is visible in a print by Martin Schongauer (inset), which likely served as an inspiration, yet the sculptor transformed this detail into an element that supports the martyr's elegant swaying posture.

The gridiron is a modern replacement—the handle and the hand are original—and the gilding of his dalmatic has been substantially restored in recent centuries, but the figure still preserves traces of its original polychromy. A superb example of Riemenschneider's stylistic language during the early years of the 16th century, the statue portrays the early third-century martyr with serene stillness and elegance, his deeply melancholic gaze seeming to transcend all earthly realities. HAK

Leonard C. Hanna Jr. Fund 1959.42

DIMENSIONS: 93.8 x 38.5 x 21.8 cm

BIBLIOGRAPHY: Gillerman 2001, 335–38, no. 245; Kalden-Rosenfeld 2001, 43, 127, no. 14; Washington 1999, 283–89, no. 32D; Bier 1982, 50–52; Wixom 1963D; Bier 1960; Wixom 1959; Schmitt/Swarzenski 1921, 28, no. 139; Tönnies 1900, 261, no. 2/3; Bode 1887, 165.

92

Mourning Virgin from a Crucifixion Group

1500–1510; VEIT STOSS (GERMAN, ABOUT 1445/50–1533)

PEARWOOD

Despite its fragmentary preservation, this delicate statuette of the mourning Virgin is a true masterpiece of late Gothic sculpture. Carved from a single block of pearwood, it is one of only two surviving small-scale statuettes that have been convincingly attributed to the German artist Veit Stoss, one of the greatest sculptors of the late 15th and early 16th centuries. A native of Swabia, Stoss is believed to have received part of his training in the Upper Rhine valley, most likely in Strasbourg, where such exceptional artists as Nicolaus Gerhaert von Leiden and Martin Schongauer were active at the time. Their works were an important source of inspiration for Stoss throughout his long career, most of which was spent in Kraków and Nuremberg, two cities that flourished in the late 15th century and attracted the greatest artistic talents of their time.

Small in scale, but monumental in conception, the figure stands in elegant contrapposto, swaying slightly toward her right. She is dressed in a high-waisted robe that is girded below her chest, a long mantle held together at the neckline, and a shoulder-length veil or headscarf. Despite the regrettable loss of the figure's arms and hands, which were originally carved free of the Virgin's body in front of her chest, the high quality of the execution is nonetheless evident in the sensuous carving of her tearful face, the subtle rendering of her long wavy hair inside the enveloping mantle, and the exaggerated treatment of her fluttering garment, which finds a close parallel in the artist's other small-scale statuette, a Virgin and Child in the Victoria and Albert Museum in London (646-1893). Unlike that work, however, the Cleveland statuette was not conceived as a single figure but formed part of a crucifixion group intended for a domestic shrine or house altar. Such ensembles served not only as objects of private devotion and meditation, they were also collected as works of art in their own right, attesting to an artist's genius and virtuosic skills in a specific medium.

While primarily known for his monumental works, Veit Stoss was not the first late medieval sculptor to execute small-scale statuettes and sculptural ensembles. Tilman Riemenschneider and Nicolaus Gerhaert von Leiden are also known for their small-scale sculptures, similarly made to satisfy the appetite of a growing number of wealthy patrons and collectors for highly refined religious works of utmost artistic merit. HAK

Purchase from the J. H. Wade Fund 1939.64

DIMENSIONS: 31 x 9.8 x 8.7 cm

BIBLIOGRAPHY: Gillerman 2001, 332–33, no. 243; Washington 1999, 297–98, no. 35; New York 1986, 243–45, no. 91; Frankfurt 1981, 200–201; Baxandall 1980, 126–28; Rasmussen 1976, 108–9; Nuremberg 1933, 23, no. 12.

248

Vesperbild (Pietà)

1515–20; MASTER OF RABENDEN (GERMAN, UPPER BAVARIA)
POLYCHROMED AND GILDED LINDENWOOD

This masterpiece of Gothic sculpture, which preserves much of its original polychromy, was carved out of two blocks of lindenwood by an anonymous German artist named the Master of Rabenden after one of his most important works, the high altar of the church of Rabenden in the Chiemgau, the foothills of the Alps. It represents the Virgin Mary holding the dead body of Christ on her lap. Commonly known as "Vesperbild" in German for its use during Good Friday vespers liturgy or as "Pietà" from the Latin *pietas* (piety, devotion), this image type originated in southern Germany during the 13th century in response to developments in late medieval piety and mystical theology.

Following the standard iconography for this apocryphal event, which is said to have taken place after Christ's deposition from the cross, Mary is shown seated on a long bench holding the lifeless body of her dead son on her knees. She is dressed in her traditional garments, a long-sleeved robe, wide mantle, and fringed headscarf that comes down to her left knee, providing a support for Christ's beaten body. Clad only in a loincloth, Christ lies across the Virgin's lap, his head falling to the side and his right arm hanging perpendicularly to the ground. Joining the Virgin in contemplating Christ's suffering, humiliation, and death on the cross, the viewer's gaze is directed on Christ's corpse, his facial features frozen in agony, his hands showing signs of rigor mortis, and the gash in his side prominently displayed. While emphasizing Christ's wounds and pain-racked features, the sculpture invites the viewer to meditate on his ordeal, the redemptive power of his death, and the miracle of salvation. It also allows the viewer to empathize with Christ's mother and contemplate her role as the most powerful intercessor on behalf of humankind.

Like most Vesperbilder, this Pietà by the Master of Rabenden was likely placed on a secondary altar in a chapel of a Bavarian church, where it would have invited the faithful to contemplate the mysteries of Christ's suffering, death, and resurrection, and pray to the Virgin, whose sorrows, pain, and anguish are believed to make her the most compassionate advocate with her resurrected son on the day of the Last Judgment. HAK

Purchase from the J. H. Wade Fund 1938.294

DIMENSIONS: 89.1 x 78.7 x 32.4 cm

BIBLIOGRAPHY: Gillerman 2001, 337–39, no. 246; Washington 1999, 152, no. 7; Rohmeder 1971, 47, no. A7; Krönig 1962, 143; Wilm 1944, 73–74; Milliken 1939; Böhler 1938, 29–30, no. 94; Wilm 1937, 41, no. 51; Halm 1926, 2: 42–43.

tur in diebus hero
dis regis iudee sar
dos quidam noie
zacharias. de uice
abia. et uxor eius de
filiabus aaron. et no
men ei elyzabeth.
Erant autem iusti am
bo ante deu inceden
tes in omnibus man
datis et iustificacio
nibus dni sine que
rela. Et non erat eis
filius. eo qd elyza
beth esset sterilis.
et ambo processissent

in diebus suis. Fatu
est autem cum sacerd
tio fungeret zacha
rias in ordine uicis
sue ante deu secdm
consuetudinem sacer
dotii. sorte exiit ut in
censum poneret. ingres
sus in templu dni.
Et omnis multitudo
ppli erat orans foris
hora incensi. Apparuit
autem illi angls dni
stans a dextris alta
ris incensi. Et zach
arias turbatus est
uidens et timor mag
nus irruit sup eu.
Air autem ad illu an
gelus. Ne timeas
zacharia. quia exau
dita e deprecacio tua
et uxor tua elizabeth
pariet tibi filiu et

❖ 94 ❖

Evangelary

ABOUT 1480–1500; MINIATURES BY THE HOUSEBOOK MASTER

(GERMAN, MIDDLE RHINE)

TEMPERA AND GOLD ON VELLUM, 216 FOLIOS

The evangelary, also known as a gospel lectionary or book of pericopes, contained the gospel readings for the Mass. Before the 12th century, such readings at Mass were usually not arranged in an evangelary but read directly from a text of the four gospels. Because an evangelary provided the full gospel reading for each feast in liturgical order, it proved a more practical volume for the altar than the gospel book. For practical purposes, gospel books ceased to be produced entirely after the 12th century. Just as the earlier gospel books, evangelaries symbolized the word of God and thus were not only lavishly illuminated with author portraits of the four evangelists, but also very often beautifully bound. This volume is remarkable for its four evangelist portraits painted by an anonymous artist of great distinction, the Housebook Master.

The Housebook Master is known principally for a large corpus of drawings in pen and ink as well as drypoint engraving, the majority of the latter preserved in the Rijksmuseum in Amsterdam. For this reason, he was formerly known as the Master of the Amsterdam Cabinet. Regarded as one of the most important artists to work in the medium of engraving before Albrecht Dürer, he was also an accomplished painter who produced dozens of panels with religious subjects, though his precise oeuvre continues to be debated by scholars. The Housebook Master was active in the Middle Rhineland, perhaps at Mainz or Heidelberg, and must have re-ceived commissions from noblemen and church authorities in this region. His identity remains unresolved, though scholars have attempted to link him, without success, to various known artists. Modern scholars have concentrated on his artistic personality, and he is now named after the Housebook, an album of his drawings preserved in Schloss Wolfegg near Ravensburg in Germany.

The Housebook Master was above all a skilled draftsman. The portraits in the Cleveland evangelary are rare examples of his work in illuminated miniatures. Characteristically German Late Gothic, they reveal an expressive use of angular drapery and realistic detail. There is a pronounced emphasis on such detail in each scene as, for example, in the construction of the furniture, the scribe's tools and paraphernalia, the colorful floor tiles, and the draping of each evangelist's garments. The facial types, with their heavy-lidded downcast eyes, as well as the treatment of the hair and beards are highly characteristic of the Housebook Master's style. He was occasionally noted for his humor. In the portrait of John, the saint is depicted erasing an error in his text with his pen knife held in his left hand. He holds a quill pen in the right.

The manuscript lies in its original blind-tooled leather binding with brass clasps; the multipage textile book markers are rare. The skillful burnished initials with vine scrolls are the work of another illuminator. SNF

Mr. and Mrs. William H. Marlatt Fund 1952.465

DIMENSIONS: 23.7 x 18.4 x 5.4 cm

BIBLIOGRAPHY: Hess 1994; Amsterdam 1985; Filedt Kok 1983, 427–36; Wixom 1964, 58–60; Stange 1934–60, 7: 105, 120, pl. 286.

The 14th century is often characterized as an age of catastrophe in Italy. The first of many outbreaks of plague hit Europe in 1348, killing one-third of the population. The papacy was wracked with instability: from 1305 until 1377, the popes resided in Avignon in southern France, in self-imposed exile from Rome, and at one point rival antipopes reigned concurrently in Rome and Avignon, backed by different political factions. The Italian peninsula was the theater of war in which the Holy Roman Empire and the papacy played out a lengthy and bloody conflict. Nonetheless, the arts thrived and prospered as the promises of the 13th century were realized and consolidated in the 14th. Indeed, that the efforts of artists working in the 13th century and through the adversity of the calamitous 14th would culminate in the beginnings of the Renaissance is a profound testament to the spirit of those artists and to the vision of the patrons who continued to commission works of art in late medieval Italy.

During the 13th and 14th centuries, cities became Italy's pre-eminent domains of power and knowledge, eclipsing monasteries and the manors of the feudal nobility as strongholds of culture and civilization. Thanks to the growth of international banking, commerce, and trade, small towns throughout central and northern Italy developed into thriving urban centers teeming with wealth and ever-growing populations in which bankers, merchants, tradesmen, and craftsmen constituted an emergent middle class.

At these cities' cores, immense cathedrals and imposing town halls were constructed. Built by ambitious bishops, the cathedrals were typically simple columnar basilicas of colossal proportions with lofty interiors. Executed at the behest of communal governments or aristocratic rulers as symbols of authority and wealth, town halls housing government offices and audience chambers often took the form of towered fortresses beside large public squares. At the cities' peripheries, new monastic orders, notably the Franciscans and the Dominicans, built massive churches to accommodate the large congregations to which they ministered, preaching against heresy and promoting the values of poverty, charity, and a highly spiritualized brand of personal piety.

Around and in these grand edifices and public spaces, civic pride and religious fervor swelled, as did the need for and production of works of art. The interiors and exteriors of seats of secular power were adorned with frescoed or sculpted decorations. In cathedrals, every available surface both inside and out was embellished with sculptural carving in a classicizing style, while extensive fresco programs were favored in mendicant church interiors. All churches required a variety of furnishings, including crosses, chalices, and textiles to fulfill the liturgical needs of their altars, as well as clerical vestments, sets of prayer and choir books (see no. 105), pulpits, and reliquaries (see no. 99). Panel paintings also became an important element of church decoration. Monumental images depicting the crucified Christ or the Madonna and Child served as awe-inspiring focal points of communal devotion. At the Fourth Lateran Council in 1215, the Catholic Church codified the doctrine of transubstantiation, asserting that during the Mass, the bread and the wine become the body and blood of Christ. Previously unparalleled drama evolved around the performance of the Mass, and the Holy Eucharist was now elevated for all to see and venerate: ever more elaborate painted altarpieces were produced as backdrops to this part of the rite (see no. 96).

While many of these works of art resulted from the patronage offered by the clergy or confraternities attached to a church or by a civic government or local rulers, wealthy private citizens played an increasingly prominent role in artistic patronage. Prosperous families built commanding fortified palaces, many crowned by towers asserting their presence on the urban skyline and providing them with a bird's-eye view of all that lay below. Prominent symbols of power and prosperity, palaces were outfitted and ornamented with frescoes, tapestries, furniture, and a variety of other luxury goods. The affluent also studded the walls of churches with imposing tomb monuments memorializing themselves and their family members. In mendicant churches, they endowed private burial chapels and filled them with liturgical furnishings, altarpieces, tomb monuments, and frescoes. Conspicuous displays of wealth and piety, sepulchral and funerary commissions were also created to care for the souls of the commemorated dead in their potentially perilous postmortem journeys through purgatory toward salvation in heaven. Individuals also strove to perfect their souls throughout the course of earthly life, many commissioning small but lavish panel paintings, prayer books, and other precious objects to aid in self-ameliorative private devotions.

In order to sate the growing demand for works of art, artists became more organized, forming specialized guilds to regulate and protect artistic practice; leading masters amassed large workshops, training successive generations of artists. These ateliers also rendered art production a cooperative venture, many hands coming together to realize the master's overarching vision. In the case of large-scale projects, this collectivity could create climates of intense artistic ferment and interchange. Artists also achieved a social status higher than in previous centuries, with painters, sculptors, and architects enjoying the most exalted place. Ultimately, though, artists labored in the service of Christ and the saints: by bestowing their artistic gifts on the portrayal of the divine, artists hoped to ensure their own salvation.

Italian art of the 13th century is deeply indebted to the achievements of Byzantium. Until the Norman conquest of 1071, southern Italy and Venice were the empire's western borders. Both before and after this date, the region maintained strong links to the east through trade, importing works of art and welcoming itinerant craftsmen. When Christian armies sacked Constantinople in the Fourth Crusade in 1204, Italy was further flooded with precious objects from Byzantium. By the end of the 13th century and throughout the 14th century, however, a variety of other idioms, ideas, and concerns took root, and Italian art evolved into a style uniquely its own.

Looking closely at classical sculpture, artists in Pisa and in Florence began to depict the human figure more naturalistically than ever before, portraying it with new-found volume, dynamism, and three-dimensionality. Artists, particularly those in Siena, absorbed the forms of the refined, courtly Gothic style prevalent in northern Europe, for example, an enriched and more subtle color palette, an attention to naturalistic detail, and an interest in delicate ornamentation and intricate decorative patterning derived from the visual language of architecture and manuscript illumination.

Iconography became more complex and varied. This in part stemmed from the founding of the mendicant orders, the canonization of new saints, and the institution of new doctrines, all of which demanded that artists be ever more inventive in formulating iconography, their works being the chief conduit by which the new sacred narratives and ideas were communicated to the largely illiterate faithful. This new complexity was also the result of the new diversity of art patrons, each requiring that the works they commissioned be personalized to suit their own specific needs. Texts also played a role in this burgeoning complexity. The ideas contained within recently discovered classical treatises transformed secular imagery concerned with government, justice, learning, and astrology. The love poetry of the French courts also informed profane imagery, and may, in part, be responsible for the transformation of the stern Byzantine Madonna into the lovely, blonde Queen of Heaven frequently found in Sienese painting, an embodiment of the literary lover's ideal lady (see nos. 97, 98). The work of Dante, Petrarch, and Bocaccio, written in the vernacular and addressing the lived experience of the medieval Italian, may account for artists situating remote biblical and hagiographical narratives and figures in contemporary settings and costumes and punctuating their works with an abundance of often charming references to everyday life.

Artists also began to infuse their works with an unprecedented and irresistible appeal to the viewer's emotions. Gradually, they abandoned the distant deities gazing imposingly and impenetrably from remote golden realms and the stylized, cartoon-like narrative scenes characteristic of the hieratic style of the Byzantine east. They were replaced with images of the Madonna and Child ripe with a mother's tender love and fears for her newborn child, pictures of Christ's Passion inciting viewers to suffer along with their Savior, and depictions of saints and angels in which these beings are proposed as mankind's helpmates, poised between earth and heaven. Thus, the human experience of the divine through art became more immediate, palpable, and full of feeling than ever before, perhaps the greatest triumph of Italian art in these late medieval centuries. VB

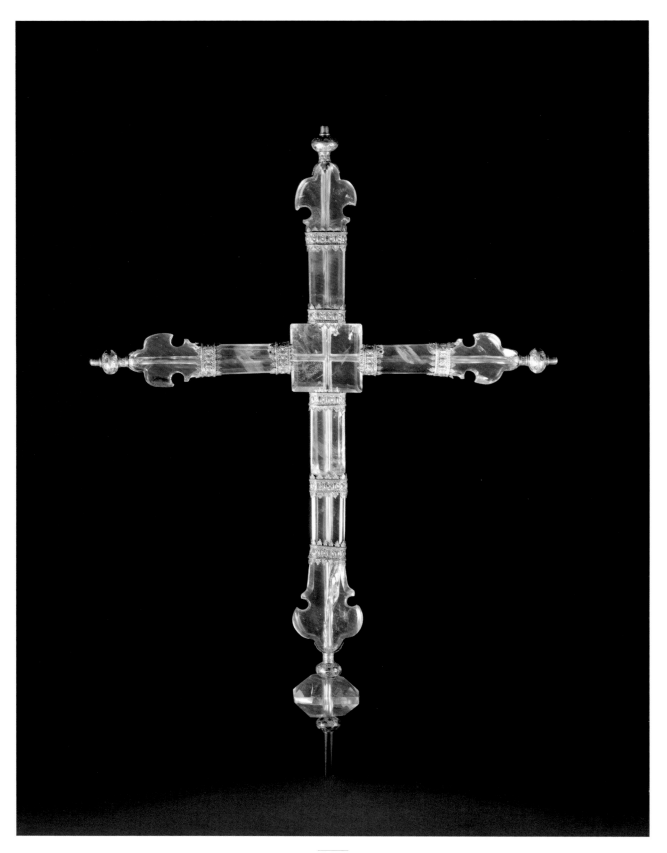

95

Cross

ABOUT 1280–1300; ITALIAN, VENICE
ROCK CRYSTAL WITH PAINTED GOLD MOUNTS

The practice of endowing churches with precious objects, widespread in western Europe by the late eighth or early ninth century, arose from the conviction that only the finest materials were suitable in service to God, the Virgin, or the saints. Rock crystal's rarity and preciousness, as well as its association with purity, made it particularly desirable for use in church furnishings, and surviving examples and inventories attest to the popularity of rock crystal crosses in church treasuries amassed between the 12th and 15th centuries throughout Europe.

This tall, slender cross consists of several pieces of rock crystal drilled through their centers and fastened together by a golden rod visible through the transparent stone. Where they join, the pieces of crystal are bound with decorative bands of gold and enamel that may date to the 12th century or mark a 16th-century refurbishment of the object. At each terminal, the crystal is fashioned into a fleur-de-lis shape, and scepter-shaped gold and enamel knobs finish the terminals. At some point in the cross's history, a figure of Christ may have hung crucified upon it. Made in Venice, which, along with Paris and Cologne, was the pre-eminent center for crystal cutting in the 14th century, this cross came from the royal treasury of Saxony and allegedly first belonged to Rudolph I of Habsburg (r. 1273–91). Undoubtedly intended for prominent display, it probably adorned an altar and may also have been carried in ecclesiastical or royal processions.

Objects fashioned from precious stones could transcend their mere liturgical or ceremonial functions and induce flights of spirituality. In his famous account of the rebuilding and refurbishment of the abbey church of Saint-Denis (written about 1144–48), Abbot Suger wrote eloquently of the sublime effect many objects fashioned from different kinds of precious stones would have had when placed upon an altar:

When, out of affection for the Church, we contemplate these new and old ornaments, seeing that admirable cross of St. Eloi, the lesser crosses, and that incomparable ornament commonly called "the crest" all placed on the golden altar, I say, sighing right down to my heart, "Thou has been in the paradise of God, every precious stone was thy covering, the sardius, topaz, and the diamond, the beryl, the onyx, and the jasper, the sapphire, the emerald, and the carbuncle, and gold. [Ezekiel 28:13]"
VB

Purchase from the J. H. Wade Fund 1927.169

DIMENSIONS: 70.2 x 52.2 x 6.6 cm

BIBLIOGRAPHY: Hahnloser/Brugger-Koch 1985, 111, no. 96; Cleveland 1936, 19, no. 14. For the quote, see Suger 1979, 62–63.

96

Virgin and Child with Saints

BEFORE ABOUT 1317; UGOLINO DI NERIO (ITALIAN, SIENESE, ACTIVE 1317–27)
OIL ON PANEL

In the first quarter of the 13th century, St. Francis of Assisi founded a new monastic order active in the evangelization of the masses through emphasizing ideals of poverty and charity. Throughout the following century, the Franciscans settled in cities throughout Italy and immediately attracted impressive numbers of followers. In order to accommodate such large congregations, the Franciscans punctuated the hilltop towns of Tuscany with immense, barn-like churches. The creator of this panel, the Sienese painter Ugolino di Nerio, made a career of providing Franciscan churches with the polyptychs that adorned the altars of late medieval Italy, of which this panel is a typical and well-preserved example.

Many ideas important to the Franciscans find expression here. At the work's center, the Virgin tenderly cradles the Christ child, who, in turn, tugs on her veil. This gesture echoes the bittersweet words of a popular Franciscan devotional text, "The Meditations on the Life of Christ," which recounts that Christ, on seeing his mother cry at her foreknowledge of his Passion, "put his little hand to her face as he would that she should not weep." The pair is flanked by images of saints Francis and John the Baptist to the left and James and Mary Magdalene to the right. Francis displays, typically, the stigmata in his hands and side. In his left hand, he holds a book and with his right gestures toward Christ. John holds a thin cross in his left hand and motions with his right in the same direction as Francis. Together, these gestures indicate the saints' status as forerunners of Christ, as St. Bonaventure, minister general of the Franciscan order, described them in the prologue to his "Life of St. Francis." Other saints—Bartholomew, Paul, Peter, and John the Evangelist or possibly Andrew—are depicted above in small triangular pinnacles. The four apostles, along with James below, assert an institutional presence, alluding to the order founded by Francis. Above the Madonna and child, in a further pinnacle, is a Crucifixion in which the cross is isolated in a barren landscape. This, together with the images of Francis himself and Mary Magdalene holding her ointment jar, is a reference to penitence, a key Franciscan doctrine. The overall austerity of the altarpiece, each niche formed by sturdy, squared pilasters joined with semi-circular arches, very appropriately reflects the order's strong profession of poverty. VB

Leonard C. Hanna Jr. Fund 1961.40

DIMENSIONS: 122.2 x 200.3 x 8.9 cm (framed)

INSCRIBED: next to St. Francis: S·FRANCISCU[S]; next to St. John the Baptist: S·IO[A]NES BAPT[ISTA]; next to St. James: [S] IACOBUS; next to St. Mary Magdalene: S MARIA MAG[D]ALENA

BIBLIOGRAPHY: Cook 1999, 86, no. 53; Hanson 1983, 34–35; Stubblebine 1979, 1: 160–61; White 1979, 73; Francis 1961, 194–205.

97

Madonna and Child

ABOUT 1350; ATTRIBUTED TO LIPPO MEMMI

(ITALIAN, SIENESE, ACTIVE 1317–ABOUT 1350)

TEMPERA AND GOLD ON POPLAR PANEL

On the eve of the Battle of Montaperti in 1260, Buonaguida Lucari dedicated Siena to the Virgin. This event proved seminal in the city's history. The miraculous victory of the Sienese over their Florentine opponents on the following day confirmed Siena's unique status as Civitas Virginis (City of the Virgin) and fostered among her citizens a fervent devotion to their heavenly protectress. This devotion manifested itself in an efflorescence of Marian imagery in Siena throughout the 13th and 14th centuries, and thus in the many altarpiece polyptychs with images of the Madonna and Child at their centers. This panel once belonged to such a work.

Here, hovering on the pure golden ground that in early Italian paintings denotes the realm of heaven, the Madonna cradles the Christ child. Every available detail and surface of this admirably well-preserved panel is rich with ornamentation. Embossed and tooled foliate decoration articulates the pilasters and trefoil cusping along the interior edge. Extensive gilding picks out the fine lines of the star on the Madonna's shoulder, creates the illusion of brocade in her underdress and the child's swaddling cloth, and illuminates the border of her blue mantle. The haloes and edge of the underdress are heavily punched and tooled. Even the curls of the child's hair seem more a decorative patterning than a natural feature.

This image is at once a tender celebration of maternal love and a melancholy foreshadowing of Christ's Passion. While the faces of mother and child are pressed affectionately together, their distant gazes betray their knowledge of the grief to come, when the Madonna will again press her face to her child's as he is lowered into his tomb. Christ tugs at her mantle as any mortal child might, but the motif also recalls the idea that she wrapped both her newborn child and his dead adult body in her clothing. The child's scroll alludes to the redemptive significance of his forthcoming sacrifice. The "stella maris" (star of the sea) emblazoned on the Madonna's shoulder refers to the words of a hymn sung at vespers and on feasts days honoring her. Thus, this panel offered its Sienese viewers the chance to contemplate many aspects of their beloved patron saint. VB

Gift of the Hanna Fund 1952.110

DIMENSIONS: 71.3 x 44 x 5.7 cm

INSCRIBED: on scroll: Egosu via / veritas et vita [Ego sum via et veritas et vita nemo venit ad Patrem nisi per me.] (I am the way, and the truth, and the life. No man cometh to the Father, but by me.) (John 14:6)

BIBLIOGRAPHY: Martindale 1988, 56; De Benedictis 1979, 22, 90; Francis 1953, 59–61; Sandberg-Vavalà 1937, 177; Weigelt 1931, 13.

98

The Adoration of the Magi

ABOUT 1440–45; GIOVANNI DI PAOLO (ITALIAN, SIENA, ACTIVE 1417–82)

TEMPERA (AND OIL?) AND GOLD ON PANEL

Giovanni di Paolo was one of the leading painters in 15th-century Siena. First recorded in 1417 as decorating a manuscript for the Sienese church of San Domenico, in later years he provided several panel paintings for altars at that church and others throughout Siena and its environs. He also painted miniatures, famously illuminating the *Paradiso* of Dante's *Divine Comedy* (British Library, London, Yates Thompson Codex). Giovanni is often called a conservative painter because he preserved the previous century's gold backgrounds and altarpiece format when his Florentine contemporaries were experimenting with new, more naturalistic idioms. He is, however, renowned for his iconographical inventiveness, as well as for painting in a style all his own, creating pictorial worlds out of idiosyncratic imaginings. His panoramic chessboard landscapes and fragile fairytale architectural confections veritably burst with charming details and eccentric figures. Indeed, as John Pope-Hennessy once wrote: "Few experiences in Italian painting are more exciting than to follow Giovanni di Paolo as he plunges, like Alice, through the looking glass."

Throughout the 15th century, artists considerably expanded on the bare biblical account of the Magi, who, having found Jesus by following a star, lay gifts before him. In particular, artists devoted unprecedented amounts of space to the Magi's procession to Bethlehem and to the bustling entourages accompanying them, which provided the opportunity to depict contemporary aristocratic life in all its splendor. One such painting was the 1423 altarpiece the *Adoration of the Magi* (Galleria degli Uffizi, Florence, 1890, n. 8364) by Gentile da Fabriano, the leading Italian artist of the international courtly style. Giovanni's *Adoration*, one of four versions of the subject painted by him, clearly looks to Gentile's. Giovanni, however, simplifies Gentile's composition. Instead of Gentile's sumptuous cavalcade traversing seas and circling forbidding fortifications, Giovanni depicts a modest, hilly countryside dotted with peasants, and focuses the viewer's attention on the Magi in their brocaded garments supplicating before Christ, held in the arms of the highly sculptural Virgin swathed in the undulating folds of her brilliant blue mantle. Opposite this main group, the Magi's courtly entourage with their carefully individuated facial expressions and garments, as well as their retinue of animals ordinary and exotic, provides an exuberant visual diversion typical of Giovanni's oeuvre.

Formerly joined to *The Annunciation with the Expulsion of Adam and Eve from Paradise* (National Gallery of Art, Washington, 1939.1.223), *The Nativity* (Pinacoteca Vaticana, 40130), *The Crucifixion* (Gemäldegalerie, Berlin-Dahlem, 1112), and *The Presentation of Christ in the Temple* (Metropolitan Museum of Art, New York, 41.100.4), the *Adoration of the Magi* once formed part of a predella, a strip of narrative scenes running along the base of an altarpiece. Although the main section of the altarpiece has not been identified, this single panel alone provides a glimpse into the courtly atmosphere pervading the arts of 15th-century Italy, and into the oeuvre and mind of one of its most distinctive and highly individual painters. VB

Delia E. and L. E. Holden Funds 1942.536

DIMENSIONS: 38.4 x 44.3 cm

BIBLIOGRAPHY: New York 1988, 191; *CMA European Paintings* 1974, 102–4, no. 37; Sterling 1974, 350–59; Francis 1942. For the quote, see Pope-Hennessy 1947, 13.

99

Frame for a Reliquary Icon

In the Middle Ages relics were thought to possess extraordinary power and value, and were thus enshrined in lavish vessels called reliquaries, typically crafted of or covered with gold, silver, ivory, gems, and enamel. Reliquaries not only paid homage to the preciousness of the objects they contained, but also, through the powerful visual impact they exerted when their costly materials glittered in candlelight on an altar or in sunlight during a procession, ensured that those relics attracted the veneration they deserved.

This double-sided reliquary's decoration is atypical in that humble materials and unusual technique were used to emulate the appearance of precious metals and stones. The reliquary rests on a gilded rectangular base decorated with a foliate *pastiglia* pattern, inset glass cabochons, punching, and four heraldic panels made of *verre églomisé*. The base supports a polygonal plinth, which in turn supports a gilded and gabled rectangular frame adorned with pastiglia and inset with rosettes containing 17 carefully labeled relics whose organic quality contrasts with their carefully wrought frame. Carved crockets curl from the gable's outer edge. Thin buttresses inset with strips of foliate and geometric patterned verre églomisé flank the frame, which originally enclosed two other pieces of verre églomisé. One de-

picted the Virgin and Child enthroned and flanked by saints above the Annunciation (Fitzwilliam Museum, Cambridge, M.56, A-1904); according to documentary evidence, the other piece, now lost, portrayed the Crucifixion.

This reliquary originally resided in the Ospedale de Santa Maria della Scala (Hospital of Santa Maria della Scala) in Siena. During the 14th century it was common for the hospital's directors to offer the foundation a gift decorated with the coats of arms of the hospital and the director's family. This reliquary was such a work. On its base, two coats of arms containing golden ladders surmounted by crosses on black backgrounds refer to the hospital, and two others, diagonally quartered, refer to the Cinughi family, to which one Mino di Cino, named as the work's patron by an inscription and director of the hospital from 1340 until 1351, belonged.

The ospedale owned an impressive collection of relics housed in a dedicated chapel in their church in the 14th century, a likely original location for the reliquary. While it probably resided chiefly on an altar, that it has two sides implies that complete viewing can only occur in the round, which would have occurred if, like most reliquaries, it was carried aloft in processions on the feast days of the saints whose relics it contained. VB

Gift of Ruth Blumka in memory of Leopold Blumka 1978.26

DIMENSIONS: 66.7 x 51.3 x 25.3 cm

INSCRIBED: on the base of the reliquary frame: obverse: HOC/OPUS : FACTUM . FUIT . SUB . ANNO . DO/MINI; reverse: [M]/CCC . XLVII .TEMPORE . DOMINI . MINI/CINI. (This work was made in

the year of the Lord [1]347 in the time of the Lord Mino [di] Cino); on the obverse and reverse of the supporting base: LUCAS ME FECIT. (Luke has made me)

BIBLIOGRAPHY: Gauthier 1983, 173, no. 100; Gordon 1981, 148–53; Moran 1979; Wixom 1979A, 128–32.

❖ 100 ❖

Madonna and Child

ABOUT 1340S; GIOVANNI DI AGOSTINO (ITALIAN, SIENA, ABOUT 1310–48?)
MARBLE WITH TRACES OF PAINT AND GILDING

Beneath a Gothic-arched canopy, the Virgin, her arm encircling the Christ child, sits enthroned on a raised dais supported by two lions. To the Virgin's proper right is St. Catherine of Alexandria, standing on her usual attribute, the wheel on which she was tortured before being martyred. St. John the Baptist, clad in a hair shirt and heavily bearded, stands to the Virgin's left. A rectangular frame encloses the divine apparition. Most likely from a Sienese church interior, this marble panel is a fragment of a larger sculptural program, possibly a tomb. Crowning such a sepulchral conception, it would have denoted the fondest hope of the soul post mortem, namely, to join the saints in heaven.

Sienese sculptural style of the 14th century was dominated by the crowded spaces and bulky forms of Giovanni Pisano, who had been summoned from Pisa to direct the construction of the facade of Siena's cathedral between 1284 and 1299. Giovanni di Agostino, however, rejected Pisano's manner in favor of the highly refined style for which contemporary Sienese painters, particularly Simone Martini, were celebrated.

Giovanni di Agostino's painterly treatment of sculpture is manifest in this work in several ways. The sculptor frequently translated the principles of spatial organization that Simone established on panel and in fresco into a three-dimensional format. By situating each figure discretely below one of the arcade's arches, the composition echoes the format standard in Simone's altarpieces. Articulated in stone in the arcade's elegant embellishments are the idioms of French Gothic architecture recently imported into Italy and rendered in miniature in the engaged frames surrounding panel paintings. The small features of the protagonists' faces, the complex linear rhythms of the draperies, and the slurred, smooth treatment of the marble parallel Simone's figure style. The throne's curiously animated lion feet recall his many imaginative details: for example, in an image of St. Luke (J. Paul Getty Museum, Los Angeles, 82.PB.72), the saint's typically static attribute—the ox—is instead a live, bellowing beast charged with guarding his inkpot.

The panel's resonance with contemporary painting is enhanced by the likelihood that it was once brilliantly colored. Although traces of paint and gilding remain in several areas of the mottled and stained cream and brown stone, this polychromy does not for the most part appear to be original. Polychrome decoration of sculpture deteriorates rapidly, however, and restorative repainting was a common occurrence. The hints of color thus probably intimate the work's intended appearance. And indeed, within a dark church illuminated only by candlelight, the divine would have seemed palpably present in this solidly three-dimensional ensemble, glowing with color. VB

Given in memory of Henry G. Dalton by his nephews, George S. Kendrick and Harry D. Kendrick 1942.1162

DIMENSIONS: 70.5 X 52.5 X 5.9 cm

BIBLIOGRAPHY: Bartalini 2005, 286; Gillerman 2001, 324–44, no. 250; Kreytenberg 1993, 16; Garzelli 1969, 199–200; Milliken 1943, 23–25; Valentiner 1924, 18.

101

Madonna and Child

BY 1461; MINO DA FIESOLE (ITALIAN, FLORENCE, 1429–84)
MARBLE WITH TRACES OF GILDING

In 1459, the Tuscan sculptor Mino da Fiesole journeyed to Rome to work on the ciborium for the high altar of the church of S. Maria Maggiore, commissioned by the French Cardinal Guillaume d'Estouteville (1403–83). Completed in 1461 but dismantled in 1747, this structure was originally decorated with 32 sculptures carved in relief. All are now displayed throughout S. Maria Maggiore, save one, the *Madonna and Child* panel in the collection of the Cleveland Museum of Art.

The popes and cardinals of the early Renaissance are often remembered for their ongoing efforts to restore the city, which had been abandoned during the Avignon papacy (1309–77). These great clerics devoted immense resources to rebuilding aging churches, restoring residences and bridges, and redecorating the interiors of revered sites. Expressed in these numerous restorations is a growing sense of the Roman Catholic Church as heir to both the Roman Empire and the early church, and new commissions were intended to represent an ideal conjunction of the imperial and Christian city. The ciborium of S. Maria Maggiore, one of several projects d'Estouteville undertook in the church in concert with Pope Pius II's efforts to restore St. Peter's to its former glory, is part of this trend. Marble

ciboria can be traced back to the very beginnings of church architecture; this ciborium's structure evokes ancient Roman architecture, and its monumental narrative reliefs, unique in Renaissance ciboria, emulate ancient Roman reliefs.

The primary Marian church in all Christendom, S. Maria Maggiore is the first church erected in the Virgin's honor: she is said to have created the miraculous snowfall on 5 August 358 that left the ground plan for the church on the Esquiline Hill. As such, it is not surprising that an impressive image of the Madonna and Child appeared on the ciborium. Perhaps surprising, though, are the differences between this work and those representing this familiar subject made in Italy a century earlier (see no. 100). Larger and more imposing than ever before, the half-length figures fully dominate the window in which they sit, drawing near to the viewer's space. The frame rejects the Gothic forms of the previous century in favor of elegant, classicizing flower motifs. Mother and child look tenderly at each other, their gazes capturing the essence of love. No longer a divine apparition, this accessible, relatable, and palpably present rendering of Christ and his mother is characteristic of the changes in art at the beginning of the Italian Renaissance. VB

Gift of Mrs. Leonard C. Hanna 1928.747

DIMENSIONS: 93.7 x 80 x 12.7 cm

BIBLIOGRAPHY: Zuraw 1993, 672–76, no. 21; Detroit 1985, 191–92, no. 63; Middeldorf 1976, 28; Pope-Hennessy 1971, 65; Valentini 1839, 190–91.

102

Miniature from a Gradual: Initial G

ABOUT 1371–77; DON SILVESTRO DEI GHERARDUCCI (ITALIAN, FLORENCE, 1339–99)
TEMPERA AND GOLD ON VELLUM

This initial would have introduced the text "Gaude-amus omnes in Domino" (Let us all rejoice in the Lord), the beginning of the Introit for the feast of All Saints (1 November). The highly chromatic initial with punched and burnished gold represents the enthroned godhead Christ (King of Justice) with his mother, the Virgin Mary (Queen of Mercy), seated at his right. Rows of saints and angels turn toward them in adoration. Christ and the Virgin hold scepters as symbols of their sovereignty and sit on a throne of seraphim. The setting is a flowery meadow symbolizing the peace and tranquility of the heavenly realm. Below, music-making angels intensify the composition, and around the enthroned Christ and Virgin may be seen the heavenly court of All Saints. Here, the artist has brilliantly painted each figure—apostle, deacon, Old Testament hero, church father, hermit saint, and virgin—with individuality and distinct characterizations. The resulting magnificent composition rivals those of the trecento altarpiece. It is a masterpiece of Renaissance manuscript painting.

This monumental initial G, along with other dispersed fragments, has long been known to derive from a large set of choral books produced in the Camaldolese monastery of Santa Maria degli Angeli in Florence. The books were largely broken up during the Napoleonic era. The Cleveland miniature appeared on the verso of folio 155 in Corale 2 (Biblioteca Medicea Laurenziana, Florence). The decoration of these splendid choral books has traditionally been attributed to Don Silvestro dei Gherarducci, a monk who entered the monastery in 1348 at the age of nine and died there in 1399. Gherarducci, who was mentioned by Vasari for the excellence of his manuscript painting, may have spent time in Siena learning his craft; numerous illuminations from liturgical manuscripts as well as some small panels have been assigned to his hand.

The scriptorium of Santa Maria degli Angeli produced liturgical books for its own use as well as for the nearby hospital of Santa Maria Nuova throughout the second half of the 14th century. A recent re-examination of payment records and other documents has suggested that, while not a miniaturist at the monastery, Gherarducci may have held an administrative role in the production of books. Regardless of its authorship, the Cleveland miniature must be regarded as among the finest late 13th-century Florentine illuminations. SNF

Purchase from the J. H. Wade Fund 1930.105

DIMENSIONS: 38.6 x 36.5 cm

BIBLIOGRAPHY: Freuler 1997, 395; Freuler 1994, 124–55 no. 16i; D'Ancona 1993, 14–18; Bent 1992, 507–23.

103

Miniature from a Manuscript: The Crucifixion

ABOUT 1390; NICCOLÒ DI GIACOMO DA BOLOGNA

(ITALIAN, BOLOGNA, ACTIVE 1349–1403)

TEMPERA AND GOLD ON VELLUM

The leading illuminator of Bologna during the second half of the 14th century, Niccolò da Bologna was enormously successful at a time when demand for books was high. His prodigious output included legal, academic, and liturgical texts, and he was unusual in that he signed some of his works, as is the case here. Highly regarded by his contemporaries, he owned two houses in Bologna and nine pieces of land. By the late 1380s, Niccolò had been appointed illuminator to the city of Bologna and was mayor of the district of Zappolino and special counselor to the Bolognese book trade. In 1393 he was elected to the Consiglio dei Quattrocento (Council of the Four Hundred), a civic body in Bologna.

Niccolò undoubtedly painted this miniature in his official capacity as city illuminator. It features the elements of a traditional Calvary group: a crucified Christ flanked by the Virgin and St. John, Mary Magdalene at the foot of the cross, and lamenting angels above collecting the blood from Christ's wounds in chalices. The figures appear against a ground of feathered acanthus leaves in gold over black, which creates a striking visual effect. Along the bottom edge are the remnants of three shields, lost when the miniature was excised from the parent volume. Because the verso is blank, for many years the miniature was presumed to have belonged to a missal. Recent scholarship has shown that the shields depicted the arms of the city of Bologna at center, with those of the apothecaries guild on either side. Thus the miniature was intended as the frontispiece to a guild register or perhaps a statute book for the city's apothecaries guild. The choice of subject was probably to create a visual analogy with a missal and thus make it authoritative. Religious iconography combined with escutcheons was typical of the illustration of Bolognese guild registers in the 14th century.

Niccolò adopted the style of Giotto: robust figures with almond-shaped eyes and slightly green-tinged flesh tones, and draperies painted in vivid colors—pale pink, light blue and gray, dark red and deep blue with white highlights. Niccolò's figures are often highly animated and his crowded compositions have considerable energy and powers of expression. His style was in turn readily adopted by younger Bolognese illuminators who carried it throughout Italy and even to Paris. SNF

Gift of J. H. Wade 1924.1013

DIMENSIONS: 26.8 x 20.2 cm

INSCRIBED: signed, lower right: NICOLAUS F.

BIBLIOGRAPHY: Voelkle/Wieck 1992, 186–87, no. 70, pl. 46; De Winter 1983A, 333–38; Washington 1975, 55–56, no. 17; Aeschlimann 1969, 23–35; D'Ancona 1969, 1–22; for comparison see Filippini/Zucchini 1947, 175–81.

104

Miniature from a Gradual: Initial D with a Prophet

ABOUT 1409–10; LORENZO MONACO (ITALIAN, FLORENCE, ABOUT 1370–1425)

TEMPERA AND GOLD ON VELLUM

This initial belongs to a three-volume gradual (Museo Nazionale del Bargello, Florence) produced by the scriptorium of the Camaldolese monastery of Santa Maria degli Angeli for the nearby hospital church of Santa Maria Nuova around 1409–10. The miniature here introduces the Introit to the Mass for the 11th Sunday after Pentecost: "D[eus in loco sancto suo]" (God is in his holy place). It would have appeared at the top of the verso of folio 122 in the last volume (Cod. H74). The recto includes staves and fragments of text for the end of the offertory hymn for the Mass of the tenth Sunday after Pentecost. The volume to which the Cleveland miniature belonged had forty-five miniatures of which seven are missing. Most of the extant miniatures represent figures of prophets or saints, and the majority appear to be the work of Lorenzo Monaco.

Don Lorenzo entered the Santa Maria degli Angeli Monastery in 1391. He represented the next generation of monks but also overlapped by several years with the esteemed miniaturist Don Silvestro dei Gherarducci (see no. 102). Lorenzo's works include manuscript painting as well as small panels and altarpieces, and he exercised a virtual monopoly over Florentine Camaldolese commissions following the death of Don Silvestro. The Cleveland miniature is a jewel-like initial that reveals Lorenzo to be a master colorist. The initial includes pink, blue, and orange sprays of acanthus leaves on a highly burnished gold ground. The turbaned prophet enclosed within holds a lettered scroll and is emblazoned with a striking yellow, blue, and orange palette; his halo is decorated with a pattern of rosette and circular punches. The flesh-tones tend toward a brownish-green more typical of Sienese painting. Little is known of Lorenzo's training, and some scholars have speculated a Sienese origin. While the attribution and dating of this miniature have been debated over the years, the prophet's three-quarter pose, with its torsion and dramatic contrapposto as well as the use of light and shadow, is highly suggestive of Lorenzo's autograph works of this period. A scholarly consensus in favor of Lorenzo's hand has emerged during recent decades.

Other well-published cuttings are preserved in the National Gallery of Art in Washington (N.814), the Wildenstein Collection at the Musée Marmottan in Paris (5, 14, 18, 54, and 102), and the Detroit Institute of Arts (37.133), among other institutions. SNF

Purchase from the J. H. Wade Fund 1949.536

DIMENSIONS: 16.7 x 16 cm

BIBLIOGRAPHY: New York 1994, 287–96, no. 38b; D'Ancona 1993, 109–11; Eisenberg 1989, 91, fig. 207; Washington 1975, 44–46, no. 13.

105

Miniature from an Antiphonary: Initial M with the Annunciation

ABOUT 1430–38; STEFANO DA VERONA (ITALIAN, LOMBARD, ABOUT 1375–1438)

INK, TEMPERA, AND GOLD ON VELLUM

This miniature originally belonged to an antiphonary, a choir book containing the music for the daily office, the prayers sung in honor of Christ and the saints at the eight canonical hours. An image of the Annunciation appropriately decorates the folio, which contains the text and music for the first antiphon sung at vespers on the feast of the Annunciation: "Missus est Gabriel Angelus ad Miriam Virginem" (The Angel Gabriel was sent to Mary). Gabriel appears to the Virgin who sits demurely behind a desk, reading, while God the Father, leaning from an angelic burst that signifies the realms of heaven, watches as his dove, trailed by three seraphim, flies toward her. In the glowing green landscape background the leaves of each tree are picked out in gold and the crenellations of rose and blue castles and towns punctuate gently rolling hills.

The fantastic, even the bizarre, holds sway in the miniature's upper third, which contains the initial *M*. At its center is a bearded merman; the ends of his fishtail encircle an unhappy moon face, and his arms support the snouts of two extraordinary sea creatures whose scaly bodies form the bows of the *M*. The initial frames a verdant landscape much like the one below, although here, to the left, a small frigate with a plump passenger sails into the distance and, to the right, returns empty. Two rabbits munch the foreground foliage. During the medieval period, it was believed that rabbits could reproduce without the loss of virginity, and thus, they were a symbol of Mary's purity. The meaning of the strange elements surrounding them, however, remains elusive.

Although choral books were produced throughout Europe during this period, the finest were illuminated in Italy. Numbered among the most treasured possessions of a church or monastery, such beautiful books were solely the prerogative of the most wealthy ecclesiastical foundations. A 19th-century penciled inscription on the reverse notes that the miniature came from the church of "SS. Pietro e Paolo in Venice," but that structure—actually a small hospital—no longer exists. The inscription may have confused the hospital with the Dominican convent of SS. Giovanni e Paolo, which likely required a new set of liturgical books at the time of its consecration in 1430, and which could have afforded such splendid furnishings. VB

Gift from J. H. Wade, 1924.431

DIMENSIONS: 19.7 x 16.7 cm

INSCRIBED: on reverse, in pencil: SS. Pietro e Paolo in Venice

BIBLIOGRAPHY: New York 2003, 106; Berkeley 1963, 27, no. 46; Cleveland 1963, 210, no. 67; Baltimore 1962, 76–77, no. 76; Dell'Acqua 1949, 63; De Ricci 1937, 2: 1929; Milliken 1925B, 70.

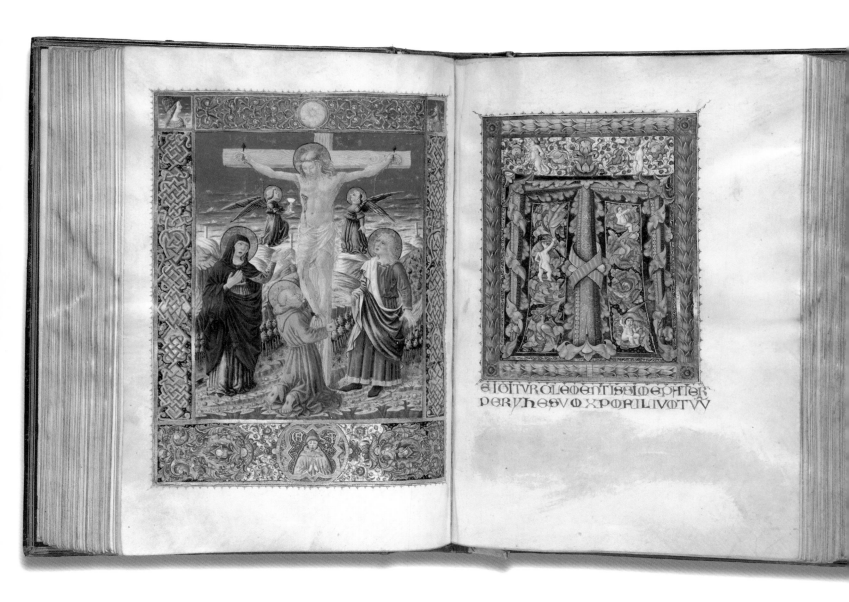

eIGITVR ClℓoeNTISSIoe PAITER
peR ℓhesvoo XPOrilivoTvoo

❖ 106 ❖

Missal

DATED 1469; MINIATURES BY BARTOLOMMEO CAPORALI
(ITALIAN, PERUGIA, ABOUT 1420–1505)
AND HIS BROTHER, JACOPO (GIAPECO) CAPORALI (ITALIAN, PERUGIA, D. 1478)
INK, TEMPERA, AND BURNISHED GOLD ON VELLUM, 400 FOLIOS

According to the colophon on folio 400, this illuminated missal (a liturgical service book for celebrating the Mass) was executed for the Franciscan male convent of S. Francesco di Montone near Perugia in Italy's Umbria region. The buildings are still extant, and the Cleveland missal was very likely intended for use on the church's high altar. The colophon provides the precise date of completion, 4 October 1469, and name of the German scribe, Henricus Haring. Also identified are the names of the convent's guardian, Presbyter Frater Stephanus Cambi, and the two procurators who commissioned the missal, Franciscus Ser Johannis de Ciurellis and Petrus Paulus de Miraculis. These individuals are depicted within the borders of the illustration on folio 185v. Such internal evidence concerning the date, place, commission, and scribe of a manuscript is exceptionally rare.

The illuminations are extensive for a manuscript missal and include a luxuriously decorated *ordo missalis* (opening page of the ordinary of the Mass) on folio 9 with elaborate borders consisting of naturalistically rendered animals and putti; the roundels show St. Francis displaying his stigmata and King David in prayer. Folios 185v–186r are the volume's masterpiece—a two-page deluxe opening to the Canon of the Mass. The recto is composed of a large decorated initial *T[e igitur]* with an elaborate extended crosspiece and highly involved foliate decoration and putti and birds. The verso is a magnificent rendering of a traditional Calvary scene with a crucified Christ flanked by the Virgin and St. John and two angels. The figure of St. Francis kneeling at the foot of the cross attests to the Franciscan usage of the volume. Elaborate use of burnished gold is visible throughout. Scattered through the volume are 31 small historiated initials with various scenes (a Nativity, Pentecost, saints Peter and Paul, and the like). Each of the small initials is further embellished with marginal floral extensions and filigree fillings within some letters.

The most excellent part of the illumination clearly falls to Bartolommeo Caporali, an important documented panel and fresco painter and miniaturist. His hand may be perceived first and foremost in the monumental full-page miniature of the Crucifixion. The corpus of Christ with its imposing musculature is carefully modeled in subtle shades of ocher, yellow, and brown and attests to intensive anatomical studies and a highly developed sense of naturalism on the part of the artist. Christ's head rests on his chest to the right at the moment of death, his face mirroring exhaustion. He wears an almost translucent loincloth beautifully draped in fine folds, suggesting softness. Bartolommeo was likely assisted by his brother, Giapeco, a Perugian miniaturist, who completed the remaining illuminations. SNF

John L. Severance Fund 2006.154

DIMENSIONS: 37 x 26.5 x 9.6 cm

BIBLIOGRAPHY: Caleca 1969; Salmi 1957, 56–57; Rome 1954, 421; Aeschlimann 1940, 37, pl. xxii; Perrott 1934, 173–84; Salmi 1933, 253–72.

Body Jewelry: European Arms and Armor

While often associated exclusively with European knighthood, arms and armor are actually among the world's most ancient crafts. In fact, fabrication techniques reached a very high level of sophistication during the Roman Empire, as can be adduced by the reliefs on the Column of Trajan (AD 114). As an expression of its owner's wealth, taste, and social standing, armor reflected the finest workmanship and materials that means would allow, just as civilian dress.

The history of European armor from the Migration Period onward can be divided into two periods, the age of mail and the age of plate, with an intervening century of transition. Around 1250 a knight was still protected in much the same way as a fifth- or sixth-century horseman who wandered across Europe. He wore a *hauberk* (mail shirt, see no. 107)—the predominant form of metal body defense until about 1350—supplemented by a metal helmet and a shield. Though little early mail has survived, it is well-represented in artistic representations from the period, chiefly in manuscript illuminations, seals, sculpture, and brass tomb effigies. By the beginning of the 13th century, a knight wore a surcoat over his mail both to protect it from rain and to provide relief from the heat of the sun. The surcoat also allowed the display of heraldic arms, which identified the knight on the battlefield. The helmet, however, is credited for the invention of heraldry: because a closed helmet hid the wearer's face, it became necessary to invent some sign by which he could be recognized, and knights mounted decorative crests (usually made of leather and later of wood) on their helmets. After about 1250, the helmet and crest were so important in Germany that they appeared on seals instead of a complete coat of arms.

While mail provided excellent defense against a sword cut and limited protection from axe blows, arrows from a longbow could punch through mail rings. A crossbow (see no. 113), which could fire bolts at three to four times the velocity of a longbow, brought about the final decline of mail armor. The armorer's solution was to devise a surface off which bolts would glance with little or no damage—plate armor. Despite its deficiencies, mail remained in widespread use for many centuries. Even during the 16th century, it was often worn under full plate armor as additional protection and continued to be made in Europe until the 17th century.

A complete suit of plate armor was constructed from numerous individual plates of steel, sometimes more than two hundred, of which no two were identical (see no.

111). Making a suit of armor was thus a tedious, labor-intensive, time-consuming, and strenuous process that required the skills of a number of artisans: an armorer to forge the plates; a polisher (or millman); a finisher to assemble the plates into a suit and fit the pieces with fasteners, pads, and straps; and finally, the decorator, usually a goldsmith or etcher, who embellished the armor for the client. The metal used in armor construction did not have to be thick and heavy in order to be effective. Strength came from the shaping of metal plates, not from their weight.

While arms and munitions armor were produced throughout Europe during the late Middle Ages, the specialty craft of making plate armor was concentrated in a few important centers with access to international trade routes and natural resources such as ore, charcoal, and running water. By the beginning of the 15th century, divergent armor styles were detectable in South Germany and North Italy. The chief armor production centers were found at Nuremberg, Augsburg, Landshut, Innsbruck, Milan, and Brescia. The products of these centers gained international renown and were exported throughout Europe. While the manufacture of low- to middle-quality plate armor flourished in other European cities such as Cologne, Genoa, and even Florence, their products did not achieve the same success or, like the Royal Armouries at Greenwich, England, not until the 16th century.

In addition to functional use in the field, specialized armor and weapons were produced for tournaments, the most popular and spectacular events staged during the Middle Ages and the Renaissance. In the 12th and 13th centuries, when contestants were training to wage war, armor was worn but weapons were blunted "for courtesy." In these "friendly" forms of combat, armored opponents fought each other as a sort of noble sport. Armor for the joust, one of the most popular of these tournament games, was constructed to offer the greatest protection where it was most needed. In the joust, mounted knights rode toward each other and, with lances, attempted to strike their opponent's targe, a kind of shield, or their breastplate. Depending on the type of joust, the goal was to unhorse an opponent, or simply to shatter one's own lance with a well-placed hit. Because the lance would make contact with a knight's left side, jousting armor is heavily reinforced on the left.

A final category of arms and armor was that designated for parade use. Fine armor was an expression of its owner's wealth and sophistication, and the prestige it bestowed upon its wearer was slow to disappear. For those who could afford it, emphasis shifted toward "dress" or "princely" armors—extravagant and costly armors decorated in various ways and intended principally to convey the owner's rank and authority as well as his consummate taste. The most popular decorative techniques were etching, gilding, blueing, and embossing. Traditionally, the styling of armor followed that of civilian costume, and armor was often worn on important social or diplomatic occasions and for official portraiture.

The period from 1450 to 1500 is regarded as the apex of the armorer's craft. During this time armor elements became slender and streamlined with sharply pointed and cusped edges, perhaps inspired by contemporary Gothic architecture. This so-called Gothic armor was not encumbered by the excessive surface decoration fashionable during the Renaissance, but was confined to smooth polished surfaces embellished by elegantly curved flutings or ornamental borders. Beauty was achieved by sublime purity of line. Armor from the Gothic Age, which may today appear drab, was originally polished mirror bright. The play of light on these steel surfaces emphasized the subtle shapes of the armor plates and offered contrast against a knight's colorful plumes and heraldic devices. Around 1500, armor styles began to depart radically from the popular Gothic harnesses and sallets. In keeping with the new Renaissance taste emerging from Italy, German armorers began to emphasize rounded forms and surface ornamentation. Throughout the 16th century armor styles continued to respond to changes in civilian costume and the ever-changing whims of the patron.

Hunting, an important part of aristocratic life, often demanded great panoply and protocol (see no. 112); specialized and beautifully wrought weapons, such as crossbows and eventually firearms, were produced as accessories. No hunting costume was complete without a distinctive hunting sword. Designed primarily to defend against dangerous game such as wild boars or bear, these side arms were also frequently used to dispatch the game at the end of the chase. It was a point of honor among aristocratic hunters to carve and section the game in the field, a further function to which these swords were well suited. They were often made as part of a set, or garniture, that included smaller knives, forks, and other implements. The hunting sword became an object of great elegance with fine detailing, sometimes using precious metals, jewels, ivory, and other sumptuous materials. During the 1600s, such swords began to be treated more as accessories or ornaments than utilitarian objects.

The decoration of both arms and armor employed virtually all the techniques used in contemporary metalwork—etching, gilding, damascening, embossing, engraving, even enameling. Such expressions of virtuosity on the part of the armorer and armor decorator (usually separate individuals) appealed to the individuality of the Renaissance princes who had the means to pay for this costly armor. At this time a stock vocabulary of ornamental motifs, often abstruse, came to be used to decorate arms and armor. These designs ultimately derived from or reflected other branches of Renaissance decorative arts, chiefly goldsmithwork, enameling, and ceramic decoration, but also to a significant degree, print etching. Frequently, the original function of armor was entirely forgotten as the medieval knight was gradually transformed into a courtier, his armor evolving into spectacular body jewelry. An essential part of this panoply were plumes and colorful fabrics attached to armor used in parades and pageants.

At its zenith, European armor reached dazzling sophistication of form and ornamentation, and as such has been referred to as body jewelry and moving sculpture. Nevertheless, the knight, fully clad in plates of steel, was truly and clearly a medieval phenomenon. SNF

107

Mail Hauberk

ABOUT 1400–1450; GERMAN?

RIVETED STEEL AND BRASS RINGS

Mail armor was the predominant form of metal body defense for European knights until about 1350. The term derives from the Old French word *maille* (mesh), implying a protective textile. Each mail garment was constructed of small linked metal rings and "woven" for a specific part of the body. Mail for the torso (a *hauberk*), the head (a *coif*), the legs (*chausses*), and the hands (*mittens*) could be made as separate pieces. A typical 13th-century hauberk reached to mid-thigh and had an integral coif with its own flap (*ventail*) that could be drawn over the mouth and closed with a strap.

Alone, mail afforded little protection. To be effective, it had to be worn over a quilted undergarment, an *aketon*, which both kept the skin from chafing and functioned as a kind of shock absorber for sword blows. To protect their mail from the elements, knights wore surcoats, which also provided relief from the sun's hot rays. A metal helmet and shield completed the costume.

Mail-makers are documented in the city of Cologne as early as 1293; a surviving charter of the mail-makers' guild of Cologne dates to 1391. We know very little about these early armorers, and few examples of mail have survived from this period. Beginning in the early 15th century, however, some drawings and engravings have survived that portray these artisans at work. The skill of mail-making lay in the final linking of thousands of metal rings into a finished product. A hauberk, for example, might include as many as a quarter million rings.

During the 14th century the appearance of the European knight steadily evolved from mailed warrior to the classic icon in full armor. Small plates were gradually added to cover the limbs, then larger ones to protect the torso. By the time King Henry V of England invaded France in 1415, mail had been either completely covered or replaced with plates of steel. SNF

Gift of Mr. and Mrs. John L. Severance 1923.1120

DIMENSIONS: h. 76.2 cm

BIBLIOGRAPHY: Fliegel 2002A, 83–97, 166, no. 92; Fliegel 1998, 35–41, 71–75; Karcheski 1995, 16–19; Gilchrist 1924, no. D1.

108

War Hat

ABOUT 1475–1500; MISSAGLIA WORKSHOP; ITALIAN, MILAN

STEEL

The period from 1450 to 1500 is considered the apex of the armorer's craft. During this time armor elements had a slender, streamlined look with pointed and cusped edges—perhaps inspired by contemporary Gothic architecture. This so-called Gothic armor was not encumbered by the excessive surface decoration fashionable later, during the Renaissance. Instead, the smooth polished surfaces were embellished with elegantly curved flutings or ornamental borders. Armor from the Gothic age may appear drab today, but originally it was polished mirror bright. The play of light on steel surfaces emphasized the subtle shapes of the armor plates and offered distinct contrast to a knight's heraldic devices and colorful plumes. After about 1500, rounded forms and surface decoration dominated armor styles. Over the course of centuries the helmet evolved from a relatively simple, bowl-shaped head shield into a complex piece of a suit of armor.

The form of this *chapel-de-fer* (war hat or kettle hat) originated in the 13th century. The open-faced, wide-brimmed hat was worn by infantry troops. Particularly useful in siegework, descendants of such hats were still in use during the 15th century and are an ancestor of today's common military helmet. The chapel-de-fer was favored by miners and other troops who stormed the battlements of a fortress. Its open face gave wearers a clear field of vision, and its wide brim provided protection from projectiles and objects dropped from above. This helmet achieves its beauty and sculptural elegance from its streamlining. The slight ridge, or comb, down the center improved deflection and increased strength. The rivets along the rim were not only decorative, but a means of attachment for a liner.

Milan was the most important center of armor production in Italy, and the Missaglia family workshop, where this hat was made, was the dominant armorer of that city. The workshop's reputation for quality was such that its commissions extended from common munitions armor to elegantly decorated princely armors. SNF

Gift of Mr. and Mrs. John L. Severance 1916.1565

DIMENSIONS: 36 x 22 x 26.6 cm

MARKS (twice repeated): MY beneath a crown and M beneath a split cross

BIBLIOGRAPHY: Baltimore 2002, 83–97; Fliegel 1998, 60, 164, no. 50; Gilchrist 1924, no. B2.

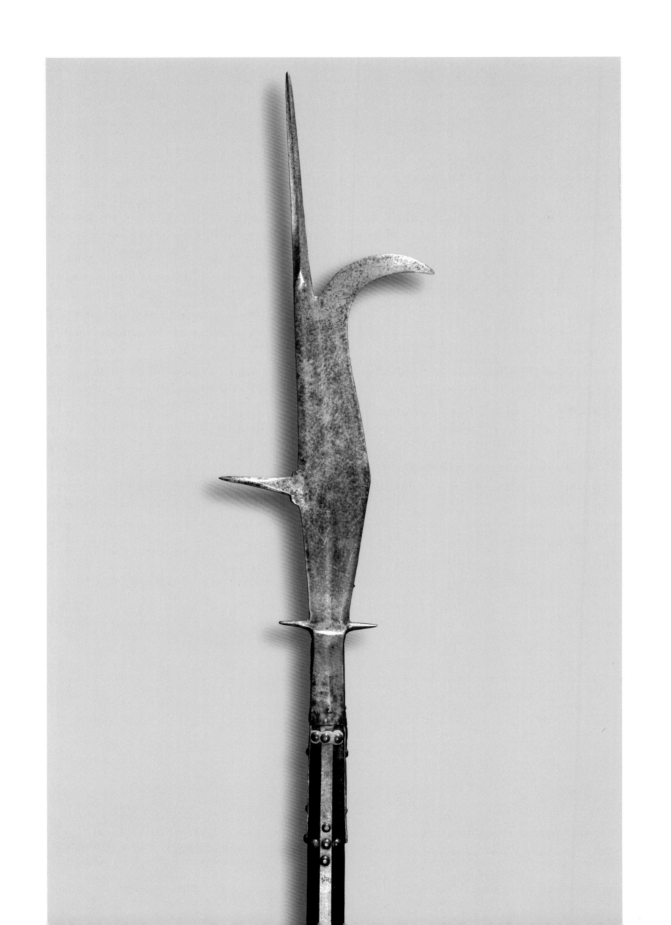

109

Bill

ABOUT 1480; ITALIAN
STEEL WITH WOOD HAFT

"Hafted weapons" is a generic term that, along with "staff weapons" and "pole arms," refers to a family of edged weapons attached to a wooden haft. With the exception of the lance, which was carried by a mounted knight, all other staff weapons were intended to be wielded primarily by men on foot.

In addition to clubs and battleaxes, the bill was one of the earliest staff weapons to be used by medieval infantries and is documented as early as the 13th century. It derived originally from an agricultural tool used to prune vines and trees, and was probably pressed into service by levied troops. With its long shaft, the bill proved effective at reaching mounted men, and a military version soon emerged. The bill's blade is essentially a large hook whose inside and outside curves have long, cleaver-like cutting edges. It is topped by a long spike. The bill was used all over Europe during the 15th century, and it was especially favored by Italian foot soldiers as late as the middle of the 16th century. In the early 16th century the English produced a bill with a shorter blade, described in 1551 by the Venetian ambassador to England:

> English bills have a short thick shaft with an iron like a peasant's hedging bill, but much thicker and heavier than what is used in the Venetian territories, with this they strike so heavily as to unhorse cavalry and it is made short because they like close quarters.

After the mid 16th century, bills were usually carried only as ceremonial weapons, and their form remained basically unchanged. Both faces of parade bills were often richly engraved and bore the insignia and coat of arms of the rulers whose guards carried them. SNF

Gift of Mr. and Mrs. John L. Severance 1916.1835

DIMENSIONS: h. 184.8 cm overall, 77.5 cm (blade)

BIBLIOGRAPHY: Fliegel 2002A, 94–95; Fliegel 1998, 124–31, 168, no. 117; Gilchrist 1924, no. H3. For the quote, see Fliegel 2002A, 95.

110

Estoc

EARLY 16TH CENTURY; GERMAN
STEEL, WOOD, AND LEATHER

The estoc, an auxiliary side arm, hung from a knight's saddle. The fairly long grip and simple cross-shaped hilt in this example are typical. The rigid blade was generally three-sided for strength. A somewhat larger version, the bastard or "hand-and-a-half" sword, was used for fighting on foot, intended to be thrust between the gaps of an opponent's plate armor. It had an elongated pommel and grip, and a rigid diamond-section blade that would not easily break under pressure. Hilts were cruciform until the middle of the 16th century, when curving quillons and ring guards came into use. Some later types have a more developed guard with knuckle bows connected by a loop, anticipating the rapier. Bastard swords were especially favored in the Germanic territories.

Until the 13th century, sword scabbards hung at a knight's left hip, suspended from a thick belt worn at the waist over a surcoat. Toward the 1350s knights began to wear heavy belts at hip level from which they could suspend a sword. The belt was usually decorated with enameled or jeweled clasps hinged together and must have been laced to the coat armor or mail to keep it in place. In the 1420s a diagonal sword belt replaced the hip belt. Both sword and dagger were kept in scabbards or sheaths made of wood covered in leather, sometimes stained a bright color and decorated with gilded appliqués and mounts. By the middle of the 14th century, knights were routinely depicted wearing daggers as accompaniments to their swords.

Medieval European swordsmiths developed different ways to make a sword, and the availability of expensive metal and the skill necessary to forge it gave rise to many jealously guarded secrets. Iron and steel held much of their mystery as the early smiths could not always produce a uniform product. They knew how to extract iron from ore, which could be forged into a bar of iron. Steel must have been produced frequently when the iron was exposed to the carbonizing action of the charcoal fire, resulting in a harder, more resilient blade. SNF

Gift of Mr. and Mrs. John L. Severance 1916.686

DIMENSIONS: h. 156.6 cm

BIBLIOGRAPHY: Fliegel 1998, 111, no. 125; Gilchrist 1924, no. E5. For related objects see Karcheski 1995, 81.

111

Partial Suit of Armor and Chanfron

ABOUT 1510–25; GERMAN, NUREMBERG

STEEL, BRASS, AND LEATHER STRAPS

Distinguished by its regularly fluted surfaces, armor in the Maximilian style was popular in South Germany and Austria during the first decades of the 16th century. Such armor was striking in sunlight, which created a dazzling effect as it reflected on the polished rippling steel. The flutings may have originated as an imitation of the pleated male costume of the day, but they were also a strengthening device similar to corrugated metal. The fluting allowed the armorer to use plates of thinner and therefore lighter steel. Such suits of armor demanded time-consuming and precise work, which drove the production costs so high that the fashion disappeared by 1540.

This partial suit of armor and *chanfron* (inset) would have been part of a garniture for man and horse. The chanfron consisted of a plate of steel contoured to the head from ears to nostrils. Normally, two holes were cut at each side of the forehead for the ears, and earpieces were sometimes riveted around their edges. This example, however, was forged in one piece and belongs in the transitional period between Gothic and Maximilian-style armors. The hinge at the top is for the attachment of the crest plate.

Holy Roman Emperor Maximilian I ruled much of Central Europe and the Low Countries from 1493 until 1519. A great enthusiast of knightly prowess, hunting, and tournaments, and a patron of fine armor, he was also a firm believer in the importance of well-stocked regional arsenals, which he is known to have furnished with arms and armor. In 1478 he established an armor workshop at Innsbruck that, after 1500, was instrumental in popularizing fluted armor throughout Austria and South Germany. Much existing armor in this style dates from the decades immediately following Maximilian's death. SNF

Gift of Mr. and Mrs. John L. Severance 1916.1714.a–j (suit) and 1916.1845 (chanfron)

DIMENSIONS: 45.2 x 37.2 x 17.8 cm (breastplate and tassets), 28.7 x 30.4 x 21.7 cm (close helmet), 59.2 x 33.2 x 10.1 cm (chanfron)

BIBLIOGRAPHY: Fliegel 1998, 70–73, 162, 166; San Francisco 1992, 44–46; Gilchrist 1924, no. A2, J2.

Hunting near Hartenfels

Elector Frederick III of Saxony (Frederick the Wise, 1463–1525), one of the seven German princes empowered to elect the Holy Roman Emperor, named Lucas Cranach the Elder court painter in 1505. Legend has it that in the early days of Cranach's tenure at the Saxon court, the artist startled the courtiers with his realistic drawings of the hunting trophies hanging on the walls of the country residences at Coburg and Locha. So striking were Cranach's depictions of game that the elector took him out to the hunting field, where he could sketch the prince and his courtiers running stags and sticking wild boar. By way of result, Cranach produced several hunt paintings recounting this sanguine courtly pastime for both Frederick and his successors, in whose service the artist also worked.

Cranach painted this scene in the rich game reserve around Schloss Hartenfels near Torgau. Praised by Emperor Charles V in 1547 as a "truly imperial residence," the castle had not been completed in 1540. Cranach must have worked from architectural drawings to produce his faithful rendering of it here, and the painting may have been commissioned to celebrate its construction. Here, the castle's distant but gleaming fairytale spires crown the background of the prickly panoramic landscape, its deep conifer forests and foaming river cut through with a rash of activity at once highly civilized and deeply primitive. Both hunt and painting were staged events, documenting life at the Saxon court as the elector wanted it to be seen. Before the hunt began, horsemen and dogs gathered the animals to be hunted into hedge pens near the river. On the day of the hunt, the gentlemen and ladies of the court arranged themselves in favorable positions to kill the stags as they were released and crossed the river, pursued by the hounds. This is the moment captured here. Elector Johann Frederick I (Johann the Magnanimous, 1503–54) stands in the foreground, resplendent in dark green hunting attire, his crossbow cocked. On the bank at the lower right, his wife, the Electress Sibylle, stands at the head of a party of ladies, poised to take the traditional first shot. The landscape is dotted with portraits of the elector's courtiers, guests, and sons. To his proper right, a young hunter accompanied by three dogs bears the Saxon motto on his sleeve: "May the Word of God Remain into Eternity." His and other hunters' garments are black and gold, the heraldic colors of the house of Saxony. In the upper right and left hand corners, boar and bear hunts, respectively, take place. VB

John L. Severance Fund 1958.425

DIMENSIONS: 116.8 x 170.2 cm

INSCRIBED: Signed lower right on boat with a winged serpent, and dated: 1540

INVENTORY NUMBER, LOWER RIGHT: 1577

BIBLIOGRAPHY: Torgau 2004, 159, no. 219; Kronach/Leipzig 1994, 310–13, no. 131; Schade 1974, 439, no. 338; Francis 1959, 198–205; Friedländer/Rosenberg 1932, 91, no. 331a; Schuchardt 1851, 1: 93.

Crossbow, Cranequin, and Bolts

ABOUT 1553–73 (CROSSBOW); 16TH TO EARLY 17TH CENTURY (BOLTS); GERMAN, SAXONY
CROSSBOW: WALNUT, BONE VENEERS, FLAX CORD, ETCHED STEEL, GILDING, AND WOOL
POMPOMS; CRANEQUIN: ETCHED, CHASED, AND GILDED STEEL; BOLTS: STEEL, WOOD, AND
LEATHER

Firearms gradually replaced crossbows in times of war during the first half of the 16th century, but they became popular weapons for hunting. Crossbows could be held or aimed ready to shoot for long periods of time without strain, and, unlike guns, they discharged silently—a desirable feature for hunting. As a sporting weapon, crossbows were clean and quiet, and fired reusable bolts.

By the middle of the 16th century, sporting crossbows had become very ornate, decorated with bone and mother-of-pearl inlays. Some crossbows, like this example, included richly carved stocks enlivened with the owner's coat of arms. They were also outfitted with complex lock mechanisms in-

corporating hair triggers and other refinements, and more powerful and longer-lasting steel bows had replaced composite bow staves. Crossbows were used as a sporting weapon across the continent, particularly among the noble classes.

This crossbow and its cranequin were made for August I, prince elector of Saxony. The stock of the crossbow is inlaid with engraved staghorn and ebony representations of trophies and musical instruments. The cranequin is engraved with flowers, leaves, masks, trophies, and the elector's coat of arms; even the cranking handle is decorated. August I was well known for his taste in elaborate objects, including rare and costly weapons. The

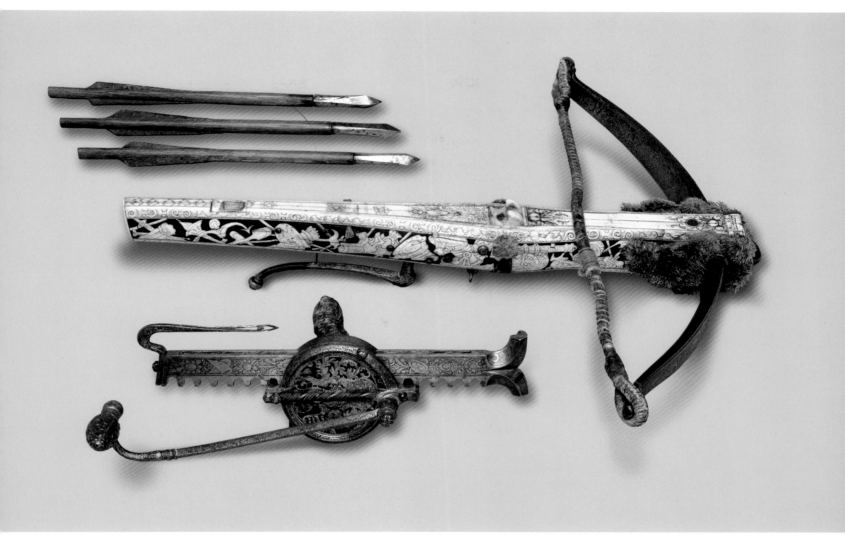

prince electors of Saxony were passionate practitioners of *parforce* hunting with dogs—elaborate, highly rehearsed occasions coordinated by signals from hunting horns. Such hunts took place in vast preserves set aside for the specific use of the ruler of the land. Hunting was not only a sport, it was essential as a source of food. The most desirable game for European nobles was the stag, often reserved for the exclusive hunting pleasure of the reigning monarch, or by special privilege to those he favored. Hunting large game by parties of aristocrats, usually assisted by packs of dogs, was known simply as "the chase."

Prowess at dispatching game and large dangerous animals was a skill to be acquired and practiced among Europe's nobles and, further, was viewed as a class privilege. It carried with it fine points of dress, vocabulary, and protocol, and it was incumbent upon the gentleman of standing to be accomplished in the use of the crossbow. SNF

Gift of Mr. and Mrs. John L. Severance 1916.1723.a–b and 1916.1742.1–5

DIMENSIONS: l. 63.5 cm, bow spread 58.5 (crossbow), l. 44.4 cm (cranequin), l. 37.2 cm (bolts, average)

BIBLIOGRAPHY: Fliegel 1998, 134–37, 173. For comparative objects, see Karcheski 1995, 50; New York 1982, 129–31 and 281–82, no. 88 and 628–30; Gilchrist 1924, no. G9.

Half-Armor for the Foot Tournament

ABOUT 1590; POMPEO DELLA CESA (ITALIAN, ACTIVE 1572–93)
ETCHED AND GILDED STEEL, BRASS RIVETS, LEATHER, AND VELVET FITTINGS

This armor was designed specifically for the foot tournament, a separate event from the equestrian jousts popularized during the Middle Ages that continued into the Renaissance. Combatants fought with swords over a barrier that separated them and protected their legs. Exchanging blows at such close quarters was particularly dangerous, and every attempt was made to protect the competitors. Foot tournament suits have a special locking mechanism that connects the helmet and gorget, the armor for the throat. The rim of the helmet overlaps a ridge on the gorget, which allows the head to turn but prevents an opponent's weapon from slipping between the armor elements.

Pompeo della Cesa, the most renowned Italian armorer of the late 16th century, maintained a large workshop in Milan's Sforza Castle, and his clients included some of the most celebrated noblemen of his day. Fine armor, like this example, was an expression of its owner's wealth, taste, and social rank. Thus it was important that a nobleman's armor be as fashionable as his civilian dress, with the best workmanship and materials his means would allow. Most wealthy patrons afforded the additional expense of embellishing their armors, choosing designs from pattern books. The most popular decorative techniques were etching, gilding, blueing, and embossing. Etching was the most frequently used; here vertical bands of etched strapwork enclose cartouches that, in turn, contain allegorical figures, classical warriors, and trophies. This type of decoration is classic Pompeo and found on more than 40 surviving suits.

The owner of this suit would have worn it with colorful puffed and slashed britches and hose; accessories such as a large ostrich feather plume (there is a brass plume holder on the back of the helmet) and red velvet pickadils between the steel plates would have provided additional dash. Traditionally, the styling of armor followed that of civilian costume. Armor became a favorite status symbol of the European nobility because of the way in which its splendor reflected the wearer's place in society. SNF

John L. Severance Fund 1996.299

DIMENSIONS: 46.5 x 33.8 cm (breastplate), 31.7 x 27.7 x 21.6 cm (helmet)

BIBLIOGRAPHY: Fliegel 1998, 58–59; Karcheski 1995, 47; Larocca 1993, 85–102; Tarassuk 1986, 18–21; Godoy 1984, 67–88; Ewald 1964, 99–105.

aedicula, *pl.* **aediculae** (Latin, "small temple" or "shrine"). A niche or opening framed by columns on either side and surmounted by an entablature and pediment.

Agnus Dei (Latin, "Lamb of God"). The representation of Christ as the lamb whose sacrifice redeemed the sins of humankind, usually shown haloed with an inscribed cross and carrying a flag, pennant, or victory banner. The image is based on John the Baptist's statement upon his first encounter with Christ: "Here is the Lamb of God, who takes away the sin of the world" (John 1:29).

alb, or **alba** (from Latin *tunica alba,* "white tunic"). A full-length, long-sleeved white linen vestment usually belted at the waist with a girdle. It is worn as an undergarment by priests celebrating the Mass.

amphora, *pl.* **amphorae.** A ceramic storage and transportation vessel of various sizes used throughout the ancient world. All have two handles and long necks narrower than their bodies. Their pointed bases, partially embedded in sand or soft ground, allowed upright storage.

ampulla, *pl.* **ampullae.** A small flask made of lead, pewter, silver, or earthenware. In the context of Christian pilgrimage, ampullae typically contained oil from lamps burning at the holy sites or other substances associated with Christian saints or pilgrimage sites.

Andachtsbild, *pl.* **Andachtsbilder** (German, "devotional image"). A type of religious image that evolved in late medieval Germany, intended for devotional contemplation and meditation.

ankh. An ancient Egyptian hieroglyph symbolizing life consisting of a T shape surmounted by a tapered loop.

antiphonary, or **antiphonal.** Used to direct the choir, this largest of all liturgical books contains the music accompanying the daily office, the cycle of devotions to Christ and the saints performed throughout the year.

aquamanile, *pl.* **aquamanilia.** Originally a basin for washing hands, later used to describe vessels from which water was poured in both sacred and secular contexts. Many take the form of beasts, both real and imagined.

arbor vitae (Latin, "tree of life"). A tree in the Garden of Eden whose fruit was reputed to offer everlasting life. In the Middle Ages, a symbolic term for the wood of the cross and also a symbol of Christ himself.

aspersorium, aspergillum (from Latin *aspergere,* "to sprinkle"). Liturgical objects used to sprinkle holy water before and during solemn ceremonies. An *aspersorium* is a bucket holding the consecrated water. An *aspergillum* is a short metal or wooden rod with a brush or metal bulb at one end that is dipped into the water and then shaken to sprinkle the water.

basse-taille (French, "low-cut"). An enameling technique in which a metal surface is engraved or carved in low relief and translucent enamel applied to cover the area.

book of hours. A private prayer book containing the daily devotions used by the laity, produced in considerable numbers during the 13th to 15th centuries. No two are the same as each was designed to fulfill the devotional needs of a specific patron, the wealthiest of whom owned lavishly illuminated versions.

breviary. A liturgical book containing the divine office. In both Eastern and Western churches all clerics must recite the divine office daily, either in church or in private.

censer. A vessel, also called a thurible, in which incense is burned during liturgical ceremonies. Burning charcoal and grains of incense are placed in a metal chamber suspended from three chains; swung by these chains, the censer produces clouds of sweet-smelling smoke.

champlevé (French, "raised field"). An enameling technique in which hollow cells are carved into the surface of a metal object and filled with vitreous enamel that, when fired at a high temperature, hardens and acquires a brilliantly colored appearance.

chasuble. The outermost garment worn by the clergy during the celebration of the Mass. Shaped like a poncho, the chasuble has a hole at its center through which the head passes, leaving the fabric free to fall over the body nearly to the feet.

Chrismon, or **Christogram.** A sacred monogram symbolizing Christ, comprising the first two Greek letters of his name, *X* (chi) and *P* (rho).

ciborium. A domed canopy covering the altar in Roman basilicas and other churches. Also a chalice-shaped vessel with a cover used to contain the consecrated Hosts reserved in the tabernacle.

cire perdue (French, "lost wax"). The metal casting procedure used in the production of hollow or solid sculpture in which a wax model is covered in clay or plaster. The void left after the wax is melted out is then filled with molten metal, and the clay or plaster shell removed to reveal the formed metal.

cloisonné (French, "partitioned"). An enameling technique in which partitions made from thin metal strips affixed to the surface of a metal object are used to separate the spaces into which enamels of different colors are placed.

collet. In metalwork, a device forming a collar around an object needing to be held in place.

colophon. An inscription or device (sometimes pictorial or emblematic) containing the scribe or printer's name and the place and date of production, placed at the end of a book or manuscript.

comes sacrarum largitionum (Latin, "master of the sacred largess"). In the Roman Empire, a powerful official who oversaw the imperial finances, controlling the mints, tax and customs duty collection, the yields of the mines, and the budgets of the civil service and army.

cornucopia (from Latin *cornu copiae*, "horn of plenty"). A symbol of abundance. The legend of the cornucopia derives from Greek mythology: Zeus gave Amalthea a goat's horn with the power to give to the person who possessed it whatever he or she wished.

dalmatic. A long, wide-sleeved tunic that is the traditional liturgical vestment worn by deacons.

Deesis (Greek, "Entreaty"). A popular Byzantine image formula representing Christ flanked by the Virgin and John the Baptist, both with outstretched hands, interceding on behalf of humankind.

Dexiokratousa. A variation on the Byzantine image formula of the Virgin *Hodegetria* in which the Christ child is held in the Virgin's right arm.

émail en ronde bosse (French, "enamel in the round"). An enameling method in which sculptural gold elements are covered with enamel.

encolpion, or **enkolpion** (Greek, "that which is worn on the chest"). A pendant often containing a sacred image or substance that is worn as a protective device by its owner with a chain around the neck.

erotes (plural of Greek *eros*, "love"). Eros is the Greek god of Love. In the Hellenistic period, love could be symbolized by manifold infants, sometimes winged, called erotes, which are the predecessors of Renaissance putti.

eulogia, *pl.* **eulogiai** (Greek, "blessing" or "benediction"). In the Byzantine world, refers to consecrated gifts including the bread of the Eucharist; the blessed bread carried away by the faithful during religious feasts; and tokens acquired by pilgrims at holy sites. Through their contact with a holy place, person, or object, they were considered to possess healing and protective powers.

evangelary. See *lectionary*.

exergue. The space at the bottom of a coin or medal, usually below the central design, which gives the date and/or place of manufacture.

folio. A sheet of paper, parchment, or other material used as a single leaf in a codex. Its faces are referred to as recto and verso (right and left).

galerie des rois (French, "gallery of kings"). A sequence of statues of biblical and historical kings located on the west facades of Gothic cathedrals, either under ornamental canopies, encircling the base of the towers, or flanking portals.

globus cruciger (Latin, "cross-bearing globe"). A globe with a superimposed cross, symbolizing Christ's domination over the world. When carried by an earthly ruler, it denotes the divinely sanctioned authority of the bearer over worldly matters.

gradual. A liturgical book containing all the musical items pertaining to the Mass.

historiated capital or **historiated initial.** A column capital or an initial letter on a manuscript page decorated with animals (both real and imaginary) and/or human figures, often combined with foliage. These decorations may be allegorical or fantastical in nature, or form part of a larger biblical or historical narrative.

Hodegetria (Greek, "She who shows the way"). The Virgin Hodegetria was a popular Byzantine representation of the Virgin holding the Christ child on her left arm and gesturing toward him with her right hand, showing that he is the way to salvation. The term itself seems to derive from the Hodegon Monastery in Constantinople, where the most important *icon* of this type resided from at least the 12th century onward.

icon (from Greek *eikon*, "image"). A representation of one or more sacred figures, such as Christ, the Virgin, or saints, or any other sacred subject that deserves veneration. Today the term is most often associated with painted panels while in the Byzantine period any representation of a sacred person or subject was considered an icon deserving veneration.

iconoclasm. The term generally used to describe the destruction of images, symbols, or monuments, usually for religious or political motives. When capitalized it refers to the period from 726 to 843, when the use and justification of religious images were heatedly debated in the Byzantine Empire.

iconophile (Greek, "icon-friendly"). Someone in favor of religious images or icons and their veneration. The term is usually used in relation to the period of Byzantine *Iconoclasm*. Also a synonym for "iconodule" (from Greek *eikon* and *doulos*, "one who serves images").

intaglio (Italian, "carving"). In jewelry, refers to incised image making. The opposite of cameo, the technique is used to make engraved seals; it leaves a raised design on the material being stamped, especially wax. Also refers to printmaking techniques in which the image is incised into a surface known as the matrix or plate.

kithara. A musical instrument of the lyre family used in ancient Greece, with seven strings of equal length and a solidly built, wooden body, usually with a flat base.

lectionary. A compendium of extracts from the gospels arranged for liturgical usage. Also called an evangelary or a book of pericopes.

locus sanctus, *pl.* **loca sancta** (Latin, "holy place"). A pilgrimage site sanctified by association with a sacred event or the presence of the remains of a saint or other sacred objects.

Logos (Greek, "word" or "reason"). An epithet and concept of Christ first used by John the Evangelist who described Christ as the "Word [logos] . . . made flesh, and dwelt among us" in his gospel (John 1:14).

maenad (Greek, "raving one"). A female worshiper of Dionysos.

mandorla (Italian, "almond"). An almond-shaped aura or halo surrounding the entire body of a holy figure, often used in images of Christ's Ascension and the Virgin's Assumption into heaven.

maphorion (Greek, "shawl" or "veil"). The long veil covering the head and shoulders of the Virgin and female saints. The Virgin's maphorion was one of Constantinople's most prized relics, preserved at the church of the Blachernae.

memento mori (Latin, "remember that you must die"). A genre of widely varied symbols and pictorial themes, all of which share the same purpose, which is to remind people of their own mortality.

Meter Theou (Greek, "Mother of God"). A term used in the Eastern Orthodox Church to refer to the Virgin Mary. Although used less frequently than *Theotokos,* an abbreviation of this epithet is often found on *icons* depicting the Virgin.

mille-fleur (French, "thousand flower"). A decorative background full of flowers and plants.

missal. A book containing all instructions and texts necessary to the celebration of the Mass.

monstrance (from Latin *monstrare,* "to show"). The vessel used in the Roman Catholic Church to display the consecrated Eucharistic Host.

niello. A method of decorating metal objects commonly used in Europe until the Renaissance but rarely after. An alloy of silver, copper, lead, and sulfur, which when rubbed into an engraved pattern on silver or gold and then fired remains dark in the crevices after the object is polished.

oculus (Latin, "eye"). A round eye-like opening or window.

opus interrasile (Latin, "embossed work"). A metalwork technique in which patterns are formed by making openings in flat metal surfaces. Frequently used in jewelry to create lacework patterns.

opus lemovicense (Latin, "Limoges work"). Objects of *champlevé* enamel produced in workshops in and around the city of Limoges in southwestern France.

orans (Latin, "praying"). Figures with both hands raised in a traditional Christian gesture of prayer.

ostensorium (from Latin *ostendere,* "to show"). A glass reliquary in which a relic could be exhibited for public veneration, now often synonymous with *monstrance*.

paludamentum. A Roman military cloak or mantle worn by soldiers and generals. The term also refers to the "scarlet robe" with which Christ was invested (Matthew 27:28).

Pantokrator (Greek, "all-sovereign" or "ruler of all"). A manner of depicting Christ, either full-length or more typically half-length, raising his right hand in blessing and holding an open or closed book in his left hand. Typically found within the central dome of Orthodox churches, also in their apses.

pastiglia. A decorative technique simulating the effects of carving in low relief, in which a thick layer of gesso is applied to a surface, modeled or tooled in low relief, and then painted or gilded.

pericopes. See *lectionary*.

phylactery (from Greek *phylakterion,* "safeguard"). Small container holding texts, relics, or other sacred substances, often worn around the neck by Christians as means of personal protection and safety.

Pietà (from Latin *pietas,* "piety" or "compassion"). A representation of the Virgin Mary mourning over the body of Christ.

pleurants (French, "those who cry"). Representations of mourners.

Prodromos (Greek, "precursor"). An epithet for John the Baptist, considered to be the forerunner of Christ.

psalter. The book of Psalms in the Old Testament, thought to be written in part by David, king of ancient Israel. Also a book containing the Psalms, usually arranged for liturgical or devotional use and sometimes richly illuminated.

pyx, or **pyxis** (Greek, "box"). In Byzantium a generic term for a small box, usually cylindrical and made of ivory. In the medieval West, a small box used to contain consecrated Hosts to be taken to the sick.

repoussé. A metalworking technique in which a malleable metal is ornamented or shaped when hammered from the reverse side.

rinceau. A decorative border or strip featuring stylized vines bearing leaves, fruit, or flowers.

sacramentary. A liturgical book containing all the prayers recited by the priest during the celebration of the Mass. The forerunner of the *missal*.

satyr. In Greek mythology, a magical creature inhabiting the woods and mountains. Half-human and half-beast, satyrs usually possess a goat's tail, flanks, hooves, and horns. Companions of Dionysos, they spend their time drinking, dancing, and chasing nymphs.

solidus (Latin, "solid"). A gold coin introduced by the Romans in 309–10 and used throughout the Byzantine Empire until the 10th century.

spolia (Latin, "spoils" or "booty"). Parts of earlier buildings, sculptures, or other materials reused in new monuments or objects.

sponsus (Latin, "bridegroom"), *f.* **sponsa** (Latin, "bride"). The mystical bridegroom and bride of the Song of Songs. A personification of God and the soul, respectively.

staurotheca (from Greek *stauros,* "cross," and *theke,* "container"). A reliquary container for one of the most sacred relics of Christendom, fragments of the material remains of Christ's cross.

steatite. A type of soapstone almost purely made of talc. Gray to green in color, it is very soft and thus easy to carve.

stigmata (Greek, "marks"). Christ's five wounds from his Crucifixion; one in each hand, one in each foot, and one in his side. Some saints, such as Francis of Assisi, have been granted the imprint of the stigmata.

stylite (from Greek *stylos,* "pillar"). An early Christian ascetic who fled the world for the desert and, perched on a pillar, spent days and nights fasting and praying in belief that the mortification of the body would ensure the salvation of the soul.

tabula ansata (Latin, "tablet with handles"). A horizontal rectangle with handle-like projections on the short vertical sides, used to frame an inscription. Many examples can be found in catacombs and in early Christian and Byzantine ivories. The form was revived in the Renaissance.

Theotokos (Greek, "God-bearer"). An epithet bestowed upon the Virgin Mary at the Council of Ephesus in 431, emphasizing that she gave birth to God, not to a man who became God.

thiasos (Greek, "Bacchic dance"). In ancient Greece a company assembled to celebrate the festival of one of the gods, especially Bacchus/Dionysos, with dancing and singing.

titulus (Latin, "title"). A conventional ancient Roman stone plaque listing an individual's honors and merits or identifying boundaries in the Roman Empire. By extension, the title affixed to Christ's cross, "INRI," an abbreviation of the Latin phrase "Iesvs Nazarenvs Rex Ivdaeorvm" (Jesus of Nazareth, King of the Jews). Also refers to certain of the oldest churches of Rome, called titular churches, and to the title of any church, or the name by which it is known and in which it has been dedicated.

trefoil (from Latin *trifolium,* "three leaves"). Ornamental cusping in the form of three-lobed leaves used in the stonework tracery that primarily decorates windows in Gothic architecture. Also used to describe the form when applied in non-architectural contexts, its tripartite structure makes it a symbol of the Trinity.

trompe l'oeil (French, "fool the eye"). A type of representation in painting in which the illusion of form, space, light, and texture are cunningly contrived to convince the viewer that what they perceive is the actual subject matter and not a two-dimensional equivalent.

vasa sacra (Latin, "sacred vessels"). The receptacles necessary to the celebration of the Mass, namely the chalice and paten, that hold the consecrated Eucharistic wine and bread, respectively.

vernis brun (French, "varnished brown"). A metalworking technique in which a brownish-red surface color is obtained by applying heated linseed oil to copper, which is heated in turn.

verre églomisé. A decorative technique in which glass is engraved, gilded, and painted. So-called in honor of the French framers Remy and Glomy, who revived its use in the 18th century.

Vesperbild, *pl.* **Vesperbilder** (German, "vespers image"). The German equivalent of *Pietà* refers to the use of these images in the Good Friday *vespers* liturgy.

vespers (Latin, "evening"). The evening prayer service in the Roman Catholic and Eastern Orthodox liturgies of the canonical hours.

Zackenstil (German, "jagged style"). A style that emerged in 13th-century Germany and was used in sculpture, painting, stained glass, and manuscript illumination. The hallmark of this style is the angularity of drapery folds taken to an extreme.

Compiled by Elizabeth Saluk and Virginia Brilliant

❖ Bibliography ❖

Aachen 1965
Aachen, Rathaus zu Aachen und Kreuzgang des Domes, 26 June–19
September. *Karl der Große. Werk und Wirkung.* Aachen, 1965.

Adams 1992
Jeremy duQuesnay Adams. "Visigothic Art." In *Spain: A Heritage
Rediscovered 3000 BC–AD 711,* 121–24. Dallas, 1992.

Aeschlimann 1940
Erardo Aeschlimann. *Dictionnaire des miniaturistes du Moyen-âge et de la
Renaissance dans les différentes contrées de l'Europe.* Milan, 1940.

Aeschlimann 1969
Erardo Aeschlimann. "Aggiunte a Nicolò da Bologna." *Arte Lombarda*
14 (1969): 23–35.

Alföldi-Rosenbaum 1996
Elisabeth Alföldi-Rosenbaum. "Women's Mantles with Decorated
Borders." In *Festschrift für Jenö Fitz,* ed. Gyula Fülöp, 105–16.
Székesfehérvár, 1996.

Amsterdam 1985
Amsterdam, Rijksprentenkabinet, Rijksmuseum, 14 March–9 June.
*Livelier than Life: The Master of the Amsterdam Cabinet or the Housebook
Master, ca. 1470–1500,* ed. Jan Piet Filedt Kok. Amsterdam, 1985.

Arensberg 1977
Susan M. Arensberg. "Dionysos: A Late Antique Tapestry." *Boston
Museum Bulletin* 75 (1977): 4–25.

Ashmoleon 1977
Ashmolean Museum Oxford. *A Summary Catalogue of the Continental
Archaeological Collections (Roman Iron Age, Migration Period, Early
Medieval),* ed. Arthur MacGregor. Oxford, 1997.

Athens 1964
Athens, Zappeion Exhibition Hall, 1 April–15 June. *Byzantine Art, an
European Art.* Athens, 1964.

Athens 2000
Athens, Benaki Museum, 16 October 2000–14 January 2001. *The
Mother of God: Representations of the Virgin in Byzantine Art,* ed. Maria
Vassilaki. Milan, 2000.

Athens 2005
Athens, Georgia Museum of Art, 14 May–6 November. *Sacred Art,
Secular Context: Objects of Art from the Byzantine Collection of Dumbarton
Oaks, Washington D.C.,* ed. Asen Kirin. Athens, 2005.

Backes/Dölling 1969
Magnus Backes and Regine Dölling. *Art of the Dark Ages.* New York,
1969.

Ball 1980
Victoria Kloss Ball. *Architecture and Interior Design. A Basic History
through the 17th Century.* New York, 1980.

Baltimore 1947
Baltimore, The Baltimore Museum of Art, organized by the Walters
Art Gallery, 25 April–22 June. *Early Christian and Byzantine Art.*
Baltimore, 1947.

Baltimore 1962
Baltimore, The Walters Art Gallery, 23 October–30 December. *The
International Style: The Arts in Europe around 1400.* Baltimore, 1962.

Baltimore 2002
Baltimore, The Walters Art Museum, 27 October–29 December. *The
Book of Kings: Art, War, and the Morgan Library's Medieval Picture Bible,* ed.
William Noel and Daniel Weiss. Baltimore, 2002.

Bank 1980
Alisa Bank. "Trois croix Byzantines du Musée d'art et d'histoire de
Genève." *Genava* 28 (1980): 97–111.

Baron 1973
Françoise Baron. "L'Annonciation de Javernant: Recherches sur un
groupe de sculptures du XIVe siècle." *Revue du Louvre,* no. 6 (1973):
329–36.

Bartalini 2005
Roberto Bartalini. *Scultura gotica in Toscana: Maestri, monumenti,
cantieri del Due e Trecento.* Siena, 2005.

Baxandall 1980
Michael Baxandall. *The Limewood Sculptors of Renaissance Germany.*
New Haven/London, 1980.

Bent 1992
George R. Bent. "The Scriptorium at S. Maria degli Angeli and
Fourteenth-Century Manuscript Illumination: Don Silvestro dei
Gherarducci, Don Lorenzo Monaco, and Giovanni del Biondo."
Zeitschrift für Kunstgeschichte 55 (1992): 507–23.

Berenson 1908
Bernard Berenson. *The Central Italian Painters.* London/New York,
1908.

Bergman 1980
Robert P. Bergman. *The Salerno Ivories. Ars Sacra from Medieval Amalfi.*
Cambridge, 1980.

Bergmann 1977
Marianne Bergmann. *Studien zum römischen Porträt des 3. Jahrhunderts
n. Chr.* Bonn, 1977.

Bergmann 1999
Marianne Bergmann. *Chiragan, Aphrodisias, Konstantinopel. Zur mytholo-
gischen Skulptur der Spätantike.* Palilia 7. Wiesbaden, 1999.

Berkeley 1963
Berkeley, University of California Art Gallery, 24 April–8 June. *Pages
from Medieval and Renaissance Illuminated Manuscripts from the Tenth to
the Early Sixteenth Centuries: An Exhibition,* ed. William M. Milliken.
Berkeley, 1963.

Bernard 1971
Bernard of Clairvaux. "St Bernard to William of St. Thierry," trans.
Caecilia Davis-Weyer. In *Early Medieval Art, 300–1150: Sources and
Documents,* 168–69. New York, 1971.

Bier 1951
Justus Bier. "Riemenschneider's St. Jerome and His Other Works in
Alabaster." *Art Bulletin* 33 (1951): 226–34.

Bier 1960
Justus Bier. "Two Statues: St. Stephen and St. Lawrence by
Riemenschneider in the Cleveland Museum of Art." *Art Quarterly*
23/3 (1960): 215–27.

Bier 1982
Justus Bier. *Tilman Riemenschneider. His Life and Work.* Lexington, 1982.

Bober 1953
Harry Bober. "André Beauneveu and Mehun-sur-Yèvre." *Speculum* 28 (1953): 741–53.

Bode 1887
Wilhelm Bode. *Geschichte der deutschen Plastik.* Berlin, 1887.

Böhler 1938
Julius Böhler. *Sammlung Georg Schuster, München.* Munich, 1938.

Böhme-Schönberger 1997
Astrid Böhme-Schönberger. *Kleidung und Schmuck in Rom und den Provinzen.* Stuttgart, 1997.

Bonaventure 1961
Saint Bonaventure. *Meditations on the Life of Christ: An Illustrated Manuscript of the Fourteenth Century, Paris, Bibliothèque Nationale, MS. Ital. 115,* trans. and ed. Isa Ragusa and Rosalie B. Green. Princeton, 1961.

Bond 1962
William H. Bond. *Supplement to the Census of Medieval and Renaissance Manuscripts in the United States and Canada.* New York, 1962.

Boston 1940
Museum of Fine Arts, Boston, 7 February–24 March. *Arts of the Middle Ages, 1000–1400.* Boston, 1940.

Brandt 1987
Michael Brandt. "Studien zur Hildesheimer Emailkunst des 12. Jahrhunderts." Ph.D. diss. Universität Braunschweig, 1986. Hildesheim, 1987.

Brandt 1998
Michael Brandt. "Aus dem Kunstkreis Heinrichs des Löwen? Anmerkungen zu Laurentius- und Apostelarm aus dem Welfenschatz." In *Der Welfenschatz und sein Umkreis,* ed. Joachim Ehlers and Dietrich Kötzsche, 353–68. Mainz, 1998.

Branner 1968
Robert Branner. "The Painted Medallions in the Sainte-Chapelle in Paris." *Transactions, American Philosophical Society,* n.s. 58, no. 2 (1968): 1–42.

Branner 1971
Robert Branner. "Rediscovering a Parisian Paintshop of the Thirteenth Century." *Boston Museum Bulletin* 69 (1971): 165–72.

Braunschweig 1995
Braunschweig, Herzog Anton Ulrich-Museum. *Heinrich der Löwe und seine Zeit: Herrschaft und Repräsentation der Welfen 1125–1235,* ed. Jochen Luckhardt and Franz Niehoff. Munich, 1995.

Bréhier 1951
Louis Bréhier. "Un Trésor d'argenterie ancienne au Musée de Cleveland." *Syria* 27 (1951): 256–64.

Brinkmann 1996
Bodo Brinkmann. "Master of Otto van Moerdrecht." In *The Dictionary of Art.* Vol. 20, 740–41. New York, 1996.

Brinkmann/Kemperdick 2002
Bodo Brinkmann and Stephan Kemperdick. *Deutsche Gemälde im Städel 1300–1500.* Mainz, 2002.

Brown 2000
Katharine R. Brown, ed. *From Attila to Charlemagne: Arts of the Early Medieval Period in The Metropolitan Museum of Art.* New York/New Haven, 2000.

Bruhn 1993
Jutta-Anette Bruhn. *Coins and Costume in Late Antiquity.* Washington, 1993.

Buckton 1983
David Buckton. "The beauty of holiness: *opus interrasile* from a Late Antique workshop." *Jewellery Studies* 1 (1983–84): 15–19.

Bullough 1965
Donald A. Bullough. "The Ostrogothic and Lombard Kingdoms." In *The Dark Ages,* ed. D. Talbot Rice, 158–74. London, 1965.

Butcher 1976
Sarnia A. Butcher. "Enamelling." In *Roman Crafts,* ed. Donald Strong and David Brown, 42–51. London, 1976.

Cahn 1975
Walter Cahn. "A Twelfth-Century Decretum Fragment from Pontigny." *CMA Bulletin* 62 (1975): 47–59.

Cahn 1999
Walter Cahn, ed. *Romanesque Sculpture in American Collections.* Vol. 2. Turnhout, 1999.

Caillet 1988
Jean-Pierre Caillet. "La croix byzantine du musée de Cluny." *La revue du Louvre et des Musées de France* 38 (1988): 208–17.

Caleca 1969
Antonino Caleca. *Miniatura in Umbria.* Vol. 1: *La Biblioteca Capitolare di Perugia.* Florence, 1969.

Cambridge 2005
Cambridge University, University Library and The Fitzwilliam Museum, 26 July–11 December. *The Cambridge Illuminations: Ten Centuries of Book Production in the Medieval West,* ed. Paul Binski and Stella Panayotova. London, 2005.

Cameron/Hall 1999
Eusebius. *Life of Constantine,* trans. with introduction and commentary by Averil Cameron and Stuart Hall. Oxford, 1999.

Camille 1998
Michael Camille. *The Medieval Art of Love: Objects and Subjects of Desire.* New York, 1998.

Caudron 1993
Simone Caudron. "Les châsses reliquaires de Thomas Becket émaillées à Limoges: leur géographie historique." *Bulletin de la Société archéologique et historique du Limousin* 121 (1993): 55–83.

Caudron 1999
Simone Caudron. "Thomas Becket et l'Oeuvre de Limoges." In *Limoges* 1999, 56–68.

Cheney 1941
Thomas L. Cheney. "A French Ivory Mirror-Back of the Fourteenth Century." *CMA Bulletin* 28 (1941): 124–25.

Christie's 1970
Christie, Manson, and Woods, London. *Ancient Jewellery, Antiquities, Gold Medallions and Coins.* Sale catalogue, 19 October 1970. London, 1970.

Christlein 1991
Rainer Christlein. *Die Alamannen: Archäologie eines lebendigen Volkes.* Stuttgart/Aalen, 1991.

Clark 1937
Kenneth W. Clark. *A Descriptive Catalogue of Greek New Testament Manuscripts in America.* Chicago, 1937.

Cleveland 1916
The Cleveland Museum of Art, 6 June–20 September 1916. *Inaugural Exhibition.* Cleveland, 1916.

Cleveland 1936
The Cleveland Museum of Art, 26 June–4 October. *The Twentieth Anniversary Exhibition. The Official Art Exhibit of the Great Lakes Exposition.* Cleveland, 1936.

Cleveland 1963
The Cleveland Museum of Art, 6 August–15 September. *Gothic Art 1360–11.* Exh. cat. "A Missal for a King." *CMA Bulletin* 50 (1963).

Cleveland 1967
The Cleveland Museum of Art, 16 November 1966–29 January 1967. *Treasures from Medieval France,* ed. William D. Wixom. Cleveland, 1967.

Cleveland 1975
The Cleveland Museum of Art. *Renaissance Bronzes from Ohio Collections,* William D. Wixom. Cleveland, 1975.

Cleveland 1986
The Cleveland Museum of Art, 10 June–27 July. *Progressive Vision: The Planning of Downtown Cleveland 1903–1930,* Holly Rarick. Cleveland, 1986.

Cleveland 1991
The Cleveland Museum of Art, 7 June–8 September. *Object Lessons: Cleveland Creates an Art Museum,* ed. Evan H. Turner. Cleveland, 1991.

Cleveland 1996
The Cleveland Museum of Art, 19 May–21 July. *Transformations in Cleveland Art 1796–1946: Community and Diversity in Early Modern America,* ed. William H. Robinson and David Steinberg. Cleveland, 1996.

Cleveland 1999
The Cleveland Museum of Art, 19 December 1999–27 February 2000. *The Jeanne Miles Blackburn Collection of Manuscript Illuminations,* Stephen N. Fliegel. Cleveland, 1999.

Cleveland Studies
Cleveland Studies in the History of Art

CMA Bulletin
Bulletin of The Cleveland Museum of Art

CMA European Paintings 1974
European Paintings before 1500. Catalogue of Paintings, pt. 1. Cleveland, 1974.

CMA Handbook 1958
The Handbook of The Cleveland Museum of Art. Cleveland, 1958. Rev. eds. 1966, 1969, 1978, 1991.

CMA Masterpieces 1992
The Cleveland Museum of Art. Masterpieces From East and West. New York, 1992.

Cook 1999
William R. Cook. *Images of St. Francis of Assisi in Painting, Stone and Glass from the Earliest Images to ca. 1320 in Italy: A Catalogue.* Florence/Perth, 1999.

Cutler 1983
Anthony Cutler. "The Dumbarton Oaks Psalter and New Testament. The Iconography of the Moscow Leaf." *Dumbarton Oaks Papers* 37 (1983): 35–45.

Cutler 1984
Anthony Cutler. "On Byzantine Boxes." *Journal of the Walters Art Gallery* 42/43 (1984–85): 32–47.

Dahmen 2001
Karsten Dahmen. *Untersuchungen zu Form und Funktion kleinformatiger Porträts der römischen Kaiserzeit.* Paderborn, 2001.

Dalton 1904
Osborne M. Dalton. "Two Medieval Caskets with Subjects from Romance." *Burlington Magazine* 5 (1904): 299–309.

Dalton 1911
Ormande M. Dalton. *Byzantine Art and Archaeology.* Oxford, 1911.

D'Ancona 1969
Paolo d'Ancona. "Nicolò da Bologna miniaturista del secolo XIV." *Arte Lombarda* 14 (1969): 1–22.

D'Ancona 1993
Mirella Levi d'Ancona. *The Choir Books of Santa Maria degli Angeli in Florence.* Vol. 1: *Illuminators and Illuminations of the Choir Books from Santa Maria degli Angeli and Santa Maria Nuova and Their Documents,* 14–18. Florence, 1993–94.

Darcel 1877
Alfred Darcel. "Exposition retrospective de Lyon." *Gazette des Beaux-Arts* 16 (1877): 180–81.

Davezac 1983
Bertrand Davezac. "Monumental Head from Thérouanne." *Bulletin, The Museum of Fine Arts, Houston* 7 (Winter 1983): 11–23.

David 1951
Henri David. *Claus Sluter.* Paris, 1951.

De Benedictis 1979
Cristina De Benedictis. *La pittura senese.* Florence, 1979.

De Coo 1965
Jozef de Coo. "L'Ancienne collection Micheli au Musée Mayer van den Bergh." *Gazette des Beaux-Arts,* 6 pér., 66 (1965): 345–70.

Dell'Acqua 1949
Gian Alberto Dell'Acqua. *Arte Lombarda dai Visconti agli Sforza.* Milan, 1949.

Deppert-Lippitz 1996
Barbara Deppert-Lippitz. "Late Roman Splendor: Jewelry from the Age of Constantine." *Cleveland Studies* 1 (1996): 30–71.

De Ricci 1937
Seymour De Ricci. *Census of Medieval and Renaissance Manuscripts in the United States and Canada.* New York, 1937.

Der Nersessian 1965
Sirarpie Der Nersessian. "A Psalter and New Testament Manuscript at Dumbarton Oaks." *Dumbarton Oaks Papers* 19 (1965): 155–83.

Destree 1902
Joseph Destree, ed. Musees Royaux des Arts Decoratifs et Industriels. *Catalogue des ivoires, des objets en nacre, en os gravé et en cire peinte.* Brussels, 1902.

Detroit 1960
The Detroit Institute of Arts, October–December. *Flanders in the Fifteenth Century: Art and Civilization.* Detroit, 1960.

Detroit 1985
The Detroit Institute of Arts, 23 October 1985–5 January 1986. *Italian Renaissance Sculpture in the Time of Donatello: an exhibition to commemorate the 600th anniversary of Donatello's birth and the 100th anniversary of the Detroit Institute of Arts,* ed. Alan Phipps Darr. Detroit, 1985.

Detroit 1997
The Detroit Institute of Arts, 7 March–31 August. *Images in Ivory: Precious Objects of the Gothic Age,* ed. Peter Barnet. Detroit/Princeton, 1997.

De Winter 1977
Patrick M. De Winter. "The Patronage of Philippe le Hardi." Ph.D. diss. New York University, 1977.

De Winter 1981A
Patrick M. De Winter. "Art, Devotion and Satire: The Book of Hours of Charles III, the Noble, King of Navarre, at the Cleveland Museum of Art." *Gamut* 2 (Winter 1981): 42–59.

De Winter 1981B
Patrick M. De Winter. "A Book of Hours of Queen Isabel la Católica." *CMA Bulletin* 68 (1981): 342–427.

De Winter 1983A
Patrick M. De Winter. "Bolognese Miniatures at the Cleveland Museum." *CMA Bulletin* 70 (1983): 314–38.

De Winter 1983B
Patrick M. De Winter. "Visions of the Apocalypse in Medieval England and France." *CMA Bulletin* 70 (1983): 396–417.

De Winter 1985A
Patrick M. de Winter. *La Bibliothèque de Philippe le Hardi, Duc de Bourgogne (1364–1404).* Paris, 1985.

De Winter 1985B
Patrick M. De Winter. "The Sacral Treasure of the Guelphs." *CMA Bulletin* 72 (1985).

De Winter 1987
Patrick M. De Winter. "Art from the Duchy of Burgundy." *CMA Bulletin* 74 (1987): 405–49.

Diehl 1922
Charles Diehl. "L'evengélaire de l'impératrice Catherine Commène." In *Comptes Rendus de Séances de l'Académie des Inscriptions et Belles-lettres,* 243–48. Paris, 1922.

Diehl 1927
Charles Diehl. "Monuments byzantins inédits du onzième siècle." *Art Studies: Medieval, Renaissance and Modern* 5 (1927): 3–9.

Dijon/Cleveland 2004
Dijon, Musée des Beaux-Arts, 28 May–15 September; The Cleveland Museum of Art, 24 October 2004–9 January 2005. *Art from the Court of Burgundy (1364–1419),* ed. Stephen N. Fliegel and Sophie Jugie. English ed. Paris, 2004.

Dixon 1976
Philip Dixon. *Barbarian Europe.* London, 1976.

Dodd 1973
Erica Cruikshank Dodd, *Byzantine Silver Treasures.* Monographien der Abegg-Stiftung Bern 9. Bern, 1973.

Donceel-Voûte 1988
Pauline Donceel-Voûte. *Les pavements des églises Byzantines de Syrie et du Liban. Décor, archéologie et liturgie.* Publications d'histoire de l'art et d'archéologie de l'université catholique de Louvain 69. Louvain, 1988.

Downey 1953
Glanville Downey. "The Dating of the Syrian Liturgical Silver in the Cleveland Museum." *Art Bulletin* 35, no. 2 (1953): 143–45.

Downey 1963
Glanville Downey. *Ancient Antioch.* Princeton, 1963.

Durrer 1901
Robert Durrer. "Die Maler-und Schreiberschule von Engelberg." *Anzeiger für Schweizerische Altertumskunde,* Neue Folge 3 (1901): 42–55 and 122–176.

Duval 1973
Noël Duval, "Un grand medallion monétaire du IVe siècle." *La revue du Louvre* 6 (1973): 367–74.

Duval 1978
Noël Duval. "Art Chretien, exposition au Metropolitan Museum de New York." *Archeologia* 120 (1978): 40.

Eastman 1927
Alvan C. Eastman. "Byzantine Ivories in American Museums." *Art in America* 15 (1927): 157–68.

Egbert 1970
Virginia Wylie Egbert. "The Reliquary of Saint Germain." *Burlington Magazine* 112 (June 1970): 359–63.

Ehlers/Kötzsche 1998
Joachim Ehlers and Dietrich Kötzsche, eds. *Der Welfenschatz und sein Umkreis.* Mainz, 1998.

Eisenberg 1989
Marvin Eisenberg. *Lorenzo Monaco.* Princeton, 1989.

Eisler 1977
Colin Eisler. *Paintings from the Samuel H. Kress Collection, European Schools Excluding Italian.* Oxford, 1977.

Elbern 1969
Victor E. Elbern. "Neue Funde goldener Geräte des christlichen Kultes in der Frühchristlich-byzantinischen Sammlung Berlin." In *Akten des VII. Internationalen Kongresses für Christliche Archäologie, Trier 5–11 September 1965.* Vol. 1, 493–97. Studi di Antichità Cristiana 27. Vatican City/Berlin, 1969.

Engemann 1972
Josef Engemann. "Anmerkungen zu spätantiken Geräten des Alltagslebens mit christlichen Bildern, Symbolen und Inschriften." *Jahrbuch für Antike und Chistentum* 15 (1972): 154–73.

Engemann 1973
Josef Engemann. "Palästinensische Pilgerampullen im F. J. Dölger-Institut in Bonn." *Jahrbuch für Antike und Christentum* 16 (1973): 5–27.

Engemann 2002
Josef Engemann. "Palästinensische Pilgerampullen. Erstveröffentlichungen und Berichtigungen." *Jahrbuch für Antike und Christentum* 45 (2002): 153–169.

Ewald 1964
Gerhard Ewald. "Ein unbekanntes Bildnis von Salomon Adler." *Anzeiger des Germanischen Nationalmuseums* (1964): 99–105.

Falke 1930
Otto von Falke. "Hildesheimer Goldschmiedewerke des 12. Jahrhunderts im Welfenschatz." *Pantheon* 5 (1930): 266–74.

Falke/Schmidt/Swarzenski 1930
Otto von Falke, Robert Schmidt, and Georg Swarzenski. *Der Welfenschatz.* Frankfurt am Main, 1930.

Filedt Kok 1983
J. P. Filedt Kok. "The Prints of the Master of the Amsterdam Cabinet." *Apollo* 117 (1983): 427–36.

Filippini/Zucchini 1947
Francesco Filippini and Guido Zucchini. *Miniatori e pittori a Bologna: Documenti dei secoli XIII e XIV.* Florence, 1947.

Fillitz 1967
Hermann Fillitz. *Zwei Elfenbeinplatten aus Süditalien.* Monographien der Abegg-Stiftung Bern 2. Riggisberg, 1967.

Fliegel 1990
Stephen N. Fliegel. "A Little-Known Celtic Stone Head." *CMA Bulletin* 77 (1990): 82–103.

Fliegel 1998
Stephen N. Fliegel. *Arms and Armor: The Cleveland Museum of Art.* Cleveland, 1998.

Fliegel 2002A
Stephen N. Fliegel. "The Art of War: Thirteenth-Century Armor." In Baltimore 2002, 83–97.

Fliegel 2002B
Stephen N. Fliegel. "The Cleveland Table Fountain and Gothic Automata." *Cleveland Studies* 7 (2002): 6–49.

Fliegel 2004
Stephen N. Fliegel. "Patronage and the Burgundian Court." *Magazine Antiques* (October 2004): 142–51.

Florence 1989
Florence, Museo Nazionale del Bargello, 20 March–25 June. *Arti del Medio Evo e del Rinascimento: Omaggi ai Carrand, 1889–1986.* Florence, 1989.

Förster 1856
Ernst Förster. *Denkmale deutscher Baukunst, Bildnerei und Malerei von der Einführung des Christenthums bis auf die neueste Zeit.* 2 vols. Leipzig, 1856.

Forsyth 1986
William H. Forsyth. "A Fifteenth-Century Virgin and Child attributed to Claus de Werve." *Metropolitan Museum Journal* 21 (1986): 41–63.

Francis 1932
Henry S. Francis. "A German Primitive of the Swabian School." *CMA Bulletin* 19 (1932): 127–31.

Francis 1936
Henry S. Francis. "A Panel by the Master of Heiligenkreuz. A Memorial to John Long Severance." *CMA Bulletin* 23 (1936): 153–56.

Francis 1942
Henry S. Francis. "An Adoration of the Magi by Giovanni di Paolo." *CMA Bulletin* 29 (1942): 166–68.

Francis 1943
Henry S. Francis. "The Lovers: A Swabian Gothic Picture of Secular Life in the Fifteenth Century." *Gazette des Beaux-Arts* 30 (1943): 343–54.

Francis 1952
Henry S. Francis. "The Schlägl Altarpiece." *CMA Bulletin* 39 (1952): 213–15.

Francis 1953
Henry S. Francis. "A Sienese Madonna and Child by Lippo Memmi." *CMA Bulletin* 40 (1953): 59–61.

Francis 1955
Henry S. Francis. "A Fourteenth-Century Annunciation." *CMA Bulletin* 42 (1955): 215–19.

Francis 1959
Henry S. Francis. "The *Stag Hunt* by Lucas Cranach the Elder and Lucas Cranach the Younger." *CMA Bulletin* 46 (1959): 198–205.

Francis 1961
Henry S. Francis. "An Altarpiece by Ugolino da Siena." *CMA Bulletin* 48 (1961): 194–205.

Francis 1966
Henry S. Francis. "Jean de Beaumetz: Calvary with a Carthusian Monk." *CMA Bulletin* 53 (1966): 329–38.

Frankfurt 1981
Frankfurt, Liebieghaus–Museum alter Plastik, 1 November 1981–17 January 1982. *Dürers Verwandlung in der Skulptur zwischen Renaissance und Barock,* ed. Herbert Beck. Frankfurt am Main, 1981.

Frankfurt 1983
Frankfurt, Liebieghaus–Museum Alter Plastik, 16 December 1983–11 March 1984. *Spätantike und frühes Christentum,* ed. Dagmar Stutzinger. Frankfurt am Main, 1983.

Freiburg 1978
Freiburg, Augustinermuseum, 10 September–22 October. *Mystik am Oberrhein und in benachbarten Gebieten,* ed. Hans H. Hofstätter and Dietmar Lüdke. Freiburg im Breisgau, 1978.

Freuler 1994
Gaudenz Freuler. "Don Silvestro dei Gherarducci." In New York 1994, 124–76.

Freuler 1997
Gaudenz Freuler. *Tendencies of Gothic in Florence: Don Silvestro dei Gherarducci.* Sec. 4, vol. 7, pt. 2, pp. 273–550 of *A Critical and Historical Corpus of Florentine Painting,* ed. Miklós Boskovits. Florence, 1997.

Friedländer/Rosenberg 1932
Max J. Friedländer and Jakob Rosenberg. *Die Gemälde von Lucas Cranach.* Berlin, 1932.

Frinta 1965
Mojmír Frinta. "An Investigation of the Punched Decoration of Medieval Italian and Non-Italian Panel Paintings." *Art Bulletin* 48 (1965): 261–65.

Fritz 1998
Johann Michael Fritz. "Der Rückdeckel des Plenars Herzog Ottos des Milden von 1339 und verwandte Werke." In Ehlers/Kötzsche 1998, 367–85.

Frolow 1966
Anatole Frolow. "Le Médaillon Byzantin de Charroux." *Cahiers Archéologiques* 16 (1966): 39–50.

Fuchs 1997
Karlheinz Fuchs, ed. *Die Alamannen.* Stuttgart, 1997.

Galavaris 1966
George Galavaris. "Brotstempel." In *Reallexikon zur Byzantinischen Kunst,* ed. Klaus Wessel. Vol. 1, 747–52. Stuttgart, 1966.

Galavaris 1970
George Galavaris. *Bread and the Liturgy: The Symbolism of Early Christian and Byzantine Bread Stamps.* Madison, 1970.

Ganz 1960
Paul Ganz. *Geschichte der Kunst in der Schweiz.* Basel, 1960.

Garzelli 1969
Annarosa Garzelli. *Sculture toscane nel Dugento e nel Trecento.* Florence, 1969.

Gauthier 1966
Marie-Madeleine Gauthier. "Une châsse limousine du dernier quart du XIIe siècle, themes iconographiques, composition, et essai de chronologie." In *Mélanges offerts à René Crozet,* ed. Pierre Gallais and Yves-Jean Rion, 937–51. Poitiers, 1966.

Gauthier 1972
Marie-Madeleine Gauthier. *Émaux du moyen âge occidental.* Fribourg, 1972.

Gauthier 1983
Marie-Madeleine Gauthier. *Les routes de la foi: reliques et reliquaries de Jerusalem à Compostelle.* Fribourg, 1983.

Gauthier 1987
Marie-Madeleine Gauthier. *Catalogue international de l'Oeuvre de Limoges.* Vol. 1: *L'Époque romane.* Paris, 1987.

Gerstenberg 1941
Kurt Gerstenberg. *Tilman Riemenschneider.* Vienna, 1941.

Gibbons/Ruhl 1974
Donald F. Gibbons and Katherine C. Ruhl. "Metallurgical Examination." *CMA Bulletin* 61 (1974): 268–69.

Gilchrist 1924
Helen Ives Gilchrist. *A Catalogue of Arms and Armor Presented to The Cleveland Museum of Art by Mr. and Mrs. John Long Severance.* Cleveland, 1924.

Gillerman 2001
Dorothy W. Gillerman. *Gothic Sculpture in America.* Vol. 2: *The Museums of the Midwest.* Turnhout, 2001.

Glaber 1981
Radulfus Glaber. "Miracles of Saint-Benoit," trans. Elizabeth Gilmore Holt. In *A Documentary History of Art.* Vol. 1: *The Middle Ages,* 18. Princeton, 1981.

Godoy 1984
José A. Godoy. "Emmanuel-Philibert de Savoie (1528–1580): un portrait, une armure." *Genava* 32 (1984): 67–88.

Goldschmidt 1914–26
Adolph Goldschmidt. *Die Elfenbeinskulpturen.* 4 vols. Berlin, 1914–26.

Goldschmidt/Weitzmann 1979A
Adolph Goldschmidt and Kurt Weitzmann. *Die byzantinischen Elfenbeinskulpturen des X. bis XIII. Jahrhunderts.* Vol. 1: *Kästen.* Berlin, 1930; reprint 1979.

Goldschmidt/Weitzmann 1979B
Adolph Goldschmidt and Kurt Weitzmann. *Die byzantinischen Elfenbeinskulpturen des X. bis XIII. Jahrhunderts.* Vol. 2: *Reliefs.* Berlin, 1934; reprint 1979.

Gonosovà/Kondoleon 1994
Anna Gonosovà and Christine Kondoleon. *Art of Late Rome and Byzantium in the Virginia Museum of Fine Arts.* Richmond, 1994.

Gordon 1981
Dillian Gordon. "A Sienese verre eglomisé and its setting." *Burlington Magazine* 123 (1981): 148–53.

Gosebruch 1979
Martin Gosebruch. "Die Braunschweiger Gertrudiswerkstatt. Zur spätottonischen Goldschmiedekunst in Sachsen." *Niederdeutsche Beiträge zur Kunstgeschichte* 18 (1979): 9–42.

Gotha 1998
Gotha, Schloss Fiederstein, 7 June–20 July. *Jahreszeiten der Gefühle- Das Gothaer Liebespaar und die Kunst der Hohen Minne im Spätmittelalter,* ed. Allmuth Schuttwolf et al. Stuttgart, 1998.

Grabar 1958
André Grabar. *Ampoules de Terre Sainte (Monza–Bobbio).* Paris, 1958.

Graeven 1899
Hans Graeven. "Adamo e Eva sui cofanetti d'avorio byzantini." *L'Arte* 2 (1899): 297–315.

Green 1948
Rosalie B. Green. "Daniel in the Lions' Den as an Example of Romanesque Typology." Ph.D. diss. University of Chicago, 1948.

Green 1986
Miranda Green. *The Gods of the Celts.* Gloucester, 1986.

Grimme 1965
Ernst G. Grimme. " 'Die Lukasmadona' und das 'Bustkreuz Karls des Großen'." In *Miscellanea Pro Arte. Hermann Schnitzler zur Vollendung des 60. Lebensjahres am 13. Januar 1965,* ed. Peter Bloch and Joseph Hoster, 48–54. Düsseldorf, 1965.

Grimme 1972
Ernst G. Grimme. *Der Aachener Domschatz (Aachener Kunstblätter 42 [1972]).* Aachen, 1972.

Gumbert 1974
Johan Peter Gumbert. *Die Utrechter Kartäuser und ihre Bücher im frühen fünfzehnten Jahrhundert.* Leiden, 1974.

Gustafson 1999
Eleanor H. Gustafson. "Museum Acquisitions." *Magazine Antiques* 156, no. 6 (1999): 778.

Hahnloser/Brugger-Koch 1985
Hans R. Hahnloser and Susanne Brugger-Koch. *Corpus der Hartsteinschliffe des 12.–15 Jahrhunderts.* Berlin, 1985.

Halle 2001
Halle, Landesmuseum für Vorgeschichte, 11 December 2001–28 April 2002. *Schönheit, Macht und Tod. 120 Funde aus 120 Jahren Landesmuseum für Vorgeschichte Halle,* ed. Herald Meller. Halle, 2001.

Halm 1926
Phillip Maria Halm. *Studien zur Süddeutschen Plastik.* 2 vols. Augsburg, 1926–27.

Hand/Mansfield 1993
John O. Hand and Sally E. Mansfield. *German Paintings of the Fifteenth through Seventeenth Centuries: The Collections of the National Gallery of Art Systematic Catalogue.* Washington/Oxford, 1993.

Hannestad 2007
Niels Hannestad. "Late Antique Mythological Sculpture: In Search of a Chronology." In *Statuen und Statuensammlungen in der Spätantike,* ed. Franz Alto Bauer and Christian Witschel, 275–307. Wiesbaden, 2007.

Hanson 1983
June M. R. Hanson. "An Examination of the Evidence for Ugolino di Nerio's Participation in the Workshop of Duccio di Buoninsegna and Collaboration during the Painting of the Maestà Altarpiece." Ph.D. diss. California State University, Long Beach, 1983.

Harck 1889
Fritz Harck. "Quadri di Maestri Italiani in possesso di privati a Berlino." *Archivo storico dell'arte* 2 (1889): 206.

Haseloff 1905
Arthur Haseloff. "Die mittelalterliche Kunst." In *Meisterwerke der Kunst aus Sachsen und Thüringen,* ed. Oscar Doering and Georg Voss, 87–118. Magdeburg, 1905.

Hasseloff 1990
Günther Hasseloff. *Email im frühen Mittelalter.* Hitzeroth, 1990.

Hattatt 1987
Richard Hattatt. *Brooches of Antiquity, A Third Selection of Brooches from the Author's Collection.* London, 1987.

Hattatt 1994
Richard Hattatt. *Ancient and Romano-British Brooches.* Ipswich, 1994. First published in 1982.

Hedeman 1995
Anne D. Hedeman. "Roger van der Weyden's Escorial *Crucifixion* and Carthusian Devotional Practice." In *The Sacred Image East and West,* Robert G. Ousterhout and Leslie Brubaker, 191–203. Urbana, 1995.

Henderson 1970
George Henderson. "An Apocalypse Manuscript in Paris: B.N. Ms. Lat. 10474." *Art Bulletin* 52 (1970): 22–31.

Hess 1994
Daniel Hess. *Meister um das mittelalterliche Hausbuch: Studien zur Hausbuchmeisterfrage.* Mainz, 1994.

Hess 2002
Kristine M. Hess. "The Saint's Presence and the Power of Representation: A Reliquary Box Depicting the Life of St. John Prodromos." M.A. thesis. Pennsylvania State University, 2002.

Hildesheim 1993
Hildesheim, Diözesanmuseum and Roemer- und Pelizaeus-Museum, 15 August–20 November. *Bernward von Hildesheim und das Zeitalter der Ottonen,* ed. Michael Brandt and Arne Eggebrecht. 2 vols. Mainz, 1993.

Hildesheim 2001
Hildesheim, Diözesanmuseum. *Abglanz des Himmels: Romanik in Hildesheim,* ed. Michael Brandt. Regensburg, 2001.

Hindman 1992
Sandra Hindman. "Two Leaves from an Unknown Breviary: The Case for Simon Marmion." In *Margaret of York, Simon Marmion, and the Visions of Tondal,* ed. Thomas Kren, 223–32. Malibu, 1992.

Hindman 1997
Sandra Hindman et al. *The Robert Lehman Collection Illuminations.* Vol. 4: *Illuminations.* New York/Princeton, 1997.

Holladay 1995
Joan A. Holladay. "The Willehalm Master and His Colleagues: Collaborative Manuscript Decoration in Early Fourteenth Century Cologne." In *Making the Medieval Book: Techniques of Production; Proceedings of the Fourth Conference of The Seminar in the History of the Book to 1500, Oxford, July 1992,* ed. Linda L. Brownrigg, 67–91. Los Altos, 1995.

Hubert 1969
Jean Hubert, Jean Porcher, and Wolfgang Fritz Volbach. *Europe in the Dark Ages.* London, 1969.

Huchard 2004
Viviane Huchard. "Un feuillet du Lectionnaire de l'abbaye de Cluny." *Revue du Louvre et des musées de France* 54, no. 5 (2004): 13–15.

Hutchinson 1958
Jane C. Hutchison. "The Development of the Double Portrait in Northern European Painting of the Fifteenth Century." M.A. thesis. Oberlin College, 1958.

İnan/Alföldi-Rosenbaum 1979
Jale İnan and Elisabeth Alföldi-Rosenbaum. *Römische und frühbyzantinische Porträtplastik aus der Türkei: Neue Funde.* 2 vols. Mainz, 1979.

Ithaca 1968
Ithaca, Andrew Dickson White Museum of Art, Cornell University, 8 October–3 November. *A Medieval Treasury,* ed. Robert Calkins. Ithaca, 1968.

Ivanchenko/Henderson 1980
Oxana Ivanchenko and George Henderson. "Four Miniatures from a Thirteenth Century Apocalypse: A Recent Discovery." *Burlington Magazine* 122 (1980): 97–106.

Jackson 1973
Sidney Jackson. *Celtic and Other Stone Heads.* Shipley, 1973.

James 1924
Montague R. James. *The Apocryphal New Testament.* Oxford, 1924.

Jean 2004
Jean of Jandun. *A Treatise on the Praises of Paris,* trans. Robert W. Berger. In *Old Paris,* 12–13. New York, 2004.

Jirousek 2001
Carolyn S. Jirousek. "Christ and St. John the Evangelist as a Model of Medieval Mysticism." *Cleveland Studies* 6 (2001): 6–27.

Jopek 1988
Norbert Jopek. *Studien zur deutschen Alabasterplastik des 15. Jahrhunderts.* Manuskripte zur Kunstwissenschaft in der Wernerschen Verlagsgesellschaft 21. Worms, 1988.

Kalaverezou-Maxeiner 1985
Ioli Kalaverezou-Maxeiner. *Byzantine Icons in Steatite.* 2 vols. Vienna, 1985.

Kalden-Rosenfeld 2001
Iris Kalden-Rosenfeld. *Tilman Reimenschneider und seine Werkstatt. Mit einem Katalog der allgemein als Arbeiten Riemenschneiders und seiner Werkstatt akzeptierten Werke.* Königstein im Taunus, 2001.

Kaminski-Menssen 1996
Gabriele Kaminski-Menssen. *Bildwerke der Sammlung Kaufmann.*
Wissenschaftliche Kataloge, Liebieghaus–Museum Alter Plastik. Vol.
3: *Bildwerke aus Ton, Bein und Metall.* Kassel, 1996.

Karcheski 1995
Walter J. Karcheski Jr. *Arms and Armor in The Art Institute of Chicago.*
Chicago, 1995.

Kavrus-Hoffmann 1996
Nedezdha Kavrus-Hoffmann. "Greek Manuscripts at Dumbarton
Oaks: Codicological and Paleographic Description and Analysis."
Dumbarton Oaks Papers 50 (1996): 289–312.

Kienbusch 1963
Carl Otto von Kienbusch. *The Kretzschmar von Kienbusch Collection of
Armor and Arms.* Princeton, 1963.

Kitzinger 1993
Ernst Kitzinger. "The Cleveland Marbles." In *Atti del IX Congresso
internazionale di archeologia cristiana, Roma 21–27 settembre 1975.*
Rome, 1978. Reprinted in *Art, Archaeology, and Architecture of Early
Christianity,* ed. Paul C. Finney. Vol. 2, 117–39. New York, 1993.

Klamt 1968
Johann-Christian Klamt. "Zum Arenberg-Psalter." In *Munuscula
Discipulorum: Kunsthistorische Studien, Hans Kauffmann zum 70.
Geburtstag, 1966,* 147–55. Berlin, 1968.

Kleinbauer 1980
Eugene Kleinbauer. "Recent Major Acquisitions of Medieval Art by
American Museums." *Gesta* 19, no. 1 (1980): 67–77.

Koechlin 1924
Raymond Koechlin. *Les ivories gothiques français.* 3 vols. Paris, 1924.

Koenen 1998
Ulrike Koenen. "Byzantinische Elfenbeine aus westliche Werktätten
und ihre Rezeption im 19. Jahrhundert." In *Chartulae: Festschrift für
Wolfgang Speyer (Jahrbuch für Antike und Christentum, Ergänzungsband
28),* 199–227. Münster, 1998.

König 1982
Eberhard König. *Französische Buchmalerei um 1450: Der Jouvenel-Maler,
der Maler des Genfer Boccaccio und die Anfänge Jean Fouquets.* Berlin,
1982.

Kötzsche 1972
Dietrich Kötzsche. "Zum Stand der Forschung der Goldschmiede-
kunst des 12. Jahrhunderts im Rhein-Maas-Gebiet." In *Rhein und
Maas, Kunst und Kultur 800–1400,* 1: 191–238. Exh. cat. 2 vols.
Kunsthalle, Cologne/Musées Royaux d'art et histoire, Brussels.
Cologne, 1972.

Kötzsche 1989
Dietrich Kötzsche. *Das Evangeliar Heinrichs des Löwen. Kommentar zur
Faksimileausgabe.* Frankfurt am Main, 1989.

Kötzsche-Breitenbruch 1984
Lieselotte Kötzsche-Breitenbruch. "Pilgerandenken aus dem
Heiligen Land. Drei Neuerwerbungen des Württembergischen
Landesmuseums in Stuttgart." In *Vivarium. Festschrift Theodor Klauser
zum 90. Geburtstag (Jahrbuch für Antike und Christentum, Ergänzungsband
11),* ed. Ernst Dassmann and Klaus Thraede, 229–46. Münster,
1984.

Kraus 1962
H. P. Kraus (Firm). *Thirty-five Manuscripts including the St. Blasien
Psalter . . . Roger Bacon (Voynich) Cipher Ms.* Catalogue 100. New York,
1962.

Kreytenberg 1993
Gert Kreytenberg. "Der Heilige Galganus und der Bildhauer
Agostino di Giovanni." *Pantheon* 51 (1993): 4–17.

Krieger 2000
Michaela Krieger. "Gerard David als Illuminator." In *Festschrift für
Konrad Oberhuber,* ed. Achim Gnann and Heinz Widauer, 215–33.
Milan, 2000.

Kronach/Leipzig 1994
Kronach, Fortress of Rosenberg, 17 May–21 August; Leipzig,
Museum der Bildenden Künste, 7 September–6 November. *Lucas
Cranach. Ein Maler Unternehmer aus Franken,* ed. Evamaria Brockhoff
et al. Augsburg, 1994.

Krönig 1962
Wolfgang Krönig. "Rheinische Vesperbilder aus Leder und ihr
Umkreis." *Wallraf-Richartz-Jahrbuch* 24 (1962): 97–192.

Kroos 1985
Renate Kroos. *Der Schrein des Heiligen Servatius in Maastricht.* Munich,
1985.

Kurmann 1987
Peter Kurmann. *La façade de la cathédrale de Reims: architecture et
sculpture des portails, étude archéologique et stylistique.* 2 vols. Paris/
Lausanne, 1987.

Lafontaine-Dosogne 1967
Jacqueline Lafontaine-Dosogne. *Itinéraires archéologiques dans la région
d'Antioche: recherches sur le monastère et sur l'iconographie de Saint Syméon
Stylite le Jeune.* Bibliothèque de Byzantion 4. Brussels, 1967.

Lampros 1966
Spiridon P. Lampros. *Catalogue of the Greek Manuscripts on Mount Athos.*
2 vols. Cambridge, Eng., 1895–1900. Reprint Amsterdam, 1966.

Lappa-Zizica/Rizou-Couroupou 1991
Eurydike Lappa-Zizica and Matula Rizou-Couroupou. *Katalogos
Hellenikon Cheirographon tou Mouseiou Mpenake (10os–16os ai.).* Athens,
1991.

Larocca 1993
Donald J. Larocca. "A Neapolitan Patron of Armor and Tapestry
Identified." *Metropolitan Museum Journal* 28 (1993): 85–102.

Lasko 1994
Peter Lasko. *Ars Sacra 800–1200.* 2d ed. New Haven/London, 1994.

Laszlo 1974
Gyula Laszlo. *The Art of the Migration Period.* London, 1974.

Leedy 1991
Walter C. Leedy Jr. *Cleveland Builds an Art Museum: Patronage, Politics,
and Architecture 1884–1916.* Cleveland, 1991.

Lehner 1871
F. A. von Lehner. *Fürstlich Hohenzollern'sches Museum zu Sigmaringen.
Verzeichnis der Schnitzwerke.* Sigmaringen, 1871.

Lille 1978
Lille, Musée des Beaux-Arts, 1978–79. *Sculptures Romanes et
Gothiques du Nord de la France,* ed. Hervé Oursel. Lille, 1978.

Limoges 1999
Limoges, Musée Municipal de l'Eveche, Musée de l'Email. *Valérie
et Thomas Becket: De l'influence des princes Plantagenêt dans l'Oeuvre de
Limoges Limoges,* ed. Veronique Notin. Limoges, 1999.

Little 1977
Charles T. Little. "The Magdeburg Ivory Group: A Tenth-Century New Testament Narrative Cycle." Ph.D. diss. New York University, 1977.

Little 1988
Charles T. Little. "Avori Milanesi del X secolo." In *La città del vescovo dai Carolingi al Barbarossa,* ed. Carlo Bertelli, 82–101. Milan, 1988.

Little 1998
Charles T. Little. "Again the Cleveland Book-Shaped Reliquary." In Ehlers/Kötzsche 1998, 77–92.

London 1984
London, The British Museum, 7 November 1984–10 March 1985. *The Golden Age of Anglo-Saxon Art, 966–1066,* ed. Janet Backhouse et al. London, 1984.

London 1994
London, The British Museum. *Byzantium: Treasures of Byzantine Art and Culture from British Collections,* ed. David Buckton. London, 1994.

Longhurst 1926
Margaret H. Longhurst. "The Eumorfopoulous Collection, Western Objects—II." *Apollo* 3 (1926): 26–63.

López 2000
Gisela Ripoll López. "Visigothic Jewelry of the Sixth and Seventh Centuries." In Brown 2000, 188–203.

Los Angeles 2003
Los Angeles, The J. Paul Getty Museum, 17 June–7 September. *Illuminating the Renaissance: The Triumph of Flemish Manuscript Painting in Europe,* Thomas Kren and Scot McKendrick. Los Angeles, 2003.

Lowden 1988
John Lowden. "Observations on Illuminated Byzantine Psalters." *Art Bulletin* 70 (1988): 241–60.

MacGregor 1977
Arthur MacGregor. *A Summary Catalogue of the Continental Archaeological Collections (Roman Iron Age, Migration Period, Early Medieval). Ashmolean Museum Oxford.* Oxford, 1997.

Magdeburg 2001
Kulturhistorisches Museum Magdeburg, 27 August–2 December. *Otto der Große, Magdeburg und Europa,* ed. Matthias Puhle. Mainz, 2001.

Mango 1958
Cyril Mango, ed. *The Homilies of Photius, Patriarch of Constantinople.* Cambridge, 1958.

Mango 1986
Marlia Mundell Mango. *Silver from Early Byzantium: The Kaper Koraon and Related Treasures.* Baltimore, 1986.

Mango 1988
Cyril Mango. "La croix dite de Michel le Cérulaire et la croix de Saint-Michel de Sykéôn." *Cahiers Archéologiques* 36 (1988): 41–49.

Martin 2000
Max Martin. "Early Merovingian Women's Brooches." In Brown 2000, 226–40.

Martindale 1988
Andrew Martindale. *Simone Martini: Complete Edition.* New York, 1988.

May 1968
Helmut May. *Weltkunst aus Privatbesitz.* Cologne, 1968.

McNally 1969
Sheila McNally. "Three Late Antique Mosaics." *MIA Bulletin* 58 (December 1969): 5–15.

Meadow 1992
Mark A. Meadow. "The Observant Pedestrian and Albrecht Dürer's Promenade." *Art History* 15 (1992): 197–222.

Melnikas 1975
Anthony Melnikas. *The Corpus of the Miniatures in the Manuscripts of Decretum Gratiani.* Vol. 1. Rome, 1975.

Mende 1998
Ursula Mende. "Zur Gestalt und Nachfolge des Braunschweiger Löwen, speziell zur Kragenform seiner Mähne." In Ehlers/Kötzsche 1998, 387–423.

Metzger 1981
Catherine Metzger. *Les ampoules à eulogie du musée du Louvre.* Notes et Documents des musées de France 3. Paris, 1981.

MIA Bulletin
Bulletin of the Minneapolis Institute of Arts

Middeldorf 1976
Ulrich Middeldorf. "A forgotten Florentine tomb of the quattrocento." *Antichità viva* 15 (1976): 11–13.

Migeon 1905
Gaston Migeon. "La Collection de M. G. Chalandon." *Les Arts* 42 (1905): 17–29.

Milliken 1924
William M. Milliken. "The Limoges Enamel Cross from the Spitzer Collection." *CMA Bulletin* 11 (1924): 30–33.

Milliken 1925A
William M. Milliken. "A Byzantine Ivory Casket." *CMA Bulletin* 12 (1925): 5–13.

Milliken 1925B
William M. Milliken. "Illuminated Miniatures in the Cleveland Museum of Art." *CMA Bulletin* 12 (1925): 61–71.

Milliken 1925C
William M. Milliken. "A Table Fountain of the 14th Century." *CMA Bulletin* 12 (1925): 36–39.

Milliken 1926A
William M. Milliken. "Early Enamels in the Cleveland Museum of Art." *Connoisseur* 76 (October 1926): 67–68.

Milliken 1926B
William M. Milliken. "The Stroganoff Ivory." *CMA Bulletin* 13 (1926): 25–29.

Milliken 1927
William M. Milliken. "A Reliquary of Champlevé Enamel from the Valley of the Meuse." *CMA Bulletin* 14 (1927): 51–54.

Milliken 1929
William M. Milliken. "A German Woodcarving." *CMA Bulletin* 16 (1929): 23–25.

Milliken 1930
William M. Milliken. "The Acquisition of Six Objects from the Guelph Treasure for the Cleveland Museum of Art." *CMA Bulletin* 17 (1930): 163–77.

Milliken 1931
William M. Milliken. "The Gertrudis Altar and Two Crosses." *CMA Bulletin* 18 (1931): 23–26.

Milliken 1934
William M. Milliken. "A Manuscript Leaf from the Time of Duke Henry the Lion." *CMA Bulletin* 11 (1934): 35–39.

Milliken 1939
William M. Milliken. "Late German Gothic Sculpture." *CMA Bulletin* 26 (1939): 43–46.

Milliken 1941
William M. Milliken. "Objects from the Samuel Mather Collection." *CMA Bulletin* 28 (1941): 36–40.

Milliken 1943
William M. Milliken. "A Memorial to Henry G. Dalton." *CMA Bulletin* 30 (1943): 23–25.

Milliken 1946A
William M. Milliken. "New Accessions of Champlevé Enamel." *CMA Bulletin* 36 (1946): 166–70.

Milliken 1946B
William M. Milliken. "*St. Jerome and the Lion* by Tilmann Riemenschneider." *CMA Bulletin* 36 (1946): 175–77.

Milliken 1947
William M. Milliken. "Byzantine Manuscript Illumination." *CMA Bulletin* 34 (1947): 50–56.

Milliken 1949
William M. Milliken. "New Accessions of Champlevé Enamel." *CMA Bulletin* 36 (1949): 167–70.

Milliken 1951A
William M. Milliken. "The Cleveland Byzantine Silver Treasure." *CMA Bulletin* 38 (1951): 142–45.

Milliken 1951B
William M. Milliken. "Four Champlevé Enamel Plaques." *CMA Bulletin* 38 (1951): 72–74.

Milliken 1952
William M. Milliken. "A Champlevé Enamel Plaque." *CMA Bulletin* 39 (1952): 7–13.

Milliken 1954
William M. Milliken. "Byzantine Goldsmith Work." *CMA Bulletin* 41 (1954): 190–92.

Milliken 1955A
William M. Milliken. "A Champlevé Enamel Châsse." *CMA Bulletin* 42 (1955): 19–22.

Milliken 1955B
William M. Milliken. "An Illumination from the 'Moralia of Gregorius'." *CMA Bulletin* 42 (1955): 183–86.

Milliken 1958
William M. Milliken. "Early Byzantine Silver." *CMA Bulletin* 45 (1958): 35–41.

Milliken 1975
William M. Milliken. *A Time Remembered. A Cleveland Memoir by William Mathewson Milliken.* Cleveland, 1975.

MMA Bulletin
Bulletin of The Metropolitan Museum of Art

Mollwo 1944
Marie Mollwo. *Das Wettinger Graduale: Eine geistliche Bilderfolge vom Meister des Kasseler Willehalmcodex und seinem Nachfolger.* Bern-Bümpliz, 1944.

Montesquiou-Fezensac 1962
Blaise de Montesquiou-Fezensac. "Le talisman de Charlemagne." *Art de France* 2 (1962): 66–76.

Moran 1979
Gordon Moran. "A 14th century Sienese Reliquary from the Spedale della Scala." Unpublished, 1979.

Morand 1991
Kathleen Morand. *Claus Sluter, Artist at the Court of Burgundy.* Austin, 1991.

Morgan 1982
Nigel Morgan. "The Burckhardt-Wildt Apocalypse." *Art at Auction* (1982–83): 162–69.

Müller/Steingräber 1954
Theodor Müller and Erich Steingräber. "Die französische Goldemailplastik um 1400." *Münchner Jahrbuch der bildenen Kunst* 5 (1954): 29–79.

Munich 1998
Munich, Prähistorische Staatssammlung, 20 October 1998–14 February 1999. *Rom und Byzanz. Archäologische Kostbarkeiten aus Bayern,* ed. Ludwig Wamser and Gisela Zahlhaas. Munich, 1998.

Munich 2004
Munich, Prähistorische Staatssammlung, 22 October 2004–3 April 2005. *Die Welt von Byzanz—Europas östliches Erbe. Glanz, Krisen und Fortleben einer tausendjährigen Kultur,* ed. Ludwig Wamser. Munich, 2004.

Musper 1970
Heinrich T. Musper. *Altdeutsche Malerei.* Cologne, 1970.

Nelson 1936
Philip Nelson. "An Ancient Boxwood Casket." *Archaeologia* 86 (1936): 91–100.

Neumann 1891
Wilhelm A. Neumann. *Der Reliquienschatz des Hauses Braunschweig-Lüneburg.* Vienna, 1891.

New York 1970
New York, The Metropolitan Museum of Art, 12 February–10 May. *The Year 1200: A Centennial Exhibition at The Metropolitan Museum of Art,* ed. Konrad Hoffmann. New York, 1970.

New York 1979
New York, The Metropolitan Museum of Art, 5 October 1977–1 March 1978. *Age of Spirituality: Late Antique and Early Christian Art, Third to Seventh Century,* ed. Kurt Weitzmann. New York, 1979.

New York 1982
New York, organized by the American Federation of Arts and The Metropolitan Museum of Art, March 1982–May 1984. *The Art of Chivalry: European Arms and Armor from the Metropolitan Museum of Art,* ed. Helmut Nickel, Stuart W. Pyhrr, and Leonid Tarassuk. New York, 1982.

New York 1986
New York, The Metropolitan Museum of Art, 8 April–22 June. *Gothic and Renaissance Art in Nuremberg.* New York/Munich, 1986.

New York 1988
New York, The Metropolitan Museum of Art, 20 December 1988–19 March 1989. *Painting in Renaissance Siena 1420–1500,* ed. Keith Christiansen, Laurence B. Kanter, and Carl B. Strehlke. New York, 1988.

New York 1994
New York, The Metropolitan Museum of Art, 18 November
1994–26 February 1995. *Painting and Illumination in Early Renaissance
Florence, 1300–1450,* ed. Laurence B. Kanter. New York, 1994.

New York 1997
New York, The Metropolitan Museum of Art, 11 March–6 July. *The
Glory of Byzantium: Art and Culture of the Middle Byzantine Era, A.D.
843–1261,* ed. Helen C. Evans and William D. Wixom. New York,
1997.

New York 1999
New York, The Metropolitan Museum of Art, 9 March–11 July.
Mirror of the Medieval World, ed. William D. Wixom. New York, 1999.

New York 2003
New York, The Metropolitan Museum of Art, 30 September 2003–1
February 2004. *Treasures of a Lost Art: Italian Manuscript Painting of the
Middle Ages and Renaissance,* ed. Pia Palladino. New Haven/London,
2003.

New York 2004A
New York, The Metropolitan Museum of Art, 15 March–5 July.
Byzantium: Faith and Power (1261–1557), ed. Helen C. Evans. New
York, 2004.

New York 2004B
New York, Miriam and Ira D. Wallach Art Gallery, Columbia
University, 14 April–12 June. *Restoring Byzantium: The Kariye Camii
in Instanbul and the Byzantine Institute Restoraion,* ed. Holger A. Klein.
New York, 2004.

New York 2005
New York. The Metropolitan Museum of Art, 20 September 2005–3
January 2006. *Prague: The Crown of Bohemia, 1347–1437,* ed. Barbara
Drake Böhm and Jirˇí Fajt. New York, 2005.

New York 2006A
New York, Bard Graduate Center, 12 July–15 October. *Lions,
Dragons, and Other Beasts: Aquamanilia of the Middle Ages, Vessels for
Church and Table,* ed. Peter Barnet and Pete Dandridge. New York,
2006.

New York 2006B
New York, The Metropolitan Museum of Art, 26 September
2006–18 February 2007. *Set in Stone: The Face in Medieval Sculpture,*
ed. Charles T. Little. New York, 2006.

Nickel 1986
Heinrich L. Nickel. "Die Hallesche Laurentiustafel." *Bildende Kunst* 5
(1986): 223–24.

Nickel 1988
Heinrich L. Nickel. "Die Hallesche Laurentiustafel, eine romanische
Grubenschmelzplatte aus dem Stadtkernbereich." *Jahresschrift für
mitteldeutsche Vorgeschichte* 71 (1988): 254–55.

Nuremberg 1933
Nuremberg, Germanisches Museum, June–August 1933. *Veit
Stoss–Ausstellung.* Nuremberg, 1933.

Oberhaidacher 1998
Jörg Oberhaidacher. "Zur kunstgeschichtlichen Herkunft und
Bedeutung des Meisters von Heiligenkreuz." *Oesterreichische
Zeitschrift für Kunst Denkmalpflege* 52 (1998): 501–17.

Oppenheim 1911
Benoit Oppenheim. *Originalbildwerke in Holz, Stein, Elfenbein usw. aus
der Sammlung Benoit Oppenheim, Berlin.* Leipzig, 1911.

Paderborn 2001
Paderborn, Erzbischöfliches Diözesanmuseum, 6 December
2001–31 March 2002. *Byzanz—Das Licht aus dem Osten. Kult und
Alltag im Byzantinischen Reich vom 4. bis 15. Jahrhundert,* ed. Christoph
Stiegemann. Paderborn, 2001.

Paris 1931
Paris, Musée des Arts Décoratifs, 28 May–9 July. *Exposition d'Art
Byzantin.* Paris, 1931.

Paris 1955
Paris, Bibliotheque Nationale, 1955–56. *Les Manuscrits à peintures en
France du XIIe au XVIe siècle.* Paris, 1955.

Paris 1981
Paris, Grand Palais, 9 October 1981–1 February 1982. *Les Fastes
du Gothique: Le siècle de Charles V,* ed. Danielle Gaborit-Chopin et al.
Paris, 1981.

Paris 2004
Paris, Musée du Louvre, 22 March–12 July. *Paris 1400: Les arts sous
Charles VI,* ed. Elisabeth Taburet-Delahaye. Paris, 2004.

Pelikan 1990
Jaroslav Pelikan. *Imago Dei. The Byzantine Apologia for Icons.* Princeton,
1990.

Perrott 1934
Emilia Perrott. "Un Messale umbro del Quattrocento." *La Bibliofilia*
36 (1934): 173–84.

Peter 2001
Michael Peter. *Der Gertrudisaltar aus dem Welfenschatz. Eine stilgeschicht-
liche Untersuchung.* Schriften des Dom-Museums Hildesheim 2.
Mainz, 2001.

Pinder 1924–29
Wilhelm Pinder. *Die deutsche Plastik vom ausgehenden Mittelalter bis zum
Ende der Renaissance.* 2 vols. Potsdam, 1924–29.

Plonka-Balus 2005
Katarzyna Plonka-Balus. *A Newly-Found Miniature from the Potocki
Psalter.* Warsaw, 2005.

Pollak/Muñoz 1911
Ludwig Pollak and Antonio Muñoz. *Pièces de choix de la collection du
Comte Grégoire Stroganoff à Rome.* 2 vols. Rome, 1911–12.

Pope-Hennessy 1947
John Pope-Hennessy. *Sienese Quattrocento Painting.* Oxford, 1947.

Pope-Hennessy 1971
John Pope-Hennessy. *Italian Renaissance Sculpture.* 2d ed. London,
1971.

Porcher 1955
Jean Porcher. "L'Homme au verre de vin et de Maître de Jouvenel
des Ursins." *Revue française de l'élite européenne* (1955): 117–24.

Princeton 1973
Princeton University, The Art Museum, 14 April–20 May. *Illuminated
Greek Manuscripts from American Collections: An Exhibition in Honor of
Kurt Weitzmann,* ed. Gary Vikan. Princeton, 1973.

Provoost 1994
Arnold Provoost. "De Cleveland-beeldengroep: Bestemd voor
een graftuin?" In *Bild- und Formensprache der spatantiken Kunst: Hugo
Brandenburg zum 65. Geburtstag,* ed. Martina Jordan-Ruwe and Ulrich
Real. Münster, 1994.

Pulver 1919
Max Pulver. "Umschau." *Das Kunstblatt* 3 (September 1919): 284–85.

Purgold 1937
Karl Purgold. *Das Herzogliche Museum [Gotha]. Mit einem Anhang: Die Herzoglichen Anstalten für Kunst und Wissenschaft seit 1934.* Gotha, 1937.

Quarré 1971
Pierre Quarré. *Les Pleurants des tombeaux des ducs de Bourgogne.* Dijon, 1971.

Quarré 1972
Pierre Quarré. *Jean de la Huerta et la sculpture bourguignonne au milieu du XVe siècle.* Dijon, 1972.

Quarré 1978
Pierre Quarré. *La Sculpture en Bourgogne a la fin du Moyen Age.* Fribourg/Paris, 1978.

Randall 1993
Richard H. Randall Jr. *The Golden Age of Ivory: Gothic Carvings in North American Collections.* New York, 1993.

Rasmussen 1976
Jörg Rasmussen. "Zum kleinplastischen Werke des Veit Stoss." *Pantheon* 3, no. 2 (1976): 108–14.

Read 1926
Herbert Read. "The Eumorfopoulos Collection: Western Objects— I." *Apollo* 3 (1926): 187–92.

Reynaud 1992
Nicole Reynaud. "Sur la Double Représentation de Guillaume Jouvenel et sur ses emblems." *Revue Bibliothèque Nationale* 44 (Summer 1992): 50–57.

Robb 1936
David M. Robb. "The Iconography of the Annunciation in the Fourteenth and Fifteenth Centuries." *Art Bulletin* 18 (1936): 480–526.

Rohmeder 1971
Jürgen Rohmeder. *Der Meister des Hochaltares in Rabenden.* Rosenheim, 1971.

Rome 1954
Rome, Palazzo Venezia. *Mostra storica nazionale della miniatura,* ed. Giovanni Muzzioli. Florence, 1954.

Ronig 1992
Franz Ronig. *Das Helmarshausener Evangeliar im Trierer Domschatz.* Paderborn, 1992.

Ronig 1999
Franz Ronig. *Ein romanisches Evangeliar aus Helmarshausen im Trierer Domschatz.* Trier, 1999.

Rosenzweig 1976
A. Rosenzweig. "A Petrographic Description of the Materials of Some Stone Sculptures at the Cleveland Museum of Art." M.A. thesis. Oberlin College, 1976.

Ross 1962
Marvin C. Ross. *Catalogue of the Byzantine and Early Medieval Antiquities in the Dumbarton Oaks Collection.* Vol. 1: *Metalwork, Ceramics, Glass, Glyptics, Painting.* Washington, 1962.

Ross 1967
Anne Ross. *Pagan Celtic Britain: Studies in Iconography and Tradition.* London, 1967.

Ross 1967–68
Marvin C. Ross. "Luxuries of the Eastern Empire." *Arts in Virginia* 8 (1967–68) 56–65.

Ross 2005
Marvin C. Ross, with an addendum by Stephen A. Boyd and Susan R. Zwirn. *Catalogue of the Byzantine and Early Medieval Antiquities in the Dumbarton Oaks Collection.* Vol. 2: *Jewelry, Enamels, and Arts of the Migration Period.* 2d ed. Washington, 2005.

Rumscheid 2000
Jutta Rumscheid. *Kranz und Krone: Zu Insignien, Siegespreisen und Ehrenzeichen der römischen Kaiserzeit.* Istanbuler Forschungen 43. Tübingen, 2000.

Rushton 2001
Pauline Rushton. "A Liverpool collector: Dr. Philip Nelson 1872–1953." *Apollo* 153 (2001): 41–48.

Russo 2000
Daniel Russo. "Les peintures de Berzé-la-Ville." *Revue Mabillon,* n.s. 11 (2000): 57–87.

Rutschowscaya 1990
Marie-Hélène Rutschowscaya. *Coptic Fabric.* Paris, 1990.

Rutschowscaya 2000
Marie-Hélène Rutschowscaya. "The Mother of God in Coptic Textiles." In Athens 2000, 219–25.

Salin 1950–52
Edouard Salin. *La civilization mérovingienne.* 4 vols. Paris, 1950–52.

Salmi 1933
Mario Salmi. "Bartolomeo Caporali a Firenze." *Rivista d'arte* 15 (1933): 253–72.

Salmi 1957
Mario Salmi. *Italian Miniatures.* London, 1957.

Sandberg-Vavalà 1937
Evelyn Sandberg-Vavalà. "Some Partial Reconstructions." *Burlington Magazine* 71 (1937): 177.

San Francisco 1992
M. H. de Young Memorial Museum, Fine Arts Museums of San Francisco, 22 February–17 May, and tour. *Imperial Austria: Treasures of Art, Arms, and Armor from the State of Styria,* ed. Peter Krenn and Walter J. Karcheski Jr. Munich/New York, 1992.

San Marino 1995
San Marino, Palazzo Pergami-Belluzzi, 4 June–5 September. *I Goti a San Marion: Il Tesoro di Domagnano.* Milan, 1995.

Sauerländer 1972
Willibald Sauerländer. *Gothic Sculpture in France, 1140–1270,* trans. Janet Sandheimer. London, 1972.

Sauerländer 1978
Willibald Sauerländer. "La sculpture du XIIe et du XIIIe siècle dans la Nord de la France." In Lille 1978, 19–21.

Sawicka 1938
Stanislawa Sawicka. "Les Principaux manuscrits à peintures de la Bibliothèque nationale de Varsovie." *Bulletin de la Société française de reproductions de manuscrits à peintures* 13 (1938): 38–44.

Schade 1974
Werner Schade. *Die Malerfamilie Cranach.* Dresden, 1974.

Schaff/Wace 1988
Philip Schaff and Henry Wace, eds. *A Select Library of Nicene and Post-Nicene Fathers of the Christian Church.* 2d series. Vol. 14: *The Seven Ecumenical Councils.* Grand Rapids, 1988.

Scheifele 1994
Eleanor L. Scheifele. "A French Romanesque Capital of Daniel in the Lions' Den." *CMA Bulletin* 81 (1994): 47–82.

Scher 1992
Stephen K. Scher. "Bourges et Dijon: observations sur les relations entre André Beauneveu, Jean de Cambrai, et Claus Sluter." In *Actes des Journées internationales Claus Sluter,* 277–93. Dijon, 1992.

Schilling 1933
Rosy Schilling. "Die Engelberger Bildhandschriften aus Abt Frowins Zeit in ihrer Beziehung zu burgundischer und schwäbischer Buchmalerei." *Anzeiger für Schweizerische Altertumskunde,* Neue Folge 35 (1933): 117–128.

Schmidt 1975
Gerhard Schmidt. "Zur Datierung des 'kleinen' Bargello-Diptychons und der Verkündigungstafel in Cleveland." In *Études d'art français offertes à Charles Sterling,* ed. Albert Châtelet and Nicole Reynaud, 47–63. Paris, 1975.

Schmidt 2005
Gerhard Schmidt. *Malerei der Gotik: Fixpunkte und Ausblicke.* 2 vols. Graz, 2005.

Schmitt/Swarzenski 1921
Otto Schmitt and Georg Swarzenski, eds. *Meisterwerke der Bildhauerkunst in Frankfurter Privatbesitz.* Vol. 1: *Deutsche und Französische Plastik des Mittelalters.* Frankfurt, 1921.

Schrenk 2004
Sabine Schrenk. *Textilien des Mittelmeerraumes aus spätantiker bis frühislamischer Zeit.* Die Textilsammlung der Abegg-Stiftung 4. Riggisberg, 2004.

Schuchardt 1851
Christian Schuchardt. *Lucas Cranach des Älteren Leben und Werk.* Leipzig, 1851.

Scillia 1995
Diane Scillia. "The Cleveland Annunciation and the Origins of Flemish Painting." In *Flanders in a European Perspective: Manuscript Illumination around 1400 in Flanders and Abroad,* ed. Maurits Smeyers and Bert Cardon, 345–56. Louvain, 1995.

Seligman 1961
Germain Seligman. *Merchants of Art: 1880–1960. Eighty Years of Professional Collecting.* New York, 1961.

Shepherd 1969
Dorothy G. Shepherd. "An Icon of the Virgin—A Sixth-Century Tapestry Panel from Egypt." *CMA Bulletin* 56 (1969): 90–120.

Shepherd 1976
Dorothy G. Shepherd. "A Late Classical Tapestry." *CMA Bulletin* 63 (1976): 307–13.

Smeyers 1998
Maurits Smeyers. *L'Art de la miniature flamande du VIIIe au XVIe siècle.* Tournai, 1998.

Solms 1995
Elisabeth de Solms. *Christs romans.* 2 vols. La Pierre-Qui-Vire, 1995.

Souchal 1967
Geneviève Souchal. "Autour des plaques de Grandmont: Une familie d'Emaux limousins champlevès de la fin du XIIe Siecle." *Bulletin Monumental* 125 (1967): 21–71.

Spatharakis 1981
Iohannis Spatharakis. *Corpus of Dated Illuminated Greek Mss to the Year 1453.* 2 vols. Leiden, 1981.

Spitzer 1890–93
Fréderic Spitzer. *La Collection Spitzer: Antiquité, Moyen-Age, Renaissance.* 6 vols. Paris, 1890–93.

Springer 1981
Peter Springer. *Kreuzfüße. Ikonographie und Typologie eines hochmittelalterlichen Gerätes.* Berlin, 1981.

Sprinz 1925
Heiner Sprinz. *Die Bildwerke der Fürstlich Hohenzollernschen Sammlung Sigmaringen.* Stuttgart, 1925.

Stange 1934–60
Alfred Stange. *Deutsche Malerei der Gotik.* 11 vols. Berlin, 1934–60.

Sterling 1955
Charles Sterling. "Oeuvres retrouvées de Jean de Beaumetz, peintre de Philippe le Hardi." *Miscellanea E. Panofsky. Bulletin des Musées Royaux des Beaux-Arts* 4 (1955): 57–81.

Sterling 1974
Charles Sterling. "Fighting Animals in the Adoration of the Magi." *CMA Bulletin* 61 (1974): 350–59.

Strong 1966
Donald E. Strong. *Greek and Roman Silver Plate.* London, 1966.

Stubblebine 1979
James H. Stubblebine. *Duccio di Buoninsegna and His School.* Princeton, 1979.

Stuttgart 1977
Stuttgart, Württembergisches Landesmuseum, 26 March–5 June. *Die Zeit der Staufer.* 5 vols. Stuttgart, 1977.

Suger 1979
Abbot Suger. *On the Abbey Church of St.-Denis and Its Art Treasures,* ed. Erwin Panofsky. 2d ed. Princeton, 1979.

Swarzenski 1921
Georg Swarzenski. "Deutsche Alabasterplastik des 15 Jahrhunderts." *Städel-Jahrbuch* 1 (1921): 167–213.

Swarzenski 1932
Georg Swarzenski. "Aus dem Kunstkreis Henrichs des Löwen." *Städel-Jahrbuch* 7/8 (1932): 241–397.

Swarzenski 1967
Hanns Swarzenski. *Monuments of Romanesque Art.* London, 1967.

Taburet-Delahaye 1996
Elisabeth Taburet-Delahaye. "Beginnings and Evolution of the *Oeuvre de Limoges.*" In New York 1996, 33–39.

Taburet-Delahaye 2002
Elisabeth Taburet-Delahaye. "Les bijoux d'Isabeau de Bavière." *Bulletin de la Société nationale des Antiquaires de France,* séance du 16 Octobre 2002. Forthcoming.

Talbot Rice 1952
David Talbot Rice. *English Art 871–1100.* Oxford, 1952.

Tanner 1990
Norman P. Tanner, ed. *Decrees of the Ecumenical Councils.* 2 vols.
London/Washington, 1990.

Tarassuk 1986
Leonid Tarassuk. *Italian Armor for Princely Courts.* Chicago, 1986.

Thoby 1953
Paul Thoby. *Les croix limousines de la fin du XII siècle au debut du XIV
siècle.* Paris, 1953.

Thomas 1979
Marcel Thomas. *The Golden Age: Manuscript Painting at the Time of Jean,
Duke of Berry.* New York, 1979.

Thoss 1978
Dagmar Thoss. *Französische Gotik und Renaissance Meisterwerken der
Buchmalerei.* Vienna, 1978.

Tietze 1913
Hans Tietze. "Ein Passionszyklus im Stift Schlägl." *Jahrbuch des
kunsthistorischen Instituts der Zentralkommission für Denkmalpflege* 7
(1913): 173–88.

Tönnies 1900
Eduard Tönnies. *Leben und Werk des Würzburger Bildschnitzers Tilmann
Riemenschneider.* Strasbourg, 1900.

Torgau 2004
Torgau, Hartenfels Castle, 24 May–10 October. *Glaube und Macht:
Sachsen im Europa der Reformationszeit,* ed. Harald Marx and Eckhard
Kluth. Dresden, 2004.

Trento 1997
Trento, Castello del Buonconsiglio, 20 June–9 November. *Ori delle
Alpi,* Lorenza Endrizzi and Franco Marzatico. Trento, 1997.

Troescher 1966
Georg Troescher. *Burgundische Malerei.* Berlin, 1966.

Troyes 1882
*Objets d'art et de curiosités orfèfrerie, bijoux, émaux byzantins et de Limoges,
bois sculptes, ivories gothiques et du 16e siècle bronzes gothiques et byzantins
etc.* Sale catalogue, 14 June 1882. Troyes, 1882.

Ultee 1981
Maarten Ultee. *The Abbey of St. Germain des Prés in the Seventeenth
Century.* New Haven/London, 1981.

Utrecht 1989
Rijksmuseum Het Catharijneconvent, Utrecht, 10 December
1989–11 February 1990, and Pierpont Morgan Library, New York,
1 March–6 May 1990. *The Golden Age of Dutch Manuscript Painting.*
Stuttgart, 1990.

Valentiner 1924
Wilhelm R. Valentiner. "Studies in Italian Gothic Plastic Art: II.
Agostino di Giovanni and Agnolo di Ventura." *Art in America* 13
(1924): 3–18.

Valentini 1839
Agostino Valentini. *La Patriarcale Basilica Liberiana Illustrata.* Rome,
1839.

Verdier 1974
Philippe Verdier. "The Cleveland Portable Altar from Hildesheim."
CMA Bulletin 61 (1974): 339–42.

Verdier 1975
Philippe Verdier. "Émaux mosans et rheno-mosans dans les collections des États-Unis." *Revue Belge d'archéologie et d'histoire de l'art* 44
(1975): 3–107.

Verdier 1980
Philippe Verdier. "A Medallion of Saint Symeon the Younger." *CMA
Bulletin* 67 (1980): 17–27.

Verdier 1981
Philippe Verdier. "A Romanesque Corpus." *CMA Bulletin* 68 (1981):
66–74.

Vikan 1980
Gary Vikan. *Gifts from the Byzantine Court. Three Illuminated Manuscript
Leaves at Dumbarton Oaks.* Dumbarton Oaks Publications 1.
Washington, 1980.

Vikan 1982
Gary Vikan. *Byzantine Pilgrimage Art.* Dumbarton Oaks Byzantine
Collection 5. Washington, 1982.

Vikan 1984
Gary Vikan. "Art, Medicine, and Magic in Early Byzantium."
Dumbarton Oaks Papers 38 (1984): 65–86.

Voelkle/Wieck 1992
William M. Voelkle and Roger S. Wieck. *The Bernard H. Breslauer
Collection of Manuscript Illuminations.* New York, 1992.

Volbach 1966
Wolfgang F. Volbach. "Zur Ikonographie des Styliten Symeon des
Jüngeren." In *Tortulae. Studien zu altchristlichen und byzantinischen
Monumenten* (*Römische Quartalschrift* Supplement 30), ed. Walter N.
Schumacher, 293–99. Freiburg im Breisgau, 1966.

Washington 1975
Washington, National Gallery of Art, 26 January–1 June. *Medieval
and Renaissance Miniatures from the National Gallery of Art,* ed. Gary
Vikan. Washington, 1975.

Washington 1991
Washington, National Gallery of Art, 12 October 1991–12 January
1992. *Circa 1492: Art in the Age of Exploration,* ed. Jay A. Levenson.
Washington/New Haven, 1991.

Washington 1994
Washington, Dumbarton Oaks, 23 September 1994–29 January
1995. *Byzantine Figural Processional Crosses,* ed. John A. Cotsonis.
Dumbarton Oaks Byzantine Collection 10. Washington, 1994.

Washington 1999
Washington, National Gallery of Art, 3 October 1999–9 January
2000. *Tilman Riemenschneider: Master Sculptor of the Late Middle Ages,*
ed. Julien Chapuis. Washington/New Haven, 1999.

Weigelt 1931
Curt Weigelt. "Minor Simonesque Masters." *Apollo* 14 (1931): 1–13.

Wentzel 1960
Hans Wentzel. "Die byzantinischen Kameen in Kassel, Zur
Problematik der Datierung byzantinscher Kameen." In *Mouseion.
Studien aus Kunst und Geschichte für Otto H. Förster,* 88–96. Cologne,
1960.

Wentzel 1961
Hans Wentzel. *Die Christus-Johannes Gruppen des XIV. Jahrhunderts.*
Stuttgart, 1961.

Werner 1961
Joachim Werner. *Katalog der Sammlung Diergardt (Völkerwanderungszei tlicher Schmuck).* Römisch-Germanisches Museum, Cologne. Berlin, 1961.

Westermann-Angerhausen 1998
Hiltrud Westermann-Angerhausen. "Die Stiftungen der Gräfin Gertrud. Anspruch und Rang." In Ehlers/Kötzsche 1998, 51–76.

White 1979
John White. *Duccio, Tuscan Art, and the Medieval Workshop.* London, 1979.

Whiting 1918
Frederic A. Whiting. "The Relation of the Museum to Local Industry." *CMA Bulletin* 5 (1918): 123.

Wilkinson 1977
John Wilkinson. *Jerusalem Pilgrims before the Crusades.* London, 1977.

Williamson 1982
Paul Williamson. "The Fifth Head from Thérouanne, and the Problem of its Original Setting." *Burlington Magazine* 124 (1982): 219–20.

Wilm 1937
Hubert Wilm. *Die Sammlung Georg Schuster.* Munich, 1937.

Wilm 1944
Hubert Wilm. *Die gotische Holzfigur. Ihr Wesen und ihre Technik.* 4th ed. Stuttgart, 1944.

Wilson 1984
David M. Wilson. *Anglo-Saxon Art from the Seventh Century to the Norman Conquest.* Woodstock, 1984.

Winternitz 1965
Emanuel Winternitz. "Musicians and Musical Instruments." *CMA Bulletin* 52 (1965): 84–91.

Wisskirchen 2002
Rotraut Wisskirchen. "Der bekleidete Adam thront inmitten der Tiere. Zum Bodenmosaik des Mittelschiffs der Nordkirche von Hüarte/Syrien." *Jahrbuch für Spätantike und Frühes Christentum* 45 (2002): 137–52.

Witt 2002
Janette Witt, ed. Staatliche Museen zu Berlin–Preußischer Kulturbesitz. Skulpturensammlung und Museum für Byzantinische Kunst. *Bestandskataloge.* Vol. 2: *Werke der Alltagskultur,* pt. 1 *(Menasampullen).* Wiesbaden, 2002.

Wittke 1966
Carl Wittke. *The First Fifty Years. The Cleveland Museum of Art, 1916–1966.* Cleveland, 1966.

Wixom 1959
William D. Wixom. "Two Lindenwood Sculptures by Tilmann Riemenschneider." *CMA Bulletin* 46 (1959): 188–97.

Wixom 1963A
William D. Wixom. "A Dutch Crucifixion Miniature." *CMA Bulletin* 50 (1963): 58–64.

Wixom 1963B
William D. Wixom. "A Fourteenth-Century Madonna and Child." *CMA Bulletin* 50 (1963): 14–22.

Wixom 1963C
William D. Wixom. "A Missal for a King." *CMA Bulletin* 50 (1963): 158–73.

Wixom 1963D
William D. Wixom. "Two Lindenwood Sculptures by Tilmann Riemenschneider." M.A. thesis. New York University, 1963.

Wixom 1964
William D. Wixom. "Twelve Masterpieces of Medieval and Renaissance Book Illumination." *CMA Bulletin* 51 (1964): 43–63.

Wixom 1965
William D. Wixom. "The Hours of Charles the Noble." *CMA Bulletin* 52 (1965): 50–83.

Wixom 1966
William D. Wixom. "Three Gothic Sculptures." *CMA Bulletin* 53 (1966): 349–55.

Wixom 1967
William D. Wixom. "Early Christian Sculptures at Cleveland." *CMA Bulletin* 54 (1967): 67–88.

Wixom 1968
William D. Wixom. "An Ottonian Ivory Book Cover." *CMA Bulletin* 55 (1968): 273–89.

Wixom 1969
William D. Wixom. "A Manuscript Painting from Cluny." *CMA Bulletin* 56 (1969): 130–35.

Wixom 1970A
William D. Wixom. "An Enthroned Madonna with the Writing Christ Child." *CMA Bulletin* 57 (1970): 287–302.

Wixom 1970B
William D. Wixom. "A Mystery Spoon from the Fourth Century." *CMA Bulletin* 57 (1970): 141–48.

Wixom 1972
William D. Wixom. "Twelve Additions to the Medieval Treasury." *CMA Bulletin* 59 (1972): 86–112.

Wixom 1973
William D. Wixom. "A Lion Aquamanile in Cleveland." In *Intuition und Kunstwissenschaft. Festschrift für Hanns Swarzenski,* 253–60. Berlin, 1973.

Wixom 1974A
William D. Wixom. "A Lion Aquamanile." *CMA Bulletin* 61 (1974): 260–68.

Wixom 1974B
William D. Wixom. "Two Thirteenth-century Walnut Angels." *CMA Bulletin* 61 (1974): 83–96.

Wixom 1977
William D. Wixom. "Leaves from a Prague Antiphonary." *CMA Bulletin* 64 (1977): 311–25.

Wixom 1979A
William D. Wixom. "Eleven Additions to the Medieval Collection." *CMA Bulletin* 66 (1979): 86–151.

Wixom 1979B
William D. Wixom. "Romanesque Sculpture in American Collections XVII." *Gesta* 18, no. 2 (1979): 42–43.

Wixom 1986
William D. Wixom. "Traditional Forms in Suger's Contributions to the Treasury of Saint-Denis." In *Abbot Suger and Saint-Denis,* ed. Paula Gerson, 294–304. New York, 1986.